THE CONSCIOUS EXPLORATION OF DREAMING:

Discovering How We Create and Control Our Dreams

THE CONSCIOUS EXPLORATION OF DREAMING:

Discovering How We Create and Control Our Dreams

by

Janice E. Brooks and Jay A. Vogelsong

Copyright © 1999, 2000 by Janice E. Brooks and
Jay A. Vogelsong
Cover art "The Process of Creativity" copyright © 1993 by
Jay A. Vogelsong
All rights reserved. No part of this book may be reproduced,
stored in a retrieval system, or transmitted by any means,
electronic, mechanical, photocopying, recording, or otherwise,
without written permission from the authors.

ISBN 1-58500-539-8

1stBooks – Rev. 6/20/00

About the Book

Dreams have drawn attention for ages, with their otherworldly, bizarre and sometimes unsettling content. Yet for all their allure, people really know little about them and how they are constructed. Everyone is familiar with various superstitious, occultist, and psychoanalytic ideas concerning dreams, yet these explanations do not really satisfy the more critically minded among us. Neuroscientific investigations of sleep and dreaming have done much to demystify dreams in recent years, but the viewpoint derived from these studies has remained unconvincing to those who consider such an approach overly reductionistic because it does not seem to connect with their own personal experiences and convictions.

The Conscious Exploration of Dreaming was written to bridge the gap between scientific and popular thinking on the subject of dreams. The authors and an additional colleague had all taught themselves to become proficient at the art of "lucid dreaming," or knowing that one is dreaming while the dream occurs. This talent enabled the trio to study dreams from the inside out, by performing a wide range of experiments designed to test the ways in which it is possible to control dreams while lucid. Such experiments gradually illuminated the natural means by which virtually all dreams may originate and unfold.

The understanding that developed out of several years' worth of experimentation and analysis of lucid dreams strongly supported a not unknown but relatively underrepresented view of dreaming, one which sees the process of dream creation as something rooted in the nature of the human perceptual system. A strong complement to the neuroscientific position, this perceptually based model has the potential to integrate a variety of perspectives and beliefs under the rubric of a single rational, commonsense approach. The present study should thus be of value to dream researchers and their students, members of the "dream community," lucid dreamers, and indeed anyone with a serious interest in dreams and human psychology.

For Ruth

Acknowledgments

We would like to thank everyone who read this book in manuscript form for their comments and insights, especially J. Allan Hobson, whose encouragement and support buoyed our efforts from the beginning, and Ruth Sacksteder, without whose correspondence, dream accounts, and assistance it could not have been completed. We also wish to acknowledge various other lucid dreamers too numerous to mention, many of whom we consider our friends or colleagues even though we may disagree on how to interpret lucid dreaming, for sharing their dream accounts, experiment ideas and perspectives. Special thanks also to Jill Gregory of the Novato Center for Dreams, Novato, California for enthusiastically providing rare reference treasures to make our work that much richer.

Contents

Foreword by J. Allan Hobson, M.D.		xiii
Introduction		xv
Chapter 1	Exploring Dreams Lucidly	1
Chapter 2	Levels of Lucidity	21
Chapter 3	The Suggestion Theory of Dreaming	43
Chapter 4	Dream Control	71
Chapter 5	Emotions, Thoughts and Memories in Dreams	101
Chapter 6	The Origins of Common Dreams	129
Chapter 7	Dream Interpretation	163
Chapter 8	The Functions of Sleep and Dreaming	201
Chapter 9	Uses of Lucidity	229
Chapter 10	Unanswered Questions	257
Notes		289
References		317
Index		333

Foreword

It is my pleasure to encourage your careful consideration of the unique body of data that forms the scientific base of this book. Authors Janice Brooks and Jay Vogelsong provide an admirably detailed set of results from their meticulous and systematic study of the conscious control of dreaming. Their work situates itself in the strong tradition of self-observation of one's dreams, the high points of which include *Dreams and How to Guide Them* (1867) by Hervey de Saint-Denys and *Studies in Dreams* (1921) by Mary Arnold-Forster.

But the new work goes far beyond its predecessors. In being far more deliberately experimental, it helps define the limits of the conscious control of dreaming as well as illuminating its fascinating capabilities. Brooks and Vogelsong are true scientists in both their adherence to value-free description and their state-of-the-art interpretation of their data.

The Conscious Exploration of Dreaming is a healthy antidote to the abundant New Age hyperbole on this important and serious subject.

J. Allan Hobson
Director, Laboratory of Neurophysiology,
Massachusetts Mental Health Center

Introduction

What is dreaming? Most people have asked themselves this question at one time or another and many have tried to answer it, usually by means of excessive speculations or elaborate theories. This book will offer evidence for a less well known but more reasonable theory of how dreaming works, evidence based largely on the experiences of three people who learned to observe and control the process of dream creation. Such controlled dreaming holds surprising significance for the nature of all dreams.

Whenever we sleep, we almost always mistakenly believe that our dreams, however bizarre or absurd, take place in reality. Only rarely do some of us realize *during* our dreams that we are, in fact, only dreaming. Such dreams have been called "lucid" because of this unusual clarity of thought. Becoming lucid enables one to clear away the dream world's typical morass of confusion and to construct a personalized reality. Lucid dreamers can escape imagined threats or tedium, and choose to fly, push through walls, work "magic," create entertaining dream adventures, and otherwise act in unusual ways in keeping with the new, more accurate assessment of their circumstances.

Lucidity also provides the ability to explore the nature of dreams by consciously experimenting *within* dreams to see how they respond to a variety of mental efforts. In our own experiments, the three contributors to this project could create dream sensations, objects, scenes, and characters merely by looking for them, manipulate them by controlling our thoughts, or make them disappear altogether. Such control seems limited only by the extent of one's own self-control and ingenuity, plus certain characteristics of the dream state itself, such as instability and incomplete access to waking memories.

Although becoming lucid sometimes disrupts a dream in progress, lucidity typically extends control rather than obliterating content. This may be due to the fact that the dreamer, despite understanding that the dream is not real, continues to interact with it *as if* it were real in some way. Ceasing this interaction and merely thinking about the dream can make the imagery disappear. Lucid dreamers therefore, whether they know it or not, end up striking a balance between action and reflection in order to keep the dream going while still maintaining lucidity. All this implies that one of the primary reasons we dream is *because* we mentally act as if we are awake, usually because we do not realize we are asleep.

Dreams do not, in this view, arise from the "unconscious," nor from the activity of any other individual part of the brain or mind assigned the task of scripting surreal dramas for some cryptic purpose. Instead we *each* create our own dreams from moment to moment as we experience them, using the same mental abilities ordinarily employed in waking to perceive, interpret, and act in the external world. Our own thoughts, feelings, and expectations about what we are experiencing so heavily influence dream content that we in effect control our dreams all the time.

The apparent lack of control experienced in ordinary dreams, and their many bizarre details as well, may largely arise from the mismatch between our reflexively applied, real-world habits of perception and behavior and the unique characteristics of dreams. Dreams lack the stabilizing force of external reality, and so have their *own* rules, much different than those governing the world where those mental habits developed. By discovering the inner workings of the dream world through direct experimentation, lucid dreamers can learn to extend the intrinsic control we all exert over our dreams. Lucid dreamers do nothing essentially different than ordinary dreamers; they merely do it with greater awareness and flexibility.

Up to this point, most investigators have missed many of the important implications of lucidity for ordinary dreams because they continue to interpret the phenomenon in terms of a variety of traditional theories. These include the belief that the striking content of many lucid dreams identifies lucid dreaming as an altered state, essentially different than ordinary dreaming. Many of these investigators' speculations concerning lucid dreaming and its possibilities seem inherently implausible, which casts serious doubts on the theoretical approaches from which such speculations grew.

The present study will address such theories and speculations to clarify why they inadequately explain not only lucid dreaming but, by extension, all dreaming.

Dream lucidity and its effects demand a different theoretical approach than any of those commonly considered by all but the most critical investigators. Hence, the following chapters will not only flesh out the alternative explanation touched on above, but will show that our personal observations as lucid dreamers accord well with modern sleep and dream research. Such research has revealed a physiological basis for the periods during which sleepers so commonly imagine themselves to be awake, as well as for the disorientation that ordinarily keeps them from realizing they are only dreaming.

Although we will describe lucid dreaming and the speculations surrounding it at some length, we ask readers to keep in mind that the discussions have an important bearing on *all* dream experience. Thoughtful readers should find this book's explanation for dreaming much different, more coherent, and simpler than any of the views derived from popular, occultist, and psychoanalytic perspectives. The book should therefore be of interest to all people who find dreams fascinating, and even to many who presently do not. They may never think of dreaming in the same way again.

Chapter 1

EXPLORING DREAMS LUCIDLY

One of the authors of this book once had a lucid dream in which she overheard a professor telling his students that the state of dream research was so bad that it would be up to them to decide what was worth studying. While a bit of an overstatement, this dream character's remark reflects some very real concerns we have about the study of dreaming in general and lucid dreaming in particular. To understand the state of lucid dream research today, one must understand the peculiarities of its history. Confusions abound in the field, not only because it is an area of study still in its infancy—at least for Western science—but because it has largely grown out of what would typically be considered occultist practices.

We would like to reclaim lucid dreaming from the wilder assumptions and speculations which currently overshadow the phenomenon, for two reasons. First, although lucid dreamers ourselves, we disagree with many popular ideas regarding lucid dreaming, ideas which have become mixed up in the field like so many weeds in a garden—weeds which many people mistake for the garden itself. Second, we believe that lucid dream observations, once they are more widely understood, will cultivate a better understanding of the nature of all dreaming and of the underlying perceptual processes of the mind as well.

In this chapter, we will give some background information about the history of lucid dreaming and the ideas surrounding it, then explain our own approach as a prelude to later chapters that will discuss our observations and conclusions in greater depth. Along the way we will introduce the standard terminology in the field and begin to address some of the common observations and misconceptions about lucid dreaming and related phenomena.

A BRIEF HISTORY

Lucid dreaming has caught the attention of theorists of many persuasions for longer than one might imagine. Scattered references to the phenomenon exist in world literature, going at least as far back as Aristotle's treatise *On Dreams*, written in the fourth century B.C. For a thousand years or more, generations of Tibetan Buddhist adepts have apparently used lucid dreaming as a spiritual exercise. St. Augustine and St. Thomas Aquinas, the Sufi spiritual master Ibn El-Arabi, the philosophers Pierre Gassendi, Thomas Reid and Friedrich Nietzsche, Society for Psychical Research founder Frederic W. H. Myers, Sigmund Freud, and a number of other thinkers discussed the possibility in their writings and sometimes explored its implications.[1]

The historical record of the last 200 years has preserved the accounts of some dedicated individuals who taught themselves to dream lucidly. In the 1800s the Marquis d'Hervey de Saint-Denys, a French aristocrat and professor of Chinese literature, not only recorded and illustrated a massive number of his own dreams in his journals, but learned to control them through the awareness he developed. He wrote a book, *Les Reves et les Moyens de les Diriger (Dreams and How to Guide Them)*,[2] about his efforts, in which he maintained that the dream theories of his day were inadequate because their promoters did not examine and experiment with their dreams directly.

A number of people appear to have been experimenting with lucid dreaming in the early decades of the twentieth century. The Dutch psychiatrist Frederik van Eeden is usually credited with coining the term "lucid dream" as one of the nine different categories into which he divided his own dreaming experiences. In 1913 he presented a descriptive paper, with special emphasis on lucid dreaming, to the Society for Psychical Research, since he thought its members would prove especially open-minded regarding his unusual ideas and reports.[3]

Van Eeden's contemporary Mary Arnold-Forster, an English gentlewoman, used the lucidity she developed through autosuggestion techniques to dream about whatever she wanted. She was especially fond of dream flying. In 1921 she published a book about her experiences, titled *Studies in Dreams*.[4]

During the same period in England, the occultist Hugh Calloway developed lucid dreaming abilities to experiment with his theories, about which he wrote under the pen name of Oliver Fox.[5] The Russian philosopher P. D. Ouspensky likewise learned to bring awareness into his dreams, largely in order to observe how dream images evolved.[6]

In 1968 parapsychologist Celia Green published the book *Lucid Dreams*, detailing some of the characteristics of such dreams with reference to the accounts mentioned above, as well as to new case material.[7] The book also compared lucid dreams to accounts of so-called "out-of-body experiences" (OBEs), or subjective impressions of leaving the body and seeing the world from outside it. *Creative Dreaming* by Patricia Garfield, first published in 1974, related concepts of dream control and lucidity to a more general audience.[8] The idea that it is possible to dream with greater awareness began to enter common knowledge.

To support a doctoral thesis on the topic, in 1978 researcher and lucid dreamer Stephen LaBerge used a prearranged eye-movement pattern to signal his awareness that he was dreaming in the sleep laboratory at Stanford University. By recording his eye movements and correlating these with his brain waves and muscle tension, he demonstrated that the signaling occurred during verifiable rapid-eye-movement (REM) periods, the recurring stages of sound sleep usually associated with the most vivid dreams.[9] This proved that he became lucid while dreaming, as opposed to when half awake or involved in other possible stages known collectively as non-REM or NREM sleep.

Along with other scientists who replicated such results—notably Keith Hearne in England, with the help of the talented lucid dreamer Alan Worsley[10]—LaBerge convinced others in the scientific community of the existence of lucid dream experiences. The field was thereby rescued at least in part from the occultist niche it had previously occupied. LaBerge has since then continued with his research and has done much to popularize lucid dreaming through giving interviews and seminars, writing articles and books on the subject,[11] and marketing various electronic lucidity induction devices.

In 1981 another researcher, Jayne Gackenbach, founded the Lucidity Association, which sponsored conferences and published a periodical called *Lucidity Letter*—later *Lucidity*—open to laymen and scholars alike. In this way interested people throughout the world, such as the German psychologist Paul Tholey, could communicate their ideas and efforts, until the periodical's demise in 1993. Gackenbach continues, on a more limited basis, to make papers pertaining to lucidity available on the Internet.

Due to popular interest in his work, Stephen LaBerge began his own organization, the Lucidity Institute, several years later. The Institute started a newsletter, *NightLight*, published from 1989 through 1996. Each issue proposed an experiment for its readers to try and reported the results of earlier experiments completed. The Institute also printed directories of members who might want to contact others to share their experiences and thoughts, but in time appeared to focus more on promotion and marketing than on research.

WHERE WE COME IN

These and similar efforts resulted in the founding of discussion groups and correspondence networks for people interested specifically in lucid dreaming, within the broader context of what has been called the "dream community," people interested in communicating with one another about dreams. The wife-and-husband authors of this book, Janice Brooks and Jay Vogelsong, are not professional scholars but ordinary people who originally contacted each other and our mutual friend Ruth Sacksteder through one such group while living in Texas, Pennsylvania and California respectively. This relationship produced an extensive correspondence, consisting of hundreds of typewritten pages over several years. We discovered that each of us had approached lucid dreaming in a different manner, that we had somewhat different opinions regarding the phenomenon, and that we had experienced somewhat different types of lucid dreams. We soon found each other's perspectives to be valuable additions to our own.

As a small child, Janice often enjoyed watching colorful imagery take shape in the air at bedtime, and she sometimes spontaneously knew when she was dreaming. In her teens she began instead to suffer from alarming incomplete awakenings from sleep during which she seemed frozen in place yet at the same time felt illusions of motion and Daliesque distortions of body image, along with other unpleasant sensations. These sleep-border phenomena could include glimpses of frightful mocking faces, a cacophony of gobbling disembodied voices, even illusions of being touched by invisibles. Having heard of only the obvious occultist interpretations of such phenomena she found them quite frightening. Other manifestations she simply considered intriguing: finding herself in strange worlds that she considered might represent other realities or consciously watching vivid "psychic visions" of various kinds.

While in college Janice fortunately came across Celia Green's book and other references which helped her make better sense of her experiences. The broken sounds and images were *hypnagogic hallucinations*, dream fragments that can replace actual sensory input at sleep onset.[12] The nasty partial awakening state was known as *sleep paralysis* and resulted simply from accidentally becoming aware of a natural inhibition of the muscles and other physiological changes associated with sleep.[13] The visits and visions, of course, were simply lucid dreams.

Fortunately, Janice lost her fears and tamed her imaginings enough to begin encouraging and directing such phenomena. She taught herself to achieve lucidity at will and began to explore its potentials, eventually satisfying herself that there was nothing supernatural about any of her experiences. Within a few years of graduating from college, Janice had her entire neighborhood remapped into a kind of oneiric arena which featured a variety of interesting sets and a lively recurrent cast of characters. The only one of us to continue having lucid dreams with any frequency—although no longer virtually daily like when she was at her peak—she approaches lucid dreaming primarily as an entertainment.

At the time we all became acquainted, Ruth had had similar experiences with sleep paralysis, hypnagogic hallucinations, and lucid dreams for most of her adult life, beginning in her twenties. Around that time she also began to study psychology, particularly Jungian theory. She worried that her experiences might indicate some kind of pathology before discovering the literature on lucid dreaming. In her case, lucidity apparently related to a persistent insomnia; she had many lucid dreams caused from lying in bed barely asleep and watching dreams take shape. She is interested in self-development and enjoys exploring the dream state in general.

Jay heard of lucid dreaming in his twenties, after having no spontaneous instances he could remember. After some effort, he had a few lucid dreams but could not focus his interest at that time, though he remained curious because of Ibn El-Arabi's endorsement of thought control during dreams.[14] Only after reading LaBerge's *Lucid Dreaming* a decade later did he focus enough to pursue continued attempts, and then primarily because of one implication of lucidity: that we are all, in our sleep, continually fooled that our dreams represent reality. He became interested in learning how far lucidity can be extended and what dreams demonstrate about human perception, which prompted the investigation and analysis that evolved into this book.

In our letters, the three of us shared our lucid experiences and proposed experiments for each other to try in our dreams. Ultimately, we managed to perform a wide range of experiments, which we had either read about or thought up ourselves as we progressed in our explorations. We recorded many similar observations, both positive and negative.

Our correspondence developed into long discussions concerning what our experiences indicated about how the mind creates dreams. At the same time, we became aware that the viewpoint developing through our experiments and discussions differed from that of many of our fellow lucid dreamers, who seemed to hold onto strong preconceptions about dreaming and what lucidity could make possible. The literature on lucidity remains—up to this point at least—dominated by opinions largely at odds with our own interpretations of our experiences.

CONVENTIONAL WISDOM? OPINIONS ABOUT LUCID DREAMING

The prevailing opinions regarding lucidity are the result of assumptions about dreaming commonly held not just by dream enthusiasts, but by the general public. People who believe in the popular theories of dream generation, when confronted by new information about lucid dreams—especially dream control—have produced a number of speculations in attempts to adapt that information to their beliefs. In this chapter, we will only briefly describe these popular models, to set the stage for more detailed discussions answering to them later in the book.

Until recently, it should be remembered, lucid dreaming was the province of those relatively few individuals who had lucid dreams and also had the time and interest to pursue them. Most worked in isolation and so were unable to compare notes with others similarly skilled and interested.[15] This contributed at times to a preoccupation with only certain kinds of the phenomena associated with lucidity, and to the creation of theories limited by the range of experience and information available to a given dreamer or researcher.

More recently the situation has improved somewhat, in that more people have learned lucidity and can easily communicate with each other. Yet many of the people interested in lucid dreaming share common preoccupations and therefore take similar approaches to the phenomenon, which limit their experimentation and especially their thought and interpretation. Some are interested in trying only very specific activities in their dreams, because of the assumptions they bring into the area. In turn, such assumptions not only color their interpretations of their lucid experiences, but largely determine the content of their dreams. That they tend to interpret their dreams selectively is evidenced by the way many repeat the accounts of some few dreams they deem especially meaningful over and over to others as "proof" of their convictions about them.[16]

The Romance of Dreams: New Age Ideologies

The majority of lucid dreamers can be considered members of the "New Age" movement, within which just about any obviously non-mainstream idea gets considered and explored. Although the preoccupations of individuals vary, such people typically pursue parapsychology, experimental mysticism, or the occult, and bring the hopes and wishes of such endeavors into the field of lucid dreaming. Indeed, such people were for some time the only people who thought lucidity possible and potentially important.

Some New Age lucid dreamers take particular interest in creating out-of-body experiences, often considering these essentially different from lucid dreams and somehow "higher" on a scale of consciousness. They borrow heavily from occult theories such as the doctrine of "astral projection" to explain what are fairly common lucid dream events.[17] In simpler terms, a person who is lightly asleep may be able to feel both a sense of the body sleeping in bed and an impression of moving a second, unconfined dream self. This dual awareness of both body images could create the illusion of "projecting" the one from the other.[18]

Those interested in OBEs offer various formalized techniques for others who do not spontaneously have them,[19] and may take the content of their OBEs quite literally, believing that they visit physical surroundings in an ethereal body, or that they are not dreaming but traveling through astral realms. Other related suppostitions include fears that the inner essence may not be able to return, that discarnate entities may try to possess the body in its absence, and that anyone encountered during an OBE could be the spirit of a dead person or of a living, fellow dreamer. Such motifs have long existed in tribal cultures worldwide, such as the Dahomey and related peoples of West Africa, whose shamans specialized in finding and returning lost dream souls.[20]

Judging by our observations of the dream community, many New Age lucid dreamers seem to be fascinated by the prospect of psychic dreaming.[21] They may experiment with telepathy, precognition, remote viewing and similar coveted talents within their lucid dreams, often coordinating their efforts with like-minded dreamers. Individuals may choose to seek knowledge of supposed past or parallel lives or to contact the dead. Some more altruistic endeavors include attempts to visualize or send out positive energy for world peace or the healing of the planet's ecological problems while dreaming.

Another, related focus of New Age lucid dreamers is "shared" or "mutual" dreaming.[22] Employing either OBE techniques or more ordinary lucid dreams, two or more dreamers will attempt to contact one another psychically and enter the "same" dream. Upon occasion, a degree of similar imagery does seem to result for whatever reason. Mutual dreamers frequently assume that this signifies successful contact, overlooking possible alternative explanations such as coincidence or similar expectations producing similar results.

Then there are the New Age explorers. Some endeavor to visit other planets or galaxies, hoping to meet highly evolved aliens. Others wish to investigate spiritual realms, seeking to contact spirit guides or angelic hierarchies or to discover higher dimensions. Yet others try to turn their lucid dreams into shamanic journeys or psychedelic trips, or to contact whales and dolphins. Finally, there are those who choose to seek the Divine through their lucid dreams, whether by meeting religious figures or by trying to induce mystical experiences such as entering the "Light" or the "Void."[23]

Of course, most New Age lucid dreamers take interest in more than one of these categories of endeavor, some perhaps even in all of them. Many have been influenced by the "Don Juan" books of Carlos Castaneda, a New Age writer who emphasized something similar to lucid dreaming.[24] Some of the "Seth" material by New Age author Jane Roberts also touches on the subjects of lucid dreaming and OBEs.[25] Although the New Age literature provides abundant imaginative material on which the dreaming mind can draw, some adherents do not seem to realize that their dreams may *reflect*, but do not necessarily *confirm*, their belief systems. The dreamer could easily set up a self-fulfilling circuit and get convinced of the reality of the dream.

A few common assumptions underlie all the preoccupations and speculations of the New Age lucid dreamers. First, they consider lucid dreaming an altered state of consciousness, superior to ordinary dreaming and perhaps to waking as well, offering new ground for their unusual explorations. Second, they believe dreams to be objective experiences, whether of the real world, the "astral world," or the psyche. This is not an uncommon idea, given the popularity of symbol dictionaries and standardized dream interpretation as a variety of diagnosis or divination. As we will discuss later, neither of these assumptions need be true to explain either lucid or ordinary dream phenomena.

The View from the Ivory Tower: Scholarly Speculations

With the recent budding interest in lucid dreaming within the scholarly community, a new set of speculations began to grow up around lucidity. Some hoped that lucid dreaming might be used to control nightmares, for instance. This line of thought led to the development of techniques for facing down fears and resolving assumed psychological conflicts: confronting or dialoguing with difficult dream characters, giving them love, and even merging bodily with them.[26] Dreamers have also been encouraged to attempt to explore their own psyches in lucid dreams for therapeutic purposes, using such techniques as requesting that their minds provide them with relevant symbols to help diagnose and offset real-life psychological issues.[27]

A yet more speculative area is the proposed use of lucid dreaming to create physical health and well-being.[28] Recommended techniques include making positive affirmations while dreaming, repairing a dream image that symbolically represents an unhealthy condition, and sending "healing energy" to an ailing or injured body part. These methods have been adapted from the practice of "creative visualization," waking imagination exercises intended for the same healing purpose.[29]

Proponents have also suggested that since dreams have sometimes been credited with creative inspiration, lucid dreams can enhance creativity, provide answers to troubling waking dilemmas, or at least enable dreamers to rehearse skills, particularly motor skills such as sports routines.[30] They likewise recommend lucid dreaming for recreation and healthy dreamtime pleasures, offering as examples the emotional highs and sexual exploits of a few lucid dreamers, as well as the adventures particular lucid dreamers with a high level of expertise have been able to maintain and enjoy.[31]

The suppositions underlying such speculations include notions that dreams are, per the most common dream theories, integral to psychological and perhaps physical well-being, to information processing, and to creativity; and, further, that these resources can be controlled or guided by lucid awareness. Again, we will show that none of these suppositions *need* be true to explain the observable characteristics of dreams.

While some pioneers in the field have tried to *promote* lucid dreaming as a means to attain various benefits, certain members of the traditional dream community, who value dreams "unpolluted" by lucidity, have warned people *away* from lucid dreaming and especially the direct control of their dreams which it enables. This concerned group includes mostly psychiatrists, analysts, therapists, and their followers, for obvious reasons. While they may consider dreams subjective, with personalized symbols to be explored by the patient, they still share many of the same notions about dreams with the people they oppose, not least that dreams are somehow of great importance. For this reason, although we have presented these as distinct approaches to lucid dreaming, there can be overlap within the categories, such as therapists who do analyze lucid dreams or encourage their clients to engage in New Age experimentation, or psychologists who mix lucid dream research with New Age interests.

Healthy Skepticism

While extravagant claims both positive and negative about lucid dreaming continue to be bandied about, the mainstream scientific community remains rightfully conservative and skeptical, since neither the positive nor the negative claims have been satisfactorily proven—or even in many cases properly articulated. If hard scientists take interest in lucid dreaming at all, they seem willing to wait for more evidence before arriving at an opinion.[32] Although the conservative approach may have its limitations when consciousness becomes the object of exploration, the skepticism of this community is understandable given the overly optimistic endorsements and the unsupported concerns that have been put forth even while knowledge about lucidity remains limited.

A VOICE IN THE WILDERNESS: PERSONAL LUCID EXPLORATIONS

In order to prevent the baby from being thrown out with the bathwater, or worse, from being drowned in *too much* bathwater, we will endeavor in this book to present a different perspective on lucid dreaming. It is based not on popular and frankly unscientific theories about dreaming, but upon our personal experiences and experimentation, careful reading of less popular but perhaps more relevant scientific research and theory, and a bit of common sense. By discussing our own carefully analyzed lucid dream experiences, and by suggesting a reasonable alternate explanation for their characteristics, we believe we will best serve our goal.

For various reasons, all three of us had the time and spare capacity to induce, recall and record incidents of lucidity; to plan experiments and work diligently at increasing our lucid dreaming skills; to examine our dreams for evidence about the lucid dreaming process; to compare notes with each other; and to study previously published material from other lucid dreamers and dream researchers. This section will discuss our approach, highlighting some of the induction methods and types of lucid dreams with which we became familiar.

Is This a Dream?

Being able to remember dreams is, obviously, a prerequisite for this kind of study, and takes a fair amount of practice all by itself. We can really say little about this other than that the more we tried, the easier it became to recall more and more dreams in more and more detail. Beyond that, the key factor involved in becoming lucid is learning to recognize what Stephen LaBerge dubbed "dreamsigns,"[33] anomalies of various kinds that can cue one in to the unreality of the situation. Bizarre elements or scenarios may mark the dream as unrealistic, or there may be oddities in one's own or another character's appearance, behavior, thoughts or feelings that indicate one might be dreaming. Even if a dream does not seem particularly unusual, after applying a bit of critical reflection numerous discrepancies between a normal waking-world setting and its dream correlate usually become apparent.

Once suspicion arises, performing a "reality test," an action designed to prove whether or not one is dreaming, helps confirm that suspicion. Our favored reality tests included attempting to turn on a light or to read print, which usually do not work well in dreams, or seeing if we could perform a feat that *only* works in dreams, such as floating in the air.

The three of us taught ourselves a number of the various lucid dream induction techniques catalogued by researchers,[34] putting up with many a sleep disturbance in the process. Deliberate autosuggestion before sleep, coupled with a strong intention to become lucid in the night's dreams, served as our most basic induction method. Even without such mental exertion, lucidity often occurred spontaneously during naps or extended stays in bed past our normal rising time.[35] Additionally, if we reviewed a dream right after waking from it, we sometimes reentered the dream state lucid.

A large proportion of Janice's and Ruth's lucid incidents began as *false awakenings*, which are experiences in which a person seems to wake up but in fact remains asleep and dreaming. Although often seamlessly realistic, false awakenings sometimes include the discomforts of sleep paralysis or disjunctive kinesthetic hallucinations—that is, "OBE" sensations. While the former can be a nuisance, the latter can be focused upon and enhanced to create a dream body for what we called "local lucids," or lucid dreams set in our own homes and environs.

Janice and Ruth were adept at remaining attentive to how their mentation altered at sleep onset, when thought can take on a fluid form teeming with dreamlike illogicality, and at pursuing the visual and auditory hallucinations that flicker at the edge of sleep. While attending to, and in some cases even controlling, these mental phenomena was fascinating in and of itself, it also often enabled us to watch dreamlets progress into full-fledged dreams which we could enter into once the scene included some sense of three-dimensionality.

Initiating either hypnagogic or OBE-type lucid dreams can be a frustrating experience. The dream limbs may not move easily, or one's whole presence may seem so tenuous that one has to exaggerate any imagined tactile contact with other dream elements in order to stabilize things. OBEs may feature the additional annoyance of their visual components taking a long time to appear. Janice's favorite means of getting around these problems was simply to *imagine* getting up and walking around, because a functional, perceiving dream body would eventually form at the new spot in mental space where she imagined herself to be. Our experiences with all such dreams were often abortive efforts since they took place in light sleep with a particularly active consciousness; in other words, we woke easily.

Stephen LaBerge uses the term WILDs, or "Wake-Initiated Lucid Dreams," for dreams entered consciously from the waking state via sleep paralysis, hypnagogic hallucinations or similar means. He refers to the more usual instances, those in which people become lucid after dreams have already started, as DILDs, or "Dream-Initiated Lucid Dreams."[36] This makes somewhat misleading terminology, since even lucidity arising during a dream may have been prompted by activities in waking, such as autosuggestion. Furthermore, dreamers do not necessarily retain lucidity during the entire transition into sleep, and may have to notice dreamsigns to clue them in once they get there, same as always. We personally have even believed ourselves to be practicing waking initiation after rousing in the night when actually deceived by false awakenings.

So although "WILD" has become familiar in the field, we would like to introduce the term *protodreaming* to describe the unformed phase between sleeping and waking, with its queer perceptions and its identification with lying in bed. Whether one falsely awakens into it from deeper sleep, or reaches it from the other direction by retaining awareness during the transition to sleep, the same techniques can be used to move from this phase into lucid dreams, and indeed all the approaches shade into one another experientially. We should mention that many of our lucid dreams that were initiated in this manner may well have occurred in NREM rather than REM sleep.[37] We of course had no laboratory equipment at hand by which to make the distinction, but it might explain why so many of our protodream incidents were vague and undeveloped, given that NREM lacks the rapid eye movements of REM that may help stimulate dream vision.[38]

What Dreams May Come: The Varieties of Lucid Experience

Not all of our lucid explorations were undertaken in the spirit of scientific investigation. We also had a great deal of fun along the way. Many lucid dreamers delight, at least some of the time, in stimulating themselves with any of a variety of pleasurable dream activities, such as romancing desirable partners, the ever-popular flying,[39] and zero-calorie feasting, and we were no exception. Janice, of course, used lucid dreaming as a form of recreation for years before becoming involved in this project, and that remained her primary motivation. She enjoyed scripting adventures of various kinds in her dreams, and went so far as to use her previously mentioned dream neighborhood as the setting for elaborate serial lucid dreams, with all the perturbations of a soap opera, which went on for years.

Jay, on the other hand, preferred to forego participating in dream scenarios and character interactions and instead to concentrate strictly on experimentation, while our friend Ruth's approach fell somewhere in between the two extremes. Despite our differing agendas and specialities we had all learned similar techniques for creating, eradicating and altering imagery. As required for a fair trial of the potentials of lucidity, we cooperated in applying these techniques to try a large variety of dream control experiments. For instance, one early, lighthearted series of experiments, proposed originally by Ruth and inspired by Alice's adventures in Lewis Carroll's *Through the Looking-Glass*, involved observing our often surprising reflections in dreams and trying to pass back and forth through dream mirrors to see what would happen. We attempted to do everything we could think of in our dreams, from walking on water to eating the moon, often with surprising ease.

In contrast, many dreamers, either because they lack the necessary skills or because of their assumptions about the medium, have relatively few lucid incidents and limit themselves to only a portion of the range of activities available. This strongly biases their interpretations of lucid dreaming, especially when they have no access to the accounts of other lucid dreamers having different kinds of experiences. The range of conscious choices available with lucidity is much wider than that available in ordinary, nonlucid dreaming or in uninformed lucid dreaming confined to narrow stylistic options. People seem to be able to find almost whatever they expect to find and to bend the medium into just about any shape they choose, although some approaches do not take lucidity very far. We therefore believe appreciating lucidity for its own sake preferable to overspecializing in a certain type of lucid dreaming without testing or at least critically assessing the alternatives.

There is also the benefit of gaining a greater perspective on what the vast range of dreaming possibilities may mean. The variety of lucid dreaming styles people have developed, along with the high degree of conscious control some dreamers have learned to exert, make good indicators of the inherent malleability of dreams. If thoughts and mental postures have such a strong influence on the character of conscious dream experiences, then dreams in general may be governed by such factors to a far greater extent than most people realize.

"Just As I Suspected"

In examining our experiences we tried to suspend our opinions about dreaming and to avoid jumping to conclusions about what lucid dreams are or what we could do with them long enough to learn *from* lucid dreaming. This stance was necessary since the dreaming mind appears to be highly susceptible to suggestion, and lucidity can be used as easily to fuel any preconceptions as to test them if one simply creates the very experiences one expects to find. Previous conceptions often interact heavily with dream content as well as prejudicing a dreamer's efforts, observations, and conclusions.

As an example, Patricia Garfield seemingly confirmed P. D. Ouspensky's assertion that speaking one's own name in a dream would disrupt the state.[40] When she tried to carve her name on a door in a dream, "the whole atmosphere vibrated and thundered, and [she] woke."[41] However, Stephen LaBerge, discerning the absence of any logical basis for this assertion, spoke his name in a dream with no resultant disruption.[42] Similarly, Celia Green, extrapolating from a limited sample, posited that lucid dreams do not exhibit any of a number of surreal effects that in fact were not at all uncommon in our own incidents: talking animals, imaginary beings, and characters unstable in appearance, to name a few.[43]

Comparing results with each other acted as another check against the unwarranted limitations which lucid dreamers commonly impose on themselves, whether based on particular models of the nature of the dream state or on conjectures regarding what constitutes possible or appropriate behavior within it. Someone influenced by certain meditative traditions, for instance, might see lucid dreaming as an exercise in developing higher consciousness and not condone any "lower," control-oriented activities,[44] ignoring the possibility that awareness of *all* options might itself constitute a more developed consciousness.

Reading accounts showing what others had accomplished broadened our conception of the range of lucid possibilities, although we had to distinguish people's interpretations of their experiences from the experiences themselves, decide when specific results came from unique associations, and be apprised of our own suggestibility. Even what other people chance to say can capture the imagination in surprising ways and influence dream content. Ruth once observed a dream cityscape as colorless as a black and white movie until her color vision gradually returned, thanks to having recently read the remarks of another lucid dreamer who professed to dreaming in black and white unless she concentrated to make colors appear. Pursuing explanations for such anomalies helped us develop a model explaining the full range of lucid and indeed virtually all dream experiences based on the concept of suggestion, to be delineated in a later chapter.

BRINGING IT ALL HOME

Although it may not currently be possible for scientists to verify in a laboratory setting many of the lucid dream observations we made, perhaps our experiential method can be viewed as valid protoscience, a relevant if preliminary approach to the conscious exploration of dreaming. Revelations, it might be said, do not so commonly strike with instant flashes of insight as develop through a great deal of hard work over time. At any rate, we hope this book and the underrepresented perspective it contains will provide solid contributions to a more well-rounded approach to lucid dreaming and to dreaming in general, as well as help interested people make real sense of their own dreaming experiences.

This book is an expansion of the ideas the three of us shared, and a digest of the examples in our own records, totaling over 2000 dreams. We should note that although Ruth generously contributed her time, thoughts and dreams, she does not necessarily share all the opinions of the authors. We have also drawn on the published accounts and ideas of other lucid dreamers and dream researchers when pertinent. Many of the fine points of our observations, particularly with regard to lucidity induction and dream control techniques, were excluded for the sake of brevity. Although all accounts of dreams, unless otherwise indicated, describe experiences with some degree of lucidity, we have included only the minimum material necessary to illustrate any given point in the text. Just as with accounts of otherwise detailed waking experiences, accounts of dreams must, by definition, be selective.

Because we wish to avoid as much as possible the self-indulgence characteristic of authors discussing their own dreams, we will not inflict personal issues on our readers except to the extent that such issues relate to the commonality of dream experience and help clarify the dreaming process. People can enjoy their own dreams because of the personal perspective that gives such constructs intelligibility and meaning. Although reading about *other* people's dreams may seem insufferably boring, like sitting through long slide shows of their vacations with droning commentary, we hope that by illuminating certain aspects of dream experience with our sometimes surprising and uncommon illustrations, we will rather be emulating the best documentary of a visit to a foreign land.

Chapter 2

LEVELS OF LUCIDITY

Many of those most interested in lucidity disagree as to what exactly lucid dreaming is. Because of its relative rarity and the enthusiasms of certain vocal devotees, some theorists have considered lucid dreaming an altered state of consciousness, discrete from ordinary dreaming. University of California psychology professor Charles Tart, to a great extent responsible for popularizing the idea of altered states,[1] argued in an early *Lucidity Letter* issue that the term "lucid dreaming" should be reserved for incidents in which one experiences a consciousness more typical of waking than dreaming.[2] He proposed another, rather cumbersome term, "dreaming-awareness dreams," for those cases that include only a *degree* of awareness of one's state, such as those described by the Orientalist George Gillespie in an earlier issue.[3] In this way he attempted to underscore the unique and separate nature of lucid dreaming.

In the next issue of the newsletter, Gillespie, a practiced lucid dreamer, answered Tart's complaint. He pointed out that while there seems to be a clear-cut difference between knowing one is dreaming and not knowing it, no such definite line exists between the levels of lucidity, and that it would be wrong to limit investigations of lucid dreaming on the basis of a narrow, preconceived definition. Therefore, he concluded, the ordinary usage of "lucid dreaming" for any instance in which one knows that one is having a dream seemed to him "the most practical distinction that can be made."[4]

Now, arguing over terminology may seem like a mere academic pastime, but how people conceptualize a phenomenon determines how they approach it. Those looking for an altered state may have very different expectations of their lucid dreams than do those not so inclined. The former may desire amazing and mystical experiences, religious ecstasy, or revelations—this, of course, aside from those who expect such things from their nonlucid dreams. But are such expectations at all warranted?

This chapter will question the wisdom of defining lucid dreaming as an altered state intellectually equal to waking consciousness. We will begin by challenging stereotypical notions of the lucid dream, then discuss the arbitrary boundaries we found it useful to draw along the lucid continuum to express varying levels of awareness. Does lucid dreaming really differ from "dreaming-awareness dreaming"? Can a clear distinction even be made between lucid and *ordinary* dreaming? How does lucid dreaming evolve over time? Our answers to such questions will clarify why lucid dream research should have an important place in the scientific study of all dreaming.

THE PUBLIC IMAGE: LUCID DREAMING STEREOTYPES

What distinguishes a lucid dream from the ordinary kind? The descriptions given by pioneers like Frederik van Eeden,[5] and on down through those of the more recent promoters, have become crystallized into something of a stereotype: that lucid dreams are hyperrealistic experiences in which dreamers possess full access to their waking faculties and engage with complete freedom in delightful adventures over which they have mastery. This represents the kind of exciting dream experience which often attracts people to lucid dreaming. However, such experiences not only do not invariably occur, they in fact comprise a strict minority of lucid dreams. In actuality, the quality of all the aspects cited, not least the quality of the lucidity itself, varies widely between individual dreamers, between one dream and another, and even between one moment and the next.

How Real Is Real?

Lucid dreams can be vividly realistic, with breathtaking clarity of vision, the smallest incidental sounds in evidence, and distinctive sensations of solidity and texture. Some people have reported their dream sensory dimensions enhancing dramatically when they become lucid,[6] to the point that they may even equate lucidity with brightness and clarity of detail. The effect can be so totally convincing that Janice, in the early days, more than once wondered if she had entered some other world.

Yet not all lucid dreams have realistic sensory qualities. Their imagery has a *range* of vividness, clarity and completeness, characteristics which to a considerable extent seem to vary proportionally with the depth of sleep.[7] Furthermore, because the dream world does not objectively exist, unrealistic effects and unstable shifts great and small can occur in a lucid dream, just as in many an unlifelike nonlucid dream. Surrealism and instability in fact serve lucidity, since without them one might judge the environment too realistic to belong to a dream and erroneously consider oneself awake. And of course, on becoming lucid the dreamer may introduce further divergences intentionally by performing fantastic feats that he or she would not think to do in a nonlucid dream mistaken for reality. Hence realism by no means characterizes lucid dreams.

Of Sound Mind?

The term "lucidity" would imply a high degree of clarity of thought. Yet one's thoughts in such dreams, too, have their instabilities and inaccuracies. Lucid dreamers often feel themselves to be in full possession of their analytical abilities and waking memories at the time, but these may well prove flawed upon awakening. It is easy, for instance, to believe that an incident from an early part of a dream sequence took place in reality despite being lucid about all the later scenes, or to judge a dream replica of a familiar setting to be completely accurate only to remember numerous discrepancies upon waking.

Contrary to popular belief, memory *of* lucid dreams can leave something to be desired as well. While lucid dreams tend to be both more memorable and more easily remembered than nonlucid dreams, we have more than once woken up knowing vaguely only that we lucidly dreamed about something or other.

The Pleasure Problem

Unusually intense levels of emotions such as fear, distress or anger while dreaming sometimes prompt lucidity, and high emotion can likewise result from it. Beginners especially may feel excitement at their lucid dream content or at the very notion of being awake in their dreams, ranging from panic to elation.[8] Over time lucid dreamers learn to cultivate detachment, since getting excited tends to wake one up or at least distract the attention, allowing lucidity to lapse. Even at her best Ruth still occasionally had dreams in which she would become lucid, exclaim delightedly, and wake up before she could do anything, or in which she focused on being lucid to the exclusion of anything more productive.

Despite the publicity that entertaining lucid dream experiences have received in the popular literature, pleasure does not automatically accompany lucidity. Indeed, many lucid dreams and other conscious sleep phenomena can be quite frightening. Nothing inherent to being more aware in one's dreams will prevent the mind from generating disturbing imagery or negative content, or keep the unsettled dreamer from doubting that he or she is really dreaming after all.

To take two extreme examples, Frederik van Eeden himself had numerous lucid nightmares which he more than half seriously attributed to the machinations of demoniacal creatures.[9] Sometimes he would dream of engaging in depraved acts that his waking self found unspeakable. In other dreams he would, as he supposed, actually see the malignant creatures which he thought were causing such imagery and trying to draw him into their debauchery, and he delighted in combating them. More recently, the Catholic monk known as Father "X," whose rather Lovecraftian elaborations on his decades of conscious sleep experiences appeared now and then in *Lucidity Letter*, had similar difficulties with morbid and malicious dream characters. He too concluded that the "beings" must exist outside his own mind, perhaps as spirits of the dead trapped in a transitional afterworld or as residents in another space-time continuum.[10] Such instances attest to the fact that lucidity does not guarantee immunity from nightmares—or from fanciful interpretations of one's dream encounters, for that matter.

Who's in Charge?

For the experienced lucid dreamer, nightmarish imagery will most likely decrease in both frequency and potency. Because of the inherent mutability of dreams, one can take control of one's nocturnal adventures and effect desired changes at will, perhaps even scare the enemy as Janice enjoyed doing by, for instance, standing unharmed through a volley of bullets. Nevertheless, even skilled lucid dreamers cannot consistently do anything they want in the private universe of their dreams. Efforts at control can be frustrated by a number of constraints, including the very instability that makes them possible.

We will be returning to the subjects of dream control and of memory, thought and emotion in lucid dreams in later chapters. For now, we mean to probe the nature and scope of lucidity itself. Just how lucid is lucidity?

A STATE OF CONFUSION: LUCIDITY BY DEGREES

Reflective lucid dreamers can identify many different grades of lucidity, many shades in the lucid spectrum. Like any technical observers, we have come to use a variety of terms for types of lucid dreams to indicate the full range of our personal experiences, since without such terms we could not easily convey our observations. The differences between the levels are subtle, though, so we intend the following typology more for illustrating lucidity's variability than for strict definitional purposes.

Nonlucidity: Not Having a Clue

People ordinarily respond to a nonlucid dream situation, whether mundane or preposterous, as if it were real. They overlook blatant disparities with reality, latch onto naive explanations and rationalizations for the incongruities they do notice, and, if they remember any of it when they wake up, probably can hardly believe they were so dense.

In one classic nonlucid dream, Janice thought she was in the process of moving house when she had in fact done so a year before, decided to enlist her father's assistance with the move without remembering that he had been deceased for some years, misremembered one of her high school teachers as an elementary school teacher, and so on. Such a concatenation of false memories and perceptions is characteristic of ordinary dreaming.

Tacit Lucidity: Not Knowing That You Know

In what might be termed "tacit lucidity," on the other hand, the dreamer acts as if he or she were lucid without actually *being* lucid. We often seemed to have an implicit awareness that we were dreaming, feeling somehow that nothing was "for keeps" and exploiting the state by thinking and behaving in ways much different than would be usual in waking. This could even include directly controlling dream events. Realizing one time that his fear was making an enemy spacecraft approach but not that he was dreaming, Jay concentrated on the idea that it had not pinpointed his location, and in a moment it veered off.

In a common subtype of the tacitly lucid dream, we would recognize what was happening as unreal, but perceive the action as a television show, movie or play that we were watching or in which we had a part. At other times, we might interpret the dream as a story we were making up, or perhaps as a fanciful experience like a delirium or a visit to another world.

Many, perhaps even most people experience a degree of tacit lucidity in their dreams from time to time without ever "realizing they are dreaming" per se. This variety may, however, become more frequent after a person has had some experience with more complete lucidity, since what would once have been ordinary dreams can be affected by practice to resemble one's lucid dreams. Our implicit knowledge of dream control skills would often arise on demand in scenarios that otherwise remained nonlucid. For instance, on one occasion Janice suddenly "remembered" that she was a magician and froze some annoying dream characters in place.

Long-term practitioners may find that sheer repetition habituates certain characteristics of their individual approaches to lucid dreaming into the rest of their dream lives. Seeing or talking about favored recurrent scenes, such as Janice's perennial outdoor concerts, or automatically acting out a typical lucid activity in a tacitly lucid way, could lead us to actual lucidity if we happened to reflect on the matter. All three of us sometimes had the experience of becoming lucid *after* unthinkingly flying, jumping out windows or performing similar stunts in accordance with our lucid habits—or even after seeing other characters doing so.

Prelucidity: Something's Wrong with this Picture

The phase in which the dreamer begins to suspect, for whatever reason, that he or she is dreaming can be called—borrowing from Celia Green[11]—"prelucidity." At this point we would often try a reality-testing technique to verify that hunch, such as the light-switch, reading, and floating tests mentioned in the last chapter. Such questioning and testing did not always provide a step up from ordinary dreaming to acknowledge that we *were* dreaming, since that can be a disruptive realization. Often the mind puts up a great deal of resistance to the truth. When Ruth noticed herself floating up a staircase and thought it strange that she could now do things she could only do in dreams before, she considered that she might be dreaming then decided against it because she believed she had not gone to sleep yet. Cases such as Ruth's thinking in the midst of a scenario that she would like to have a lucid dream and trying to figure out how to "become lucid" might qualify as somewhere between tacitly lucid and prelucid.

Postlucidity and Other Oddities

Sometimes we would become aware that we were *recently* dreaming, without being aware that we were *still* dreaming. This "postlucidity," as Jay dubbed it, could even lead to telling other characters about the interesting dream we just had. Such instances commonly occurred during false awakenings or when a scene suddenly changed.

We have actually discussed lucidity with dream characters and recounted prior *lucid* dreams to them without realizing we were concurrently dreaming. An instance of this type cannot be considered a valid lucid dream itself, though it may lead to one. In one dream Ruth explained to an interested audience that her favorite reality test was to jump into the air and see if she floated. Giving a little jump to demonstrate, to her shock and amazement she floated about ten feet off the ground.

Semilucidity: Getting the Idea

In the case of "semilucidity," we would realize we were dreaming without comprehending the full significance of that fact. In some cases the understanding about being asleep and having a dream would be diffuse and undeveloped. We might think of ourselves as sleepwalking, visiting the real world in a dream body, or having psychic visions, or perhaps recognize only some of the imagery as coming from a dream.

At other times, while not quite so confused about the difference between waking and sleeping, we understood only a select few implications of the fact that the dream was not real. These could be quite arbitrary. Jay once realized he had left his keys and wallet inside a dream house and made the keys appear in his hand so he could unlock the door to retrieve the wallet. Selective lucidity makes for many such humorous incidents.

Quite commonly we would simply continue with the scenario that had been progressing when we realized we were dreaming, perhaps now with a bit more self-assertion. Semilucid dreams thus can include play-acting like some tacitly lucid dreams, with the distinction that when semilucid one realizes one is going along with an unreal plot. This may, however, lead to a loss of lucidity if that plot becomes too involving.

Sometimes we deliberately chose to keep lucidity muted to a low level if a dream narrative proved particularly engrossing, especially in the case of pleasurable adventures or romantic interludes. We might elect to be selective in exercising lucidity, perhaps intervening just long enough to test a skill or to deal with a particular problem to further the plot. We could likewise experience variable lucidity within a dream period, so that we constantly had to remind ourselves of the fact that we were dreaming, of the implications of that fact, or of our lucid intentions. By no means did we always find lucidity easy to hold on to once achieved.

Dreams Within Dreams

To further muddle the picture, we occasionally *dreamed* about becoming lucid without really doing so, by engaging in activities that commonly entertained us when lucid and mistaking that for lucidity itself—as if jumping out a window or going through a mirror, say, were all it would take to have a lucid dream. This kind of mock lucidity can arise in the case of what we call a "frame dream," a dream in which one seems to fall asleep at a location in the imaginary world and starts a new scenario. Such dreams within dreams sometimes involved very little volition and awareness even though we thought of ourselves as lucid.

When relatively rational in quality, our frame dreams could also generate valid lucid sequences, lucid except for the delusion about our sleeping circumstances. Supposed "WILDs" actually initiated from nonlucid bedroom scenes or undetected false awakenings in this manner tended to develop unusually rapidly, since we were already asleep, but they were otherwise indistinguishable from regular WILDs.

Full Lucidity: Keeping Your Wits About You

Semilucidity occurs frequently among lucid dreamers, and may comprise the bulk of the time spent "lucid" for most people. At a certain point of practice, though, the adept dreamer should experience relatively full lucidity from time to time. This includes remaining aware that one is dreaming after becoming lucid, and keeping in mind the significance of the fact; the social conventions and physical laws of the waking world will be seen as merely optional in the dream environment. When fully lucid we sometimes decided to control the dream to a great extent to emphasize lucidity, and sometimes chose instead merely to observe and develop whatever scenario was already in progress while keeping a measure of critical detachment, depending on our mood or our waking goals.

Perfect lucidity, where nothing about one's thinking is later revealed to have been less than astute, would appear to be relatively rare, in dreams as indeed in waking life. The various forms of partial lucidity seem very common indeed, both in our own accounts and in other dreamers' descriptions that we have read in *Lucidity Letter* and elsewhere. Moreover, although the level of dream lucidity does show improvement over time, the progression is anything but steady. As frequent lucid dreamers we experienced considerable variations in critical ability from incident to incident, fully lucid in one dream but having surprising gaps in the lucidity of the next.

Protolucidity: Awake in Your Sleep

The level of lucidity varies as widely in protodreaming, the state of identifying with the dormant body at sleep onset or between scenes, as it does in regular dreaming. We could, for instance, have tacitly lucid protodreams in which we took ourselves to be interacting with ghosts or other entities, even though we normally reacted to such things only as auditory or tactile hallucinations. Sometimes, too, we might mix various interpretations of protodream experience in a muddled way, considering ourselves to be making images, or trapped awake in the sleep state, or even having some kind of seizure.

Although our protodreaming could feature all manner of hallucinations, sometimes we would be lucid without any imagery at all: merely aware of lying asleep thinking, perhaps reviewing recent dream events or, in Ruth's case, feeling a bit claustrophobic. Such "protolucidity" includes the same clarity about one's state as dream lucidity, simply with no illusory sensory perceptions occurring simultaneously. Indeed the lack of hallucinatory material may qualify these cases as the most lucid of dreams, or perhaps as lucid *sleep*.

BORDER DISPUTES: REDEFINING LUCIDITY

Other dreamers and researchers have made observations similar to ours concerning the levels of dream lucidity.[12] However, we will not propose a strict continuum of lucid experience, as some have tried to do,[13] to make a certain forced sense of the experiences available, since they are truly in confusion. What, then, *can* one usefully infer from such a range of observations?

A Dream by Any Other Name

We conclude not only that no true distinction can be made between different levels of lucidity in dreams—though they can certainly be named—but that no clear line can be drawn even between lucid and nonlucid dreams. Lucidity is embedded in ordinary dreaming. Its starting and ending points are not necessarily well defined within the dream, nor even necessarily discrete from one another in a sense, since the dreamer often carries concerns from the nonlucid portion into the lucid portion: plots, characters, scenes, emotions. Just as one can become absorbed in a book to the point of forgetting oneself, browse through it while thinking of other things, or study it with a critical eye, and yet in all cases be reading, all of the different kinds of lucid and nonlucid experiences blend together on close inspection; all count as varieties of dreaming.

This becomes especially clear when it is considered that even so-called nonlucid dreams often exhibit a certain clarity of thinking that could be termed "lucid" in the broader sense of the word. In some of our own nonlucid dreams, we know ourselves as ourselves, think and act relatively rationally, and question what happens to us in an attempt to orient ourselves, even to the point of almost recognizing our true state. Janice has found that dreams in which she does a lot of thinking and analyzing commonly precede or end up as lucid dreams.

This level of rationality comes in seeming contrast to the

stupidity of other of our nonlucid dreams in which we believe that some bizarre scenario represents reality, develop false memories of events that never really occurred, and maybe do not even remember our real identity. Yet even such muddled instances can evince a distorted, implicit sense of the simple truth that nothing we do at the moment will matter much. In one nonsensical nonlucid interlude of Jay's, when the Queen of England became angry at his lack of respect for her he shrugged it off with a sincere disclaimer that he was just Elvis Presley's dog.

Further, almost everyone learns to achieve a certain low level of lucidity as a child when his or her parents explain, "It was just a dream." Many may, as children or adults, realize this fact only *after* experiencing a nightmare and waking up. Others, though, can practice a minimum degree of intervention in their dreams when matters get out of hand: they wake themselves up, revise an ugly outcome, or simply interrupt a bad dream and continue asleep.

Lucidity is no "all or nothing" affair, since the dreamer does not always recognize the full extent of its implications;[14] and it may never be complete in dreams, since their imagery is by nature illusory. Yet awareness in general can never be completely absent from dreams either, since no one could perceive them, think during them or recall their content were they not essentially conscious phenomena. Certain people simply come to develop that awareness to whatever maturation point in their dreams. "Lucid dreams" are dreams in which the awareness has reached a decisive level of self-reflection, making lucid dreaming a natural part of the total range of dreaming experience possible. It would perhaps be better to talk of *incidents of lucidity in dreams* rather than of *lucid dreams* as such—though we will, of course, continue to refer to "lucid dreams" in deference to common usage.

Becoming Lucid About Dreaming

How can we continue to address lucid dreaming as something distinct from nonlucid dreaming, which it will no doubt still remain in the minds of many of those who experience it? Exactly by referring to lucidity as a mental phenomenon *not* confined to dreams or varieties of dreams: as critical reflection. This faculty can be directed not just towards deciding whether or not one is having a dream, but at any assumption that one wishes to understand more than reflexively or superficially. Charles Tart seemed to come to this understanding when he wrote in a later *Lucidity Letter* that the word "lucid," used technically, could apply to all states of consciousness. He wrote, "My perceptions and understandings of both my world and myself can vary in their degree of experienced lucidity."[15]

Enhancing the degree of lucidity attained in dreams requires proper reconceptualization of what is happening, and much of the groundwork for that reconceptualization occurs during waking. Reading about lucid dreaming, for instance, teaches the mind to encompass the idea of lucid dreaming and provides a glimpse of the possibilities that dreaming with greater awareness can open up. And as the divergent pursuits of lucid dreamers show, waking ideas about lucid dreaming have a profound effect on shaping the kinds of lucid dreams obtained.

However intriguing it may be, becoming lucid *during* a dream strikes us, in this light, as much less essential than becoming lucid *about* dreaming; the one does not automatically insure the other. As Janice's case history in the last chapter showed, some people begin, despite being nominally "lucid," by wrongfully interpreting their conscious sleep phenomena in paranormal terms, that being the closest frame of reference for such experiences that they know—like trading Occam's razor for Sweeney Todd's. Such people's experiences could be better illuminated by clear thinking, something hard to develop when learning about lucid dreaming in relative isolation with only arcane sources at hand.

Dreams remain dreams regardless of what people call them, regardless of the level of lucidity brought to them, and regardless of the changes lucidity may bring to their substance. The distinction lies mainly in knowing, when sufficiently lucid, that no matter what may inspire them one's own mind is responsible for the events in one's dreams. A dreamer can then choose how to interpret and react to imagery without being manipulated into emotional responses to unreal situations.

The difference between nonlucid and lucid dreaming, in other words, does not matter nearly as much as the difference the difference makes. If one's reactions remain the same in either case, or change only along the lines dictated by some unreasonable frame of reference, it does not really help much to become lucid, since the whole point of lucidity is not taking dreams at face value—understanding that they *are* only dreams, not realities of any kind.

High Hopes: The Altered State Debate

What of those who believe lucid dreaming an altered state because of having distinctive experiences in their lucid dreams, whether of unique sensual pleasures, strange sensory distortions, extremes of bliss and devotion, or mystical dissolution of self? "The less distracted I am by thoughts," runs one account, "the more intensely aware and joyous the experience becomes—what I can only describe as ecstasy."[16] These phenomena might seem to argue for defining lucid dreaming as a different state than ordinary dreaming. However, such experiences do not occur only during lucid dreaming, but reportedly in other states as well, including meditation, psychedelic drug trips, nonlucid dreams, and even waking.[17] Lucid dreaming cannot be judged unique on that basis.

Some partisans consider fantastic lucid dreams to represent a greater level of lucidity than that found in more ordinary lucid dreams. Jayne Gackenbach has represented such dreams, as well as those in which the dreamer maintains a certain detachment from the content, as virtual stepping stones to enlightenment.[18] She apparently believes lucid dreaming closely akin to meditation, both being vehicles that, in her terms, can increase awareness and ultimately lead to the experience of pure consciousness—awareness of awareness only.

This makes for a rather slanted interpretation of what lucid dreaming is, given that many people become lucid dreamers without any interest whatsoever in meditation, transcendence or ecstasy. Our own experiences with dreams in which we merely observed the action, or with becoming lucid in dreamless sleep, did not impress us as particularly "spiritual." Moreover, while the three of us did not particularly try to achieve euphoric effects, neither did such effects occur spontaneously in all our formidable number of lucid dreams, even in dreams resembling those others would consider of especial significance. Hence, they can neither be intrinsic to lucid dreaming nor be the inevitable next steps on the ladder of consciousness.

We do know that emotions, no doubt including bliss, can run high in dreams, and it may well be true that the contents of consciousness can temporarily be annihilated by meditating within them. Yet these results would seem to relate to individual expectation. Although those who incubate such dreams seem to think they let go of conscious control in order to have them, they may in effect let expectation control the dream instead. The belief that they have relinquished control to a higher force might possibly produce the emotional components and convincing aura that our more skeptical endeavors lacked.

Several implications follow from defining lucid dreaming as a type of dreaming rather than as a separate altered state. Most importantly, once it is understood that lucid dreaming is still only dreaming, and neither an altered state in its own right nor an intrusion into the dream state, then clearly any observations made by lucid dreamers *do* have a relevance to the study of how the mind creates ordinary dreams. Furthermore, those who approach lucid dreaming with grand expectations about having exceptional experiences might reflect a bit about what really goes on in their dreams and how they may be influencing them to agree with the assumptions they bring to the matter. Attaining partial lucidity while dreaming does not mean that anything one experiences or thinks at the time will necessarily be important or true, since one *is* still dreaming and subject to many of the same confusions and confabulations common to all dreams. Any initial lucidity should be considered only the starting point for greater possible lucidity.

PRACTICE MAKES PERFECT

Given some of the not-so-lucid reactions to conscious dreaming we have described, it should be clear that learning how to have lucid dreams is more than a matter of applying a particular set of induction methods. Increasing one's overall level of lucidity in dreams entails changing many assumptions, great and small, derived from waking-world experience and thought. These include some firmly entrenched expectations about how the world works. Lucid dreamers only gradually acquire the appropriate skills for working with the dream environment, for prolonging dreams, and for coping with nightmares, for instance, and to make real progress they have to identify and overcome any number of limiting beliefs along the way.

Getting By in the Dream World

Assumptions carried over from waking life help create and maintain dream imagery, with the result that dreamers continually mistakenly apply waking-world rules to the dream world and end up with only imperfect lucidity. Dreamers do not immediately realize that when lucid they can free themselves from such limitations; it takes a fair amount of experimentation to discover the new principles that govern dreaming. For instance, one gradually realizes that many physical necessities of the waking world do not pertain in the dream world. In waking life, creative solutions to problems do not employ magic. In dreams, however, one can fly or teleport away, melt through or break down walls, move or banish obstacles by will, change sizes and shapes, and otherwise overcome apparent physical limitations. Mastering such techniques greatly increases the possibilities for viable choices of action within a dream narrative.

By way of comparison, anyone trained on a standard typewriter who switches to using a full-featured word processor will probably begin by simply typing on it in the accustomed manner. Only gradually will he or she learn to use the more advanced functions built into the new system, such as making blocks of text appear and disappear at will. Similarly, the novice lucid dreamer must alter any mental models of what dream behavior should be like away from the basic waking standard to allow for a new conceptualization of dream possibilities.

There is a learning curve involved with all such activities. Beginners often think, for instance, that they must flap their arms or make other bodily efforts in order to fly in their dreams before realizing that all it takes is concentration.[19] Also, a lucid dreamer can waste time waiting around or searching for a particular goal, until he or she realizes that a literal search is less to the point than conjuring the image directly or coaxing the mind into producing it in some way. So when Janice wanted to ride a white horse in a certain dream, she simply called aloud for one despite the skeptical remarks of another character, then watched smugly as a white horse with a few tan spots on its neck came galloping gallantly along the street. Such controlled dreaming always presents some challenges, though, for while the mutable nature of the dream environment makes such magical feats possible it also introduces random instabilities that can make objects, characters and even whole scenes appear, change and disappear at inopportune moments.

Nothing Lasts Forever

When a dream scene changes abruptly, one may find oneself suddenly engaging in new activities. This distracting phenomenon can be detrimental to lucidity, because the dreamer easily becomes caught up in a new set of assumptions and preoccupations. It requires considerable wherewithal to retain full awareness during such transitory segments, which otherwise might seem like unexplained hiatuses when one tries to recall the dream.

The false awakening qualifies as a particularly common type of scene shift, in which the scene typically becomes one of the dreamer lying in bed. It takes practice not only to learn how to identify these experiences by checking for dreamsigns, but to do anything useful with them. Whenever he detected a false awakening, Jay had a bad habit of trying to wake himself up for real in order to record his previous dreams without really appreciating the fact that he was still dreaming. Janice tended to lie around waiting to wake up, until she eventually realized she could get up within the dream and explore her environs, which led ultimately to the development of her lucid soap opera.

Quite commonly in our experience, the visual component of a lucid dream would abruptly disappear. Sometimes our identifying the imagery as unreal would destabilize the scene in progress at once, or we would fail to participate enough to keep the dream going. At other times, the blank spots would occur at random. In any case, we found that if we continued to try to engage the dream environment tactiley and kinesthetically, a scene would eventually reappear. According to Stephen LaBerge, such activity helps to override the sensations of the immobile physical body that would otherwise tend to pull one awake.[20] There are important additional implications, however, which we will explore in later chapters.

My Enemy, Myself

Lucidity can offer a potent defense against nightmares and other unpleasant scenarios. Reactions to having the good fortune to become lucid during the course of a bad dream vary widely along the lucidity spectrum and tend over the course of time to reflect the dreamer's increasing mastery of the dreaming process.[21] Initially, a nightmare victim who becomes lucid will probably struggle to awaken. Later, other strategies will come to mind. The dreamer might decide to fly away from adversity, for instance, or try to confront and conquer his or her enemies, whether by fighting them, transforming them into innocuous characters, or making them disappear. The initial discovery that one can hold one's own in the formerly threatening dream world can be quite empowering.

In time we learned that alarming dream figures tend to disappear of themselves if given minimal attention. Also, when one faces them down and demonstrates their inability to inflict harm, would-be dream aggressors may, as it were, dissipate in chagrin.[22] As experience deepens, an adept lucid dreamer will develop the mental flexibility to deal with dream negativity in a variety of creative ways, selecting what seems most appropriate in the particular instance or for his or her own dreaming style. Eventually negative dream content might virtually disappear if it always brings on the lucid perspective needed to mitigate it.

Running on Empty

In certain respects, it is considerably easier to master dream characters than to master the dream self. The developing practitioner is bound to come up against certain stumbling blocks, including irrational behaviors and ideas temporarily entertained by the dreaming mind as well as a variety of more pervasive false assumptions. For one thing, on becoming lucid we would often follow our first inclination with minimal deliberation, whether that might be to push through a mirror, to fly from a negative interaction, to inform dream characters that they were part of a dream, or to find a sex partner. Only after awakening would we come to question the choice of activity, which may have been at odds with a waking agenda. To make matters worse, knowing that the lucid dream would most likely be relatively short often led us to a concern with time, sometimes to humorous effect as we flurried around, believing that the opportunity to explore the dream would end all too quickly. Such excitation, of course, could result in making the dream end even sooner than it need have.

As we have mentioned, beginning lucid dreamers may be adversely influenced by various offbeat ideas. They have to learn to reevaluate their experiences, so they can understand and work with confusing, even seemingly supernatural phenomena in a rational manner. For example, some sleep paralysis experients see or otherwise sense a menacing presence, most likely a dream projection of their own fear. In our experience, when this fear disappears with an informed interpretation of the state, any "presences" that may manifest will change character accordingly.

Even lucid dreamers who know better can suffer from time to time from naive confusions about the state, since the dreaming mind readily takes up all sorts of notions at which the waking mind might scoff. Many a nominally lucid dreamer will ascribe oneiric oddities to jumping around in time or between parallel lives. We would sometimes wonder if people in the real world could see us in some ghostly form, or imagine that someone met in a dream must literally be that person dreaming at the same time rather than a mental image. Such semilucid lapses have abashed us considerably.

An additional barrier to lucidity is the human tendency to jump to conclusions based on limited information. Prevailing expectations from earlier dream experience strongly influence what one finds possible in a lucid dream, even though the same activity that may seem impossible for some—walking through walls, say—poses no difficulty at all for other lucid dreamers. Gradually, one can learn to take expectation into account and work to counterbalance it, overcoming a variety of habitual associations. For example, Ruth was quite delighted when she finally got some dream characters to float and dance in the air with her in a lucid dream after years of laboring under the assumption that only she could fly in her dreams.

UNCOMFORTABLE TRUTHS

To conclude, since induction techniques only take one so far and since the level of lucidity varies widely from dream to dream, it is obvious that one does not just "become lucid"; one *learns* lucidity. This learning is a long, gradual process, full of trial and error, like learning to read or to ride a bicycle. Although we do not really know to what extent self-control, memory, reason, and critical ability can be sharpened in dreams, we do know that becoming lucid in a dream only constitutes the beginning, because lucidity usually starts out only partial or limited in scope.

Some dreamers further limit lucidity by carrying excess mental baggage in the form of a favored occultist, metaphysical or psychological theory into their dreams, employing it as dogma rather than investigating its validity. Those writing on the subject of lucid dreaming have overall exhibited a tendency to become attached to such ideas and to prescribe and proscribe particular dream behaviors for their readers accordingly. With time and effort, lucid dreamers can learn to question and confront their own convictions and those of others, testing the ideas of assumed authorities instead of assuming them true. Trying to debunk such notions outright within dreams does not always work, because the dreams can respond to the suggestion of the very notion one has in mind to try to counter. Nevertheless, more detached observations over time will create, we feel, a more accurate picture. Whatever one's skill at induction or even at control, it may be necessary to revise many an outmoded belief about dreaming before one's thinking on the subject clarifies enough to qualify as truly lucid.

Chapter 3

THE SUGGESTION THEORY OF DREAMING

Lucid dreaming raises some interesting challenges for dream theory. The preceding chapters have illustrated several important points that any explanation of lucid dreaming, as well as any encompassing theory of dreaming in general, should take into account. Firstly, lucid dream content so often parallels accounts of certain "paranormal" and sleep disorder-related phenomena that one must conclude that many, perhaps most of such experiences may be misinterpreted, quasi-lucid dreams. Lucid dreaming is in fact such a malleable medium that people from a range of conceptual backgrounds use it to explore their disparate and often conflicting interests. Because of the different levels of skill and thought exercised by lucid dreamers, and because of the way their personal expectations interact with the content of their dreams, lucid dream content varies widely from individual to individual and from dream to dream, to the point that distinctive styles of lucid dreaming become possible.

Secondly, lucid dreaming cannot be a discrete altered state of consciousness, because it is highly variable in quality and inextricably confused with ordinary dreaming. Moreover, the transcendental effects claimed by some by no means occur for all. Lucidity can more reasonably be seen as a difficult-to-achieve reconceptualization of dream experience which some people can learn through both dreaming and waking efforts. Such learning takes the form of gradually *unlearning* waking habits and discovering and mastering the unique rules governing dreaming.

These observations have the potential to change contemporary views of how the mind creates dreams. They do not fit popular models featuring an unconscious mind crafting dreams for its own purposes, since such models do not easily account for lucidity at all except as an intrusion by the conscious mind or as evidence of an altered state. This chapter will discuss a view of dream creation that makes better sense of lucid dreaming phenomena and of ordinary dreams as well—what might be called the "suggestion theory of dreaming." The suggestion theory is grounded in a "world-modeling" model of how the mind works, as presented in detail by William James in his 1890 *Principles of Psychology*,[1] and as more recently articulated in the work of such researchers as Robert Ornstein of Stanford University.[2] The modeling concept has enriched such fields as psychology, philosophy and anthropology, and it is such a useful paradigm that the next section will explain its broad foundations in some detail.

THE CONSTRUCTED WORLD

Every day, all day long, each of us deals indirectly with the real world. "Indirectly" because, although the real world assumably exists outside of our minds, we actually perceive and interact with that world only by means of mental models, inner maps for interpreting everything around us and guiding our own behavior. We learn these models from earliest infancy, through both direct observation and enculturation, or training by others about their ways and beliefs. The models become built up to remarkable levels of complexity during a lifetime of experience, a process which constitutes our education in the widest sense.

Partial Truths

Different species have varying capacities to receive sensations and to store information, the natural abilities which support and continually update the world-modeling function. Frogs, for instance, can perceive very few forms of stimuli and have little capacity to learn more than they react to or "know" instinctually.[3] The human range of perception and memory, on the other hand, is truly enormous.

Nevertheless, our models are based on *selecting* information of use to us from the vastly greater amount of information present in the real world. Our senses come "hardwired" to register only certain wavelengths of light, frequencies of sound, degrees of temperature, and so on, and only certain levels of detail within a given range. We further select out such information as we do receive, paying attention to what seems important to us because of genetically programmed, culturally trained, or personally evolved interests.

As an example, of all the possible sound patterns of human speech, any given language will recognize only certain ones in certain combinations as valid. An English speaker would not accept the sequence "mná" as even a potential English word, since it does not conform to our model of grammar. Yet it is a common enough word in Irish Gaelic, meaning "women." By the same principle, an art exhibit, flower show, or sporting event, say, becomes a much different and richer experience for the knowledgeable expert than for the bored novice. The novice simply has never paid the attention required to learn to perceive the often subtle distinctions that, to the expert, define various classes and quality levels within that particular frame of reference and make it especially interesting.

From this filtered input, we construct multiple interlocking pictures of the physical and social environment, a patterning of reality which comprises our total world model and upon the fitness of which our survival, social viability, and personal expertise depend. Consequently, we tend to take these learned models, including our personal values and opinions, as truths. And our perceptions, especially the simpler ones, become increasingly habituated until we no longer notice they are largely constructed or implied—unless, at a later date, some misperception, or a careful study of psychology, points this out.

Following the Perceptual Map

Because of our dependence on inner models, what we see and how we see it depend in large measure on what we look for. Once, while visiting relatives, Janice went into a room to pick up her mother's umbrella. She could not see it, even though several children pointed it out. Finally one child walked over and touched it, and it became visible—an open umbrella sitting on the floor. Janice could not initially perceive the umbrella since she had been selectively looking for a *closed* one. Similarly, one time when Jay went fishing with his family he chose a likely spot and stepped out onto a rock to cast his line into the river, only to find himself suddenly immersed in water over his head. The "rock" turned out to be only a paper bag floating on the surface.

Such misperceptions and miscalculations happen more often in all our lives than we usually like to admit. Our misplaced car keys may turn up in a place where we already looked once without seeing them; when we get in the car we may automatically start driving towards work even though we mean to go to a shopping mall in the other direction; and when we arrive we may not even recognize our dentist shopping there at first because he or she appears out of the usual context. We would notice such mismatches between model and fact even more often if we did not tend to *avoid* situations in which we would likely be embarrassed or upset by our disorientation. One can also witness world modeling in operation by "seeing" shapes in clouds, rock formations and so on—imposing familiar patterns where none really exist.

Think also of the "let's pretend" games of children in terms of developing world models. Children do not notice many of the details of the world around them until these are demonstrated or named. As they grow in sophistication their models for understanding and interacting with that world evolve to provide for greater discrimination in perception and increased flexibility of response, and also come to approximate those of the people around them more and more closely. As adults, we must constantly add details to our models—a new route to work, a new computer program, a different tax law, a variation on a recipe.

In our continual educations, we must all have our focus properly directed, so we can learn to perceive the world in the richness of detail required by the demands of our lives. Such experience as we do gather occurs only insofar as we pay the required attention. As James wrote, "My experience is what I agree to attend to. Only those items which I notice shape my mind—without selective interest, experience is an utter chaos."[4]

Experience alters the brain. Its neurons and the networks that link them encode, to whatever extent, the information to which we attend. On a more practical level, this means that perception, thought, and action produce memories or habits which guide us through our lives. Having the ability to keep so much information about the world in our heads by structuring experience in this way means we do not have to relearn it in every new situation, nor have every behavior built in as an instinct in the manner of more mechanical creatures.

The Big Picture

Relying on inner models also ensures that we do not have to take in every detail of the physical or social environment with the acuity of Sherlock Holmes. Instead we notice partial information or cues, on the basis of which we fill in the rest of our perception with assumptions and expectations based on habit. So, for example, the average driver will prepare to pull over if he or she hears a siren in the distance, expecting an ambulance or fire engine to be approaching, whereas the siren will call up quite different associations for a criminal on the run. The same signal suggests different scenarios.

In such a manner we can make complex assessments of people, places and things, and perform complex actions, based in most situations on only the briefest of cues. Only when an ambiguous situation presents itself—and when we have our wits about us—will we concentrate on what we are seeing and doing, and then only until we can make the situation fit within a preexisting picture of reality or create a new category of experience to accommodate it. Our imaginary trip to the mall, for instance, may result in our acquiring any number of marvels which, to our dismay, the spouse may take one look at and dismiss as mere "junk" thanks to categorizing things a bit differently.

Selective attention gives us remarkable adaptability, but it also makes us subject to certain classes of delusory experience. Like the proverbial blind men grasping individual parts of an elephant and picturing the unfamiliar animal as similar to a snake, a spear, a tree trunk, and so on, we all too readily jump to conclusions and confuse our models with the real world, usually when we do not pay the required attention to ambiguous signals. This propensity can be seen most strikingly in two conditions when we *cannot* properly pay attention to or test reality: dream sleep and hypnosis.

"YOU ARE GETTING SLEEPY": DREAMING AND HYPNOSIS

Hypnosis, defined as a passive conscious state in which ideas can be planted in a willing subject's mind to generate certain reactions, well demonstrates the delusory effects of using world-modeling abilities to overextrapolate from suggestive cues. As William James explained, the best hypnotic subjects become so suggestible that the hypnotist can make them believe that they are cold or hot, dirty or wet; that things eaten or drunk taste like completely different items; that everyday objects are live animals or people; and even that they have taken on an alternate personality or become an inanimate object.[5]

In his 1896 Lowell Lectures on Exceptional Mental States, James pointed out many of the similarities between hypnosis and dreaming, and apparently proposed a theory of dreaming quite similar to the one detailed here. Unfortunately, his lecture on "Dreams and Hypnotism" survived as notes only.[6] Other scientists and authors before and since James' time, including Stephen LaBerge and Emory University sleep researcher David Foulkes,[7] have proposed similar theories of dream generation.[8] The present presentation is therefore a confirmation and elaboration of a previously proposed concept, rather than a completely new and original theory as such.

Strong Associations

Although physiologically different, hypnosis and dreaming share a number of psychological characteristics.[9] Both states typically feature, despite the individual's relative mental arousal, a narrowing of attention to an attenuated focus; vivid and convincing hallucinations; forgetfulness during the state; amnesia of the state after waking; and insensibility to outward sensations.[10] The hypnotized subject's lessened sense of pain, voluntary lack of initiative, decreased self-consciousness and critical ability, and childlike reasoning are all likewise characteristic of the dreamer.[11]

The examples given earlier about everyday misperceptions suggest that the same psychological characteristics may underlie even *ordinary* perception, although usually in a much less exaggerated form.

In any case, the fact that people prove highly *suggestible* both under hypnosis and in dream sleep indicates that this effect is related to the above combination of factors. In both states, the inability to double check conflicting information against a consistent outward reality, so as to correct any faulty impressions, lets our fancies run wild. In James' terms, "Any object which remains uncontradicted is ipso facto believed and posited as absolute reality."[12]

Due to a constriction of awareness, whether imposed by a hypnotist or by the natural process of sleep, we come to react to suggestions of whatever variety as if they stood for complete realities. We perceive them as such because of the way the mind normally builds up complicated pictures from minimal cues, and react to them accordingly, like Don Quixote tilting at his windmill "giants." In our dreams, lucid or not, we respond to internally generated information just as if we were operating in the external world, mistakenly employing our usual habits of perception. As Robert Ornstein, who has similarly described dreams as resulting from world-modeling activity persisting in the absence of sensory cues, once wrote:

> Dreams are fascinating examples of the operation of the mind when isolated from the influence of the external world, in vitro, as it were. The convincing nature of dream experience shows that we see a world made for us by our brain functions, not the world "out there."[13]

Projecting Realities

In a darkened movie theater, we can focus intently on an engaging film, latching onto such stimuli as we receive until the fiction seems almost real. Similarly, when our perception of the real world diminishes after we fall asleep our own fantasies take on seeming life, so that it becomes harder to see how we are making them up, projecting them. Consider the easy method of generating a dream body and visuals in an OBE dream by imagining walking along until eventually one seems to *perceive* the world from the new location rather than just *picture* it, or how continuing to interact with a dream in the imagination will often restore a lost scene after the visuals disappear, as mentioned in a previous chapter. These simple lucid dream techniques show how thoughts and memories readily externalize into seeming perceptions under certain conditions.

More generally, when not tied to a stable outward environment the attention naturally becomes destructured and tends to wander along the paths of association or habit created by experience. We may then reflexively misinterpret any of the ideas that come to mind to represent complete realities, and without outward stimuli or a full set of memories available for comparison, our interpretations and confabulations will likely go unchecked. The dreaming brain in effect projects an imaginal environment in which its fancies can play out, an inner staging ground configured from past experience of all kinds by the world-modeling function.

This process explains both the familiarity and the strangeness of most dream scenes. They seem familiar because the images come from our own memories, yet also strange since those memories can recombine associationally to create a potpourri of new, surreal admixtures and abrupt discontinuities.

The dream ego—the character one plays in a dream—comes into existence because of habit in the same manner, since most outward perceptions depend on having a perceiving body. One may think of a door, for example, at a certain level of sleep. Soon a door appears, or appears to appear, and because doors exist in the real world, so must a real person be present to notice them. The dream ego reaches out and opens the door, the threshold is crossed, another dream has begun.

A Small Suggestion

Any factor reaching awareness should be able to influence the content of an unfolding dream exactly like a hypnotic suggestion. A wide range of such potential suggestion factors appear to govern each new step of the dream, in effect competing with one another for expression. These include thoughts and emotions, associations and expectations, and sensory and neurological intrusions. The bulk of this chapter will consider many such suggestion factors that we personally have identified, illustrating them with observations from both lucid and nonlucid dreams from our records.

WHAT'S ON YOUR MIND?

Because the perceptions have nothing physical to lock on to during sleep, one cannot easily perceive anything steadily for long in dreams. This general instability of imagery allows one's own mental activity—thoughts, emotions, and so on—to provide suggestions that affect the course of dreams, in what might be called the foreground of dream creation.

"I Think, Therefore It Is": Thoughts and Preoccupations

Although it may not always be obvious in the average half-forgotten nonlucid account, careful lucid observations demonstrate that the dreamer's shifting thoughts while dreaming can play a major role in directing content. Because people are not used to guarding against this element in mundane waking experience, it can produce completely unintended effects even in lucid dreams. For example, once when Ruth marveled at a dream tree in full spring blossom and thought about it how was really fall in waking life, the leaves of other trees nearby started to turn fall colors. Such image alterations, including whole scene shifts, often occur in response to simple thought-suggestions.

The thoughts that guide dream content do not have to take place during sleep. We often used autosuggestion *before* sleep to produce desired imagery and to help us remember particular experiments to try. The same effect can easily occur accidentally. Many people have had dreams enacting something they went to bed anticipating having to do the next day, such as getting up early to keep an appointment or make a phone call. Thus any thoughts and preoccupations immediately prior to sleep can influence one's dreams even if not remembered in the usual sense while dreaming.

Sigmund Freud introduced the term "day residues" for lingering impressions of the day's happenings that affect the night's dreams.[14] Some more modern models of dream creation also stress the importance of daily incidents in causing dreams, on the idea that the dreaming brain sorts and consolidates recent memories for long-term storage.[15] Yet such material may perhaps suggest certain imagery merely because the incidents remain on the dreamer's mind, without special processing being involved. Most dreams we can think of that have incorporated day residues have been wild concoctions not resembling the real events in any way conducive to promoting accurate memory.

We occasionally found that the *kind* of thinking performed extensively during the day, such as linear/logical or more abstract or creative mentation, had a bearing on the style of our dreams, even when their content did not reflect the day's considerations directly. This would also tend to make thoughts more important than recent memories per se in shaping dreams.

Funny Feelings: The Effects of Emotion

Emotions likewise affect dreams. Just as in the case of waking preoccupations, one's mood prior to sleep sometimes has an influence on dream content, as when some minor domestic discord turns into an exaggeratedly vitriolic dream spat. Emotions *during* dreams can equally serve as suggestion factors. When Janice, after having been laughing uncontrollably at some dream comedy skits, wanted to make up an exciting lucid story about criminals breaking into her house, the best villains her mind could come up with after all the comedic themes were Stan Laurel and Oliver Hardy armed with bottles of seltzer.

As we have already alluded, lucid dreams can prove frightening to some people for the much same reason as certain nonlucid dreams: the interpretation placed on them at the time serves as a suggestion factor, with the subsequent compliance of imagery to fit the emotion. People who have not read about lucid dreaming, or who have read mostly alarmist and occultist opinions on the subject, may be especially fearful of it and consequently create negative experiences for themselves, as with so many of Janice's early sleep paralysis incidents. But even with better information, the dreamer can set up a vicious circle of emotion and imagery, fear indulged in while awake or asleep invoking repugnant imagery which in turn sustains the fear. Janice went through a brief period of doubt and alarm regarding lucid dreaming after renewed exposure to other people's unhealthy attitudes, resulting in a number of negative incidents before she straightened out her feelings on the matter.

Most of our lucid dreams, however, have been ordinary in both emotional tone and content. Therefore the individual's particular interpretation and its emotional consequences, rather than lucidity alone, determine the ensuing positive, negative, or neutral quality of the imagery.

Here, There, and Everywhere: The Direction of Attention

Not all thoughts and emotions translate into dream imagery. It is certainly possible to think and feel, and even to imagine different scenes, without affecting dream content in the indicated direction dramatically or at all. When Jay became lucid during a dream card game, for instance, he tried to visualize a single card flying in a circle through the air, but this produced no more visible effect than would picturing it in his waking imagination.

So why do only certain thoughts and emotions influence imagery, and only at certain times? If habitual world models govern dreaming, it should come as no surprise that one can think, emote, talk to oneself, and imagine things without *necessarily* affecting dream content, since people normally do those things in waking without changing the outside world. The question then becomes, What kind of thoughts and emotions *do* change the content of waking experience, not literally perhaps but in terms of what we perceive and how it affects us?

The answer is, *those that significantly alter how we direct our attention.* Such "pre-perceptive" thoughts and emotions determine our priorities with regard to what we observe and also make the preliminary interpretations of those observations. As such they are the ones most likely to affect what happens in dreams, more so than merely picturing things happening against an already convincing background. If we hear a clopping sound out in the street in waking and think, "That sounds like a horse's hooves," when we go to the window and look out we may well find we made a mistake. But if the same sound were to occur in a dream, most of the time, the horse would be there, right on cue.

As mentioned before with regard to eliminating threatening characters, dream images generally lose coherency and disappear when attention is taken away from them and redirected elsewhere. They can become more active and start changing around when they receive too *much* attention. In one case when some workmen walked by in a dream and Janice turned to watch them, they stopped and began talking to each other, as if by her giving them attention they now had to do something. Dream images can be said to exist, in fact, only insofar as one gives them attention at all.

Janice performed a number of experiments showing how direction of attention affects dream imagery. The first time she stood around doing nothing in a dream, the locale soon filled up with an assortment of characters. When she tried this again on a later occasion, this time counting to thirty, nothing comparable happened, perhaps because she did not wait long enough or because the counting kept her mind occupied. Most of the time, if she had no special goals in a lucid dream, unexpected things would turn up vying for her attention.

Lucid dreams might be better structured overall than nonlucid dreams because the quality of attention improves when lucid. The comparative realism of scenes, objects, and characters in many lucid dreams may also be due, at least in part, to expending a higher level of critical attention on the images, which would serve to enhance and stabilize them to a point. While too much thought and attention can break up imagery, without *any* directed attention all dreams would likely be as random and unstructured as hypnagogic hallucinations, since awareness provides the cohesive element that strings a dream narrative along from moment to moment.

THE SEEDS OF THE PAST: HABIT AND POSSIBILITY

If thought, emotion and direction of attention form the foreground dimension of dream creation, then our mental habits, including perceptual habits, can be said to constitute the background. Learned narrative patterns give structure to dream plots,[16] while various associations and expectations developed from how we have directed our attention in the past form a matrix within which our present mental activity can operate. These not only make important suggestion factors but in essence control dream content for us even when we do not do so more directly.

We are seldom aware of the associative processes guiding our dreams, since such processes tend to be automatic, drummed into us by waking training. But certain strange dream images and sudden transitions that seem perplexing may nevertheless have solid bases in our personal networks of associations. Jay, for instance, once dreamed nonlucidly that his infant nephew Zachary was the size of a strawberry, complete with leaf and stem. But he could not imagine what inspired the image until Janice pointed out the rhyme link between "Zachary" and "strawberry daiquiri."

The Power of Expectation

As should be clear from previous chapters, expectations derived from waking or from prior dream experience make prime determinants of dream imagery and often limit its range. This is why developing expertise in lucid dreaming can take years of practice. The power of expectation makes it comparatively easy to recreate well-known places and people or familiar types of scenes and characters in dreams. Often reflexive in nature, expectations can be difficult to control, as when Ruth tried walking with her eyes shut in a dream, wondered if she would bump into anything, and promptly hit a chair.

The fact that dream imagery usually disappears when the dream eyes close and reappears when they open itself demonstrates expectation from waking experience at work, since those "eyes" do not really exist. The restored scene will tend to be the original one if the dream eyes do not stay shut long. If they remain closed long enough, on the other hand, a new scene might develop, especially if one has that result in mind. We often used this technique to "teleport" to new dream locations or to induce intentional false awakenings.

The frequency of *unintended* false awakenings in the experience of lucid dreamers also illustrates the effect of expectation. When they realize they are really in bed dreaming, people often naturally expect to awaken shortly. But, being solidly asleep still, they only dream of doing so. This kind of play on the expectation of waking also accounts for why trying to sleep in situations of constant disruption by others, or trying to wake up to record dreams, both tended to promote false awakenings in our experience.

On the other hand, a *lack* of guiding expectations can create blank spots in lucid dreams. When one of us did not know what to do in a lucid dream, performed certain abrupt actions like bursting through mirrors, ceilings and walls, or tried other activities with no parallel in waking experience and therefore difficult for us to picture, the lack of an immediate creative response could produce imageless discontinuities, like losing the picture on a television set.

The relatively realistic quality often associated with lucid dreams may be, besides a result of increased critical attention, yet another example of expectation at work, if becoming lucid puts one more in line with one's everyday assumptions. Stephen LaBerge has mentioned that in nearly 900 lucid dreams, he played a part other than himself in only three instances, in one of which he appeared as a magic set of china.[17] In any case, observations concerning the role of expectation in dream creation are common to many lucid dreamers, including LaBerge.[18]

Counterexpectations and Other Twists

Dreams do not always respond to one's most superficial expectations. Counterexpectations and other associations in the back of one's mind can also have their effects. This makes the picture more complex and interesting. For instance, lucid dream researcher Paul Tholey cites a dream of his in which he waited in apprehension for an "avenging figure" to come and punish him for acting violently against another character, since this fate commonly befell him after aggressive dream actions. When none appeared on this occasion, he expected to be safe for a change and elatedly made to leave the room, upon which a dire masked avenger indeed manifested.[19]

Conversely, the failure of some of Janice's dream images to live up to her initial expectations of them as hostile threats does not necessarily mean that such images had benign intents that she at first misperceived. It might indicate that, rather than responding to the suggestion of being potentially threatening, they responded to the overall context of the dream situation, or even to the suggestion that she intended to deal with them. In one example, a suspicious-looking character turned out to be only a policeman, probably because of Janice's thinking another character nearby looked like a criminal.

Suggestions from other people can also affect one's dream content. Though arbitrary outside suggestions may catch and focus the attention from time to time, as in Ruth's stray black and white dream from Chapter 1, suggestions from people one respects, including experts or authority figures, will probably have the most effect. With a bit of effort, though, we three could usually overrule outside suggestions running counter to our own experience or preferences. While Jay was running freely in one lucid dream like he usually did, he recalled Janice claiming that dream running made her tired. Then he too felt tired, but he soon got over it.

By watching out for such effects as we have been discussing, experienced lucid dreamers learn, to whatever extent, to *control* their thoughts, emotions, and expectations to guide their dream imagery and to preserve the stability of their dreams. One can concentrate to focus the will on a particular outcome, or manipulate one's reactions and direction of attention to produce a desired result. Working on both levels of dream generation, the adept lucid dreamer can commandeer the associative processes that normally propel dreams throughout an extended sequence, creating and enhancing entertaining scenarios simply by harnessing the force of suggestion. We will have much more to say about the nature of dream control in the next chapter.

OUTSIDE INFLUENCES: SENSORY AND SOMATIC CUES

External suggestion factors can likewise influence dream imagery, introducing some surprise details to the composition. These factors have long been noticed by both dreamers and dream researchers, notably French scientist Alfred Maury, who published a book on sleep and dreams in 1861.[20] Maury had an assistant place perfume under his nose, hold a burning match under his feet, tickle him with a feather, and perform other, similar experiments while he slept to see how such sensations would become incorporated into his dreams. In the above instances, he dreamed he was in a perfume shop in Cairo, walking across hot coals, and being tortured with hot pitch respectively. So although people are mostly cut off from the senses during sleep, certain sensory and somatic stimuli do intrude from time to time, and the mind can integrate these into ongoing dreams in a variety of creative ways.

Awkward Facts

The position of the body can influence dream content. Janice, a light sleeper, has often awakened in a position similar to that last taken during a dream. She could even sometimes sense correctly during a lucid dream that her dream body had taken on her actual sleeping pose. Given that bodily paralysis is a defining characteristic of REM sleep, designed to keep us from acting out our dreams,[21] it seems more likely in such cases that the dream body moves to match the physical body than that the physical body moves in parallel with the active dream body. The latter could potentially occur, though, during the occasional NREM dream, during transitions from REM to NREM sleep, or when prompted by unusually strong motor signals.[22]

Janice continually found that awkward sleep positions like having one leg bent or tucked under another impeded the movements of her dream body, making it difficult to walk, mount a horse or pedal a bicycle. This kind of problem would sometimes disappear during the course of the dream with lessened attention to it.

Not every dreamer will notice his or her body position having such clear effects on imagery, however. Mary Arnold-Forster, for instance, noted that her sleeping position apparently made "no difference whatever" with regard to her dreams of flight.[23] This distinction may indicate the greater depth of sleep of some dreamers, and their correspondingly lessened sensibility to their sleeping circumstances.

Unusual touch stimuli associated with sleeping circumstances occasionally drifted into our recorded dreams as well. A pillow pressing hard against Janice's neck created a dream in which a man kept grabbing her by the neck, and her cat's grooming itself on the bed and gently bumping into her legs led once to a protodream in which she felt sensations of being caressed.

What's That Sound?

Noises from the external world can also find their way into dreams. Many readers will have heard their phones, doorbells, or alarm clocks ring and made this information fit into their ongoing dreams instead of waking up, perhaps even transforming one kind of ring into another. Such invading noises often become modified into other, related sounds that better suit the dream context, as in the time Jay's snores translated into the sound of chalk scraping on a blackboard in Janice's school dream.

Sounds from the external world can also penetrate dreams correctly, rather than being incorporated in distorted form. Ruth heard her *own* snoring on several occasions, and Janice observed an interesting effect one time when a dream character looked up startled at the loud sound, filtering into the dream, of someone walking in the hall outside her room in reality. Occasionally, the real sounds that percolate into Janice's sleep enough to wake her up, whether direct or distorted, have seemed dramatically amplified in volume; popping noises from a fan, for instance, might magnify into explosive gunshots. This is probably because people become increasingly sensitive to small stimuli when in a quiet, still environment, and because dreams tend to exaggerate suggestions in any case.

Seeing the Light

Stephen LaBerge and other researchers have taken advantage of the mind's ability to notice small stimuli from the waking world and to weave these into the dream fabric in more or less predictable ways. LaBerge developed and marketed several portable feedback devices, the most popular of which feature a mask fitted with infrared sensors that detect the rapid eye movements characteristic of REM.[24] These devices signal with beeps and flashes when REM sleep has begun, to help the individual become lucid. Dreamers using such mechanical aids often report straight or embellished incorporations of the cues, seeing the light in their dreams as the sun, a flashbulb, or some such bright image. In one of Jay's dreams when he was trying out a prototype version, the signal took the form of a girl appearing and disappearing in a flash of light.

Janice, who often slept during the daytime, found that the brightness of her false awakening and OBE-type dreams typically varied with the amount of light present in her real external environment. Though the lighting in other kinds of dreams seemed unaffected, sleeping by day or by night almost always produced "local lucids" with the equivalent illumination. This effect seemed to relate more to sensing the light level than to remembering the time of day she went to bed, because several times she saw imagery with only one dream eye, and awakened to find the other one occluded by a pillow. Again, such effects probably reflected her tendency to sleep lightly.

When Nature Calls

Hunger, thirst, a full bladder, sexual arousal, and other physical needs and desires commonly alter the course of dreams. An intruding sensation of this sort usually leads to scenes of trying to satisfy the particular need, often successfully suggesting the sensation away while the dream lasts.[25] Bodily discomforts of various kinds, from a stuffy nose to aches and pains to an uncomfortable body temperature, can affect dream content as well. For instance, being too cold or too hot might induce dreams of snowy streets or summery beaches respectively, or, as Janice found, false awakenings in which the dreamer attempts to adjust bedclothes, a window or a thermostat.

We do not know what proportions of dream content the various common suggestion factors—mental activity, mental habits, and sensory intrusions—create or influence. Such proportions probably vary from dreamer to dreamer and from incident to incident. Sensory cues, for instance, may intrude rarely, but the likelihood of their intrusion should vary with the soundness of the sleep and the strength or novelty of the sensation. Awareness also seems to select out those external suggestion factors that best fit the context of the dream event or which the dreamer has come to notice as a matter of course. With lucidity, critical thought presumably exerts a greater influence than usual, since one can choose to ignore the emotion-laden content, habitual situations, or stray intrusions around which whole dreams might otherwise be built.

THE BRAIN AS DREAM GENERATOR

There remains yet another class of potential suggestion factors to examine: the electrical and chemical activity of the dreaming brain. This section will introduce a key scientific model of dream creation that emphasizes this physiological aspect of dreaming, the "activation-synthesis" hypothesis proposed by Harvard sleep researchers J. Allan Hobson and Robert McCarley. Their model created quite a stir when first introduced, since it implied that people could dismiss dreams as almost completely meaningless productions of the central nervous system.

The Case for Activation-Synthesis

Hobson and McCarley postulated that neurophysiology not only controls our cycling in and out of REM sleep, but determines the content of our dreams. In the near absence of external stimuli, they suggested, the brain makes a brave attempt to synthesize the disjointed information generated by the patterned activation and random firings of its own neurons, as initiated by the brainstem, the part attached to the spinal cord. Erratic eye movements stimulate the brain's visual system and make dream scenes move in a quirky fashion; streams of motor impulses inhibited from being physically acted out instead propel the dream body; and the critical faculties of the brain lag in too much of a chemical slump for us to know the difference.[26]

It is hard to say, from an *experiential* point of view, when any sleep-specific brain functioning might suggest specific dream images. Certain sensations that Janice has felt seem related to the neurological findings that Hobson and his associates have studied, although they occur more commonly at sleep onset than in what we would judge to be REM sleep. For instance, while falling asleep one time she felt an impression that her dream self, although no realistic body or scene had formed yet, was walking along, when suddenly her ankles jerked. The jerk may have been an ordinary bedtime muscle twitch and unrelated to the imagery, but possibly her brain had been sending out movement impulses and her mind translated those into the walking hallucination just before waking enough to carry out the impulses.

The high incidence of flying dreams experienced by narcoleptics in some studies indicates that a physiological determinant of some sort might be suggesting this particular image,[27] though of course many normal individuals report flying as a popular dream image too. Unusual interruptions of controlled lucid dreams imply that such factors may be involved in other instances, such as the time Jay flew into an invisible barrier in midair and had to pull himself over it, or the time Janice's dream steed spooked at some vague apparitions ahead and, refusing to go that direction, turned back the way they had come.

Since the brainstem mostly generates electrical and chemical signals *without* conscious control or modulation, we picked the above examples of unexpected impediments to control as likely cases of such signals influencing dream content. Any incomprehensible signaling detected within the brain would probably be glossed as bizarre imagery, strange sensations or uncontrolled happenings, creating the more random elements of dreams. However, a much larger class of imagery might be created by such signals. In particular, any of the many dream actions seen as external to the dream ego may well be influenced or created by the electrical activity and neurochemistry peculiar to REM, especially when such external actions run contrary to the expectations of the dreamer. For example, visitors intruding in one's bedroom, hardly an everyday occurrence in reality, are annoyingly commonplace in false awakenings, perhaps because the poorly coordinated activity of the dreaming brain suggests the presence of others.

This is not to say that dreamers lack control of how they *interpret* such signaling. Automatistic brain activity would assumably be read in the context of the dream scenario, though it might tend to suggest, in general, some form of external activity or movement. This interpretation of the activation-synthesis hypothesis would be in accordance with the general feeling of control associated with lucid dreams, as well as with the feeling that we and at least some other people have in our ordinary dreams of controlling, to a large extent, our own thoughts, reactions and activities.

A Two-Way Street

Dreams seem, in our experience, more consciously controlled than the Hobson/McCarley theory would allow as presently formulated. Were they only reflexive interpretations of electrical activity, our lucid dreams would not show such a range of control possibilities as they obviously do. We would not be able to lose scenes just by closing dream eyes or jumping through dream ceilings were an underlying physiological determinant governing all imagery. Nor, without influencing dreams by our conscious thoughts and learned mental structures, could we craft stories that advance relatively coherently *at the time* rather than being stitched together in memory after the fact from patchwork images. Discriminating between control and the lack thereof is a fairly elemental skill, even given the potential distorting effects of rationalization.

Other researchers have likewise critiqued the one-way bias of activation-synthesis. "The way the brain is actually put together," says LaBerge, "would require a two-way street as a model, allowing forebrain control of brainstem activation, and therefore allowing higher cortical functions such as thinking and deliberate action to influence the dream."[28] So while Hobson and McCarley intended their model as a theory of dream generation in its own right, we propose that random neurological activity is just one of many sources of input screened by the world-modeling function during dreaming. Such activity would most likely seem like complete nonsense were it not structured in this way. This is not to deny, of course, that all suggestion factors, including thoughts, involve neurological impulses of some kind.

Although particular extrapolations of the activation-synthesis hypothesis may be overextended, modern scientific research, and specifically Hobson's work, can be seen as consistent with our own theoretical approach. The two formulations in fact complement one another. We have simply fleshed out the "synthesis" side of the equation from a psychological rather than a physiological perspective, in the process including several additional suggestion factors we consider too important to overlook.

AUTHORITY AND OPINION: OTHER MODELS OF DREAM CREATION

Before the advent of Hobson and McCarley's theory, most professionals seem to have accepted one or another model of dream creation involving the action of an "unconscious" mind. The popular imagination embraced these formulations, as well as retaining notions that dreams represent spiritual planes of existence or come from supernatural agencies. Extended into waking thought *about* dreams, the principle of suggestion even accounts for the seeming validity, in certain instances, of these other models themselves, since the opinions of experts can affect expectation and consequently dream content.

The Eye of the Beholder: Belief as Suggestion

Given the various opinions about the nature of dreaming and lucidity, it is no wonder that different lucid dreamers experience different varieties of lucid dreams, or change styles at different stages in their development. Whether intending to exercise control or not, once the dreamer attains lucidity his or her expectations of lucid dreaming will have some control over what subsequently happens. The dreamer's beliefs about lucidity will inform the outcome of his or her lucid dreams—although within the limits of dream possibilities.

People with the vague, fantastical notions about conscious dreaming promoted by literary and occultist models of dreams as magical realities will tend to get the kind of strange experiences suited to their mindsets, as Janice once did. Similarly, altered state enthusiasts who expect lucidity to bring ecstatic dreams, healing dreams, dreams that tell the future, wise dream figures who give sage advice, mandala and white light patterns, and so on, not surprisingly at times find what they expect to find, or something which resembles what they expect. One study, for instance, found a statistical correlation between various conceptions of what an encounter with the Divine would be like and the actual lucid dreams the subjects produced.[29] It would, per the suggestion theory, be unusual if this were not the case, since one's models of dreaming should influence dream content to a certain extent.

Some people, of course, will fail to have the particular exotic types of lucid dreams they crave despite their strong desires and preoccupations. They may lack the talent for effectively programming themselves for such dreams, making their expectations eventually wane. Still, the "deep" and "mystical" lucid dreams seem to occur mostly for those highly interested in such things, although the hopes for transcendence, healing, special intuitions and sage advice may go unmet. Even if they *are* met, the individual may not be giving himself or herself enough credit for the accomplishment, instead attributing it to some source outside the ordinary self.

Cutting the Freudian Knot

The extravagant expectations of the altered-state partisans have been fostered in part by theories positing dream generation by the unconscious, that part of the psyche which supposedly processes experience independently of conscious awareness and opinion. Two major schools of thought have diverged on this matter. Classical Freudians, for one, see the unconscious as a turbulent sewer filled with unacceptable desires and repressed feelings and memories that from time to time flood forth in dreams, emotional upheavals and physical symptoms, despite the conscious mind's frantic efforts to dam them back.

Undeniably, instinctual drives, along with negative personal traits, psychiatric conditions and the desperate needs underlying them, count as suggestion factors and can manifest in dreams in various ways. However, the psychodynamic approach that Freud promoted, which stated that base impulses underlie *all* dream creation while being protectively disguised by puzzling dream symbols, cannot be true. Such needs obviously control only a minority of dreams, and are certainly not usually disguised. The beliefs and motivations that guide our thinking and behavior, in dreaming as indeed in waking, may be numerous and often contradictory, but we may as well admit them all to be ours, even if some may be only dream-specific and would seem out of character in ordinary life.

Later, Jungian-based conceptualizations transformed the unconscious from a hydraulic reservoir to a sacred well of knowledge—a "higher" or "deeper" inner self. With our spiritual betterment as its objective, the argument runs, this wise unconscious fashions meaningful messages encrypted in the language of dream symbols. If another, truer level of ourselves created dreams expressly for our enlightenment, then expectations of the miraculous like those promoted by the dream community could be warranted.

It may indeed be true that psychological complexes, intuitions, or creative inspirations, like any other thoughts or emotions, from time to time suggest specific dreams from which people can learn about themselves and the world. We can potentially have new insights while dreaming, even though we do not usually think as clearly then as when awake. However, if a significant number of people do *not* dream of suppressed, deeper or higher levels of experience, and, more importantly, if a significant proportion of *dreams* do not contain such insights—which certainly seems to be the case—then any theory which purports to encompass all the phenomena of dreaming must take into account its more general characteristics instead of overemphasizing its anomalies.

Economy of theory would argue that the mind creates all dreams in essentially the same manner. Since lucid dreams undoubtedly qualify as dreams, since they are observed and recalled better than most ordinary dreams, and since their evidence strongly upholds the suggestion theory, not the unconscious model, we personally believe this explanation of dream creation more probable. The suggestion theory of dream generation accords with the observations of lucid and nonlucid dreamers alike, including members of the dream community. The mind's habitual world modeling can stand in for the "unconscious" of the common theories, and explain the same phenomena without invoking any mysterious psychological or metaphysical operations.

"It's a Knockout": Habit vs. the Unconscious

Could it not be claimed that the parts of the brain or mind that reproduce the world while dreaming, even while attention guides more specific content, are *in effect* the unconscious of the psychoanalysts? Unfortunately to do so, although it would appeal to people who believe in such ideas, would sidestep the fact that such modeling systems, while byproducts of awareness, do not act from some motive of their own as in the psychodynamic theories, but in a strictly reflexive, mechanical manner. Our observations indicate not only that dream generation is largely automatic, driven by personal and perceptual habits, but that the only motivated element involved is one's own directed attention. Even that gets caught in a spin, taking its fancies for externalities like a cat chasing its tail for a mouse.

A wise unconscious is neither conclusively observable nor necessary for explaining the workings of the psyche. William James noted that instinctive, reflexive, and habitual acts could all *appear* as if guided by awareness.[30] He proposed that "the pursuance of future ends and the choice of means for their attainment are . . . the mark and criterion of the presence of mentality in a phenomenon,"[31] to help differentiate automatic behaviors from those truly motivated by awareness.

James also noted that any supposed "unconscious mental state" may, in fact, be explained as one of several conscious or habitual processes. Conscious ideas can be forgotten only to spring up anew disguised as insights; results similar to reasoning can be produced by habit or ingrained structural patterns; and some ideas become successively clearer with continued thought, until eventually one feels one must have understood them all along.[32] As far as more cutting-edge scientific opinion on the idea of the unconscious goes, in his *The Dreaming Brain* Hobson states flatly that he believes Freudian dream theory to be unscientific. He points out that not only was the notion of an internal censor disguising unpalatable dream content based solely on observations of patients whom Freud judged to be pathologically repressed, the concept of repression was itself based on a false model of the nervous system.

The idea did not come to an unbiased Freud after he had systematically collected dream reports from many subjects. Psychoanalytic dream theory is thus largely a speculative, *a priori* theory. And even as such it is based upon almost no evidence.[33]

The psychodynamic approach did lead to certain real progress in psychology, by indicating that biological and nonverbal mental impulses might affect thinking and behavior. However, such ideas are today better embodied in other disciplines, such as sociobiology and cognitive psychology. And despite these contributions, psychoanalysis never came close to being on proper terms with dreaming, largely because of its reliance on the concept of the unconscious.

SOUND AND FURY, SIGNIFYING . . . WHAT?

Some partisans may protest that knocking out the unconscious as the source of dreams would sacrifice the idea that dreams can be meaningful. We do not maintain that dreams must be meaningless, but suggest that a different process creates dreams than people usually consider—that dreams mean something *different* than commonly thought. Rather than dismissing the various potential influences on content, from thoughts and expectations to sensory and neurological intrusions, as pollutions of the dreaming process, we say simply that anything reaching awareness can generate dream imagery. What matters is not the particular suggestion factor, but the *mechanism* by which such suggestions translate into the hallucinations of dream experience; and that mechanism is the filtering of experience through learned patterns of perception in a state of consciousness disengaged from the outside world.

The suggestion theory has several advantages over other, better known physiological, psychological and metaphysical models of dreaming, whose originators selectively singled out specific types of cues to construct what they took for complete theoretical platforms. Not only does our perspective accord well with scientific theory, it is inclusive, explaining the particular effects emphasized by each approach—and many other effects besides—in a rational, internally consistent manner. We also like to think it makes a certain amount of intuitive sense.

We will return to a detailed consideration of the suggestion theory and perceptual habits, as well as discuss the implications of our viewpoint for dream interpretation systems, modern sleep and dream research, and the belief systems of lucid dreamers, in the second half of the book. First, we aim to clear up the confusions surrounding one of the most striking yet least understood aspects of lucidity: dream control.

Chapter 4

DREAM CONTROL

Dream control has sparked considerable controversy in the ongoing discussion surrounding lucid dreaming. Because lucidity often brings about a marked increase in control over various dream elements, some consider dream control unnatural, even potentially harmful to the psyche, while others see it as a valuable therapeutic resource. Since our own viewpoint provides a rather different vantage on the matter, this chapter will review and in large measure refute arguments from both sides of the rift. We intend to show how, *within the dream context*, control is practical, even unavoidable, but not necessarily relevant to psychodynamics. We will also draw on our own expertise to introduce the scope of the interesting experimentation that lucid control enables.

THE DREAM CONTROL CONTROVERSY

Most of the debate concerning possible effects, positive or negative, of control has taken place among members of the dream community, people who dedicate themselves to the study of dreams because they believe such experiences especially meaningful and important. These include dream interpreters of various persuasions, dream researchers, authors of books on dreaming, and interested lay people, many of whom form groups and societies to exchange dreams and their thoughts about them. Having vested interests in dreams, such people not surprisingly hold strong opinions about them, making for some lively disputation.

Expert Witnesses? Lucidity on Trial

Many traditional clinicians believe that the unconscious mind both keeps track of crippling complexes and provides the means to repair them. They argue that control interferes with a dream's natural interpretability and with the work of the unconscious in producing dreams. "From my clinical standpoint," claims one psychoanalyst, "lucid modification of uncomfortable dreams can obscure the clarifying possibilities of the dreams—and can offer the dreamer little more than the joy of extraordinary control or reassurance."[1] Such people may see flying away from or manipulating unpleasant situations in dreams as escapist avoidance of the mental difficulties they think are symbolized in dream predicaments. This escapism would be detrimental to the psychological healing and personal development potentials assumed of dreams.

Others in the dream community, usually those experienced with lucidity themselves, take the opposite stance and argue that control can *enhance* dreaming's supposed integrational and problem-solving functions. Some believe that lucidity fosters the resolution of inner conflicts and psychological issues, because the conscious ego can participate actively and willingly in uniting with the contents of the unconscious as presented in dreams.[2] Others, such as Patricia Garfield, encourage lucidity since it allows the pursuit of creative answers to a dreamer's questions right at the assumed source of creativity.[3]

Even those in favor of dream control impose restrictions on the extent and kind of control permissible.[4] This is because both the "pro" and "con" points of view, while superficially contradictory, nevertheless argue from similar assumptions. These include the ideas that dreams perform some useful function and that their specific contents must be important; that dreams supply pertinent data about one's past and present psychological states, usually in symbolic form; that dreams wholly or largely arise from an unconscious mind; and that ordinary dreaming is essentially different than lucid, controlled dreaming.

Objections Overruled

Even without considering the results of controlled dreams themselves, several objections can be raised at once to these assumptions, especially as construed to paint control in a negative light. First, no one has yet proven what the natural function of dreaming is. Many of the functions considered, psychological and physiological alike, seem highly speculative, as later chapters will show. In any case, lucid dreams comprise only a small part of remembered dream output and an even smaller portion of the total number of dreams a person actually has. "Normal" dreaming patterns and whatever function they possibly perform will not be altered to any significant extent by dreamers becoming lucid from time to time or by exercising greater control during lucid incidents, and there should be no dearth of unaltered dreams for therapists to analyze.

Second, there are numerous schools of dream interpretation and potentially as many interpretations of a particular dream as there are analysts to analyze it, not to mention the diverse folkloric interpretations a given dream might evoke worldwide. "Interfering with interpretability," then, must be considered a concept largely in the eyes of the would-be interpreter. The question of why lucid or controlled dreams cannot themselves be interpreted remains inadequately addressed, perhaps because relatively few people experience them, or because few psychoanalytic authorities understand them. Lucid dreams have many spontaneous elements, and the lucid aspect itself *could* be considered to reflect a dreamer's desire for knowledge, control, and self-mastery, for instance—or to reflect the dreamer's disregard for certain opinions regarding dreams.

Third, the notion that an unconscious mind or other higher source within the psyche puts together intentional, vital messages for the conscious mind—or that of an accommodating therapist—has been questioned even within psychiatric circles.[5] Some researchers, like Stephen LaBerge, say that both the conscious and unconscious minds have to be involved in the dream-creation process, since if dreams were completely unconscious phenomena people would not be *able* to exert any kind of control over them, let alone remember them.[6]

The previous chapter presented a different theory of dreaming, the suggestion theory, which eliminates the idea of the unconscious mind altogether. This theory depends not on the traditional psychoanalytic view of discrete conscious and unconscious processing of reality, but on a perceptual or habit-based model of how the brain constructs reality using its world-modeling function—the acquired, interrelated mental structures that interpret input, guide our responses, and shape experience. From such a perspective, dream control need not be posited as destructive at all. It could even be a developmental breakthrough for patients in therapy to start taking responsibility for their dreams rather than remain the victims of their own entrapping mental habits.[7]

Fourth and finally, one should not automatically assume lucidity and control particularly unnatural. Consider that, in general, most people *naturally* forget most of their dreams, yet few in the dream community object to people making extra efforts to remember, record, and mull over dreams. Surely these activities could be construed as unnatural, so where should the line be drawn? To remember dreams is to start along the road to control, since any attention turned towards dreams, whether asleep or awake, can end up affecting them.

Although many people find the concept of lucid dreaming quite baffling, others, including young children, spontaneously have lucid dreams with a fair frequency. The ability to become lucid and even to control dreams with great skill may therefore be part of our *natural* human endowment, just like the capacity to write literature, though few may do either. To argue that people should not learn to become lucid and control their dreams would then be similar to maintaining that they should not learn to read and write because of course the natural state of affairs *must* be better.

The Popular Judgment

Interestingly, in our own survey of some sixty lucid dreamers, we found that almost 100 percent considered experimentation with control justified. A few respondents, especially spokespeople within the dream community, did qualify their agreement, maintaining, for instance, that people should try it "only if they want to." These results would seem to make fears about control more typical of theorizers than of ordinary people interested in lucid dreaming.

We can see why analysts might still have reservations about a phenomenon as new to scientific inquiry as lucidity. After all, they are used to working with imbalanced individuals, for some of whom lucid dreaming might not be a good idea for one reason or another. This does not mean, however, that the population at large has to accept their clinical cautions, since not all share their particular doctrinal biases and concerns.

GONE TO THE DOGMAS: DREAM CONTROL AND PSYCHOTHERAPY

Some mental health professionals, most notably Paul Tholey,[8] have taught their clients to use lucid dream control as part of an overall course of treatment. From this point of view, interpretation becomes possible *within* a dream, perhaps more effectively than within an analyst's office. In the dream milieu, the lucid individual can dialogue with dream characters directly about various personal issues. The dreamer can also pose questions to the imaginal situation at hand or otherwise take an active part in the dream's interpretation while still dreaming. For instance, in one dream Janice came across a console that she decided to take to be the control board of her mind, and reset its levers for regulating emotional circuitry to produce maximum happiness. Though we do not consider the results more meaningful than any other arbitrary interpretations we might impose on dream content, we have sometimes found such techniques interesting to try.

Control Yourself, Not Your Dreams?

Stephen LaBerge exemplifies the perspective of those who believe lucid dreams important and control potentially of benefit. Trying to strike a reasonable stance on the control issue, LaBerge has suggested that dreamers resolve rather than attempt to escape from dream conflicts, but that they control the reactions of their own dream egos rather than "magically" manipulate any of their imagery, adding that the latter type of control does not always work. He writes:

> We are free to regulate our responses to dream content, and what we learn in so doing readily applies to our waking lives as well . . . . For this reason, among others, I would advise the lucid dreamer who would be wise: "Control yourself, not your dreams."[9]

This "hands-off" approach to control presents certain problems, however. For example, LaBerge recommends changing one's attitude rather than controlling characters by, say, turning them into vermin because the latter would not be practical in waking life. Yet in waking life people commonly save face by doing just that, not literally perhaps but in the imagination—such as calling an obnoxious boss a "pig" under one's breath. Such reconceptualization is not so impractical, then, though maybe not so mature.

LaBerge also expresses concern that those who learn to solve problems magically in dreams might come to hope to do so in waking as well. This seems unlikely for most people, given that lucidity means being able to tell the difference between dreams and waking. Besides, every day we all employ situation-specific behaviors, some of which would be completely inappropriate in other settings, without any such confusion. We know we can safely shout in indignation at a baseball game but not at the office, for instance. Dreamers should, therefore, be able to control their imaginary aggressors while realizing that they cannot do so quite so magically in the waking world.

Moreover, in dreaming, changing one's attitude often *constitutes* controlling the characters because it prefigures their responses. Janice discovered that she had a moment of leverage during which she would assess the appearance of a newly arriving character, then react according to her interpretation of it. The character, in turn, usually responded in accordance with those expectations. So when a Frankenstein monster appeared in a dream mall one time, Janice knew that her reaction would determine how it behaved. Rather than running away and being chased as in similar dream situations in the past, this time she went right up to the creature and shook its hand, and it acted like a friendly, sophisticated gentleman, walking and talking with her and proposing a business partnership.

Lucidity permits volitional manipulation of the interpretive process in whatever way seems appealing at the time. By minding our thoughts and actions we could strongly influence a character's behavior, even to the point of deliberately fabricating danger where none necessarily existed just for the fun of it. If Janice were to decide in a later lucid dream that she *wanted* to be chased by a Frankenstein monster for a thrill, she could arrange it with little difficulty.

Dream Control as Self-Control

Other, more subtle flaws mar the "control yourself, not your dreams" approach too. It does seem more lucid to control one's reactions to troublesome dream characters, whether by ignoring them or modulating one's expectations of them, than to waste time and effort in conflict with them. However, dream control is, at bottom, self-control, since dreams come from our own minds. If controlling "them" or "it" does not always work, as LaBerge maintains, it is precisely because we often falsely conceptualize dream imagery as external to ourselves. Not only can we not control our dream selves without affecting dream imagery too, we cannot control the imagery without affecting ourselves, since such control *requires* monitoring our own thoughts and perceptions. It makes little difference, then, whether the dreamer wrestles the fear to master the monster or wrestles the monster to master the fear, since both come down to essentially the same thing; the one is a projection of the other.

In other words, although the things we perceive in dreams may be fashioned at least as much from our memory stores and ingrained mental constructs as from our immediate thoughts and feelings, and so seem convincingly independent, virtually all of their source suggestions ultimately lie in our heads. Particular characters, images and situations occur due to habits, beliefs, fears, assumptions, associations and expectations *of our own*. One aspect of self-control must therefore be control of dream characters and the dream environment—though dream characters, not surprisingly, sometimes seem to have different ideas.

One wonders, however, how many lucid dreamers practicing extensive control experience difficulty with dream characters rebelling against that control before such a possibility gets put into the dreamers' heads. Jay had no such problem, and Janice's soap opera characters started asserting independence only after some of her correspondents suggested that she let them make their own decisions. While most of the characters Ruth polled seemed averse to the very concept of dream control, and some have actually attacked her over the issue, she has also gotten them to find control quite agreeable simply by expecting and willing them to say "yes."

On a related note, many lucid dreamers report that their characters act decidedly indignant at being dismissed as mere figments.[10] Of course one would expect beings with sentience, a quality that people impute onto dream characters just as they do onto puppets, to feel insulted at being snubbed, which would tend to engender such responses. Yet while we certainly experienced similar reactions, we also came across characters who fully accepted being dependent on us. So if one alters one's expectations of independent intelligence, one might find characters quite amenable to the idea of being unreal or different than the dreamer in essential ways, much as they seem amenable to just about every other suggestion thrown their way.

Have You Hugged Your Monster Today?

The ease of changing the behavior of characters has profound implications for the psychological-integration school of lucid dream theorists, which maintains that dreamers should show love and respect to any inner enemies as personified in contrary dream characters. Via this dream conflict resolution, the story goes, one can symbolically assimilate repressed or unaccepted aspects of oneself, and solve the psychological issues that inspired the dramatized conflict in the first place. Far more likely, from our perspective, the change in attitude simply has an equivalent, reflexive effect on the characters, with no psychodynamic implications whatsoever.

One does not have to have enemies with whom to battle and reconcile in lucid dreams at all, if one gains control of one's reactions early enough to shape an encounter positively from the outset, as in Janice's "Frankenstein" example. Can a dream conflict represent anything if it takes place or not only on the basis of a particular choice of dream behavior? Moreover, a direct effort of will and imagination, without any kind of interaction that might be taken as symbolic, can likewise change hostile character behavior dramatically, as when Jay successfully willed a dream woman to stop choking him and be friendly.

The outlook LaBerge and others promote also recognizes the efficacy of altering imagery by "magical" means, such as purifying a menacing zombie with holy water or making a deadly serpent into a beautiful butterfly. It further presumes that to change a dream image directly in this way will somehow change the undesirable underlying pattern of thought, which will be mastered permanently by one's actions.[11] Transforming negative dream images to positive, it is believed, symbolically transforms negative personality traits to positive or otherwise solves real psychological problems. LaBerge further argues that the dreamer does not even have to interpret the dream to achieve integration by either the reconciliation or alteration methods. Citing personal examples featuring each technique, he asserts that while the dream conflicts he resolved may have depicted actual personality conflicts, he "was able to resolve them without even having to know what they represented"; his "acceptance or transformation of the dream characters represented a symbolic acceptance or transformation of whatever unidentified emotion, behavior, or role they stood for."[12]

To say that personal integration can be attained outside awareness and with such facility strikes us, we must say, as a rather facile assumption, based on the further assumption that dream images symbolize psychological affects in the first place. Dream images readily shift around on their own, after all, due to instability prompted by the vagaries of association, mixed emotions, neural activity, and so on. Why should deliberate change make any difference?

The whole notion that dream control can have any direct effect on reality comes down, we fear, to magical thinking. As far as we can tell, changing one dream image into another only changes it on the level of emergent thought and perception, and only temporarily at that. Consider the following analogy. If Jay were to drive by a farm one day and see a cow, then later dream about the scene and deliberately change the cow into a horse, he could be quite confident that he would not forever alter his conception of cows as distinct from horses, nor even alter the specific memory of the barnyard scene. The only effect on his memory would be that now he would recall having changed one animal into another in a dream and know he could do that—a new dream control accomplishment.

If Jay's memory processes would barely be affected by his dream action, his psyche would be even less so. It seems highly unlikely that his nurturing instincts, represented by the cow, would be replaced by aggressive, horselike urges when he woke up, as the "transform your dream symbols" school would suggest, since the three of us have never seen such changes occur. It is even more far-fetched to suggest that the real cow would change into a horse or that the farmer would mysteriously decide to swap livestock because of Jay's actions. Yet the second line of magical thinking is the reductio ad absurdum of the first, and not at all uncommon among dreamers, given the popularity of attempts at healing and psychic contact through dreams.

Our personal experience with recurrent dream settings fatally contradicts such assumptions. Damage that Ruth and Janice on impulse inflicted on their local lucid dream sites did not even reappear in later *dreams*, let alone affect their psyches or the outside world. Janice often demolished whole buildings in her dream neighborhood and found them intact on her next dream visit, even if that occurred only a few minutes later. When a change of whatever sort *did* recur in subsequent serial dreams, the effect seemed to hinge on what she wanted or expected. This evidence again strongly supports the suggestion theory rather than the standard psychodynamic models of dreaming.

In sum, the problems resolved by the reconciliation and alteration techniques described above are *dream* problems. Even if they have been inspired by real ones, resolving them will not automatically cure the real ones. Whatever increase in well-being some adherents may have experienced as a result of their endeavors, we did not notice any lasting changes in our psyches from sentimentalizing characters or from manipulations of what we pretended to be symbolic imagery, let alone the vastly greater quantity of imagery we did not consider in such terms. Any correlation between dream elements and psychological issues has to be assumed and imposed by the dreamer, because it is by no means necessarily obvious or internally consistent. The whole premise would also seem to contradict LaBerge's other advice regarding *not* controlling one's dreams.

Character Assassination

Aggression against dream characters does not go down well at all in certain circles. Those theorists who issue mandates to lucid dreamers to befriend or positively transform their dream enemies tend to admonish that violent behavior against imaginary imagery will alienate corresponding components of the psyche. Robert Van de Castle, formerly of the University of Virginia Medical School, has gone so far as to write, "To murder a dream character would be to commit a form of intrapsychic suicide."[13]

Such concern seems to be based on a combination of waking-world ethics and what amounts to superstitious deification of the unconscious. We feel that any code of behavior in lucid dreams should be a matter of personal taste and principle—and context-specific taste and principle at that—rather than of wariness regarding unproven psychological aftereffects. Some lucid "aggression," after all, occurs only to affirm that one indeed recognizes the difference between dreams and reality. Jay demonstrated this concept quite strikingly when he stepped on a dream dog and pressed down until his foot met the ground, then made the dog melt back together again and petted it.

One might equally argue, if positing that dream actions have any psychological aftereffects at all, that aggressive behavior would beneficially subdue the negative personal qualities encoded in dream elements. Indeed, not all dream psychologists have towed the pacifist line. Upon a time some instead adopted approaches that hearkened back to certain shamanistic perspectives, based on the writings of anthropologist Kilton Stewart concerning the Senoi people of Malaysia. Stewart noted that, according to the Senoi, "every person should and can become the supreme ruler and master of his own dream or spiritual universe, and can demand and receive the help and cooperation of all the forces there."[14]

Stewart's work informed a highly popular approach to dreamwork before later investigations showed his accounts to bear little resemblance to the actual beliefs of the culture he professed to have studied.[15] Patricia Garfield, for one, published an extensive set of prescriptions following the "Senoi" system.[16] She recommended fighting and even killing aggressive dream characters, thereby converting their negative energies to positive and making allies of their spirits or essences. Garfield also encouraged indulging in sexual relations in dreams as often and intensely as possible, as a means to connect with parts of oneself in need of integration.

As it turns out, though, we have inflicted damage on dream characters with no demonstrable effect on ourselves, negative *or* positive, which the theorists would have trouble taking into account except as evidence of our own opacity. And although we have defeated our share of dream aggressors, none ever rose to vow allegiance as a result, and we see no reason to take sex acts in dreams at anything more than face value either. Any seeming confirmations of such idealistic hypotheses may tell more about one's belief system than actuality, since even supposedly "lucid" dreams can reflect back one's own mind to oneself—or what certain authorities have put into it.

To take a simple example, the idea that dream characters can be supernatural beings of various kinds, from devils, angels and exalted guides to denizens of the astral plane or the abode of the dead, has by no means disappeared in contemporary society. Imagination and expectation can produce characters that don any such excitatory guise. These manifestations more firmly etch the source ideas in the minds of some people, who may not consider that dream entities of a type in which they strongly believe may be no more real than the vampires or other discounted monsters haunting their nightmares. Such widespread motifs can also influence dream content from time to time even when in opposition to one's everyday beliefs, as we personally can attest. Moreover, the dream world will respond equally well to entirely idiosyncratic and temporary notions regarding the nature of its inhabitants. Janice's characters often professed to be the fairies of European folklore, and one time some characters reacted as if a secret had gotten out when she accused them of being self-organizing networks of brain cells.

As we have already pointed out with reference to OBEs, some people see the dream-world populace as composed of the spiritual doubles of living individuals, a notion with roots in shamanistic thought.[17] Dream characters can be quick to take up this notion as well. Given the prevalence of nonlucidity, probably more often than not dream characters simply react to the default assumption that they are real people in the real world. The point of all this, then, is that dream characters are heavily influenced, and thus to whatever extent controlled, by the expectations of the dreamer. If they can react in accordance with all these wild notions, they could certainly from time to time reflect back, without really proving, more commonly accepted ideas that they represent parts of the psyche. The principle of suggestion limits the validity of psychotherapeutic ideas of dream characters just as it does many more obviously questionable folkloric and New Age perspectives.

EVERYTHING'S UNDER CONTROL

One member of the dream community has stated that "control somewhat violates the existential nature of the dream, the fundamental nature of dreaming."[18] The suggestion theory would argue that, given the nature of world modeling, it is impossible to *avoid* control in the broad sense, because we all endeavor to interpret, comprehend and react to everything we perceive in dreams, as indeed we do in real life. This, in turn, inescapably affects dream content, to the extent that even believing that one is not controlling a dream would itself be a form of control with certain effects on content. Therefore, from this perspective, dreams are *already* controlled, and lucidity merely fosters greater awareness of this basic fact.

The Hidden Dimension

Dream control occurs as a matter of course in nonlucid as well as lucid dreams. To travel from one place to another, to look for and find an item, or to use an object in a dream all constitute control. Nonlucid dreamers nevertheless lack the perspective which would enable them to exercise such control beyond certain limiting factors. Generally, because dreamers believe in the reality of what they experience, they try to control the dream world just as they would the waking one—through physical efforts.

In dreams these take the form of actions by the dream ego, the character the dreamer plays. Such efforts do not always succeed very well, exactly because the dream is *not* real and therefore responds in ways typical of dreams, not in ways typical of the real world. Images change or disappear in the space of a thought; an unresolved dream body or slowly responding visuals make progress difficult; a clouded memory creates confusions; an anomalous situation enhances anxiety. So the average dreamer cannot read a book or even find it a moment later, cannot see well or turn on a light, cannot remember what happened yesterday or what year it really is, and cannot figure out how he or she got into such a mess.

This sorry state of affairs does not, however, mean we do not influence our dream content. Per the suggestion theory, dreams are conscious experiences created by our own awareness interacting with whatever suggestion factors happen to present themselves while we sleep, as mediated by ordinary habits of perception. Dream control thus exists at the most fundamental level in the form of processing information through the filters of our subjective expectations and assumptions. Our habitual associations guide and propel dream development, and we further steer this development by direction of attention and choice of reaction if nothing else.

Moreover, the comparative ease of controlling images mentally after attaining and practicing lucidity implies that all dreams operate to a large extent under the influence of the dreamer's thoughts, erratic though those may be. In other words, we cannot help but control our dreams, but we do not as easily control our thoughts and their effects, which would make the process more precise. So when Janice ran up her driveway in one lucid dream and thought about how doing so in reality would set all the neighborhood dogs to barking, her dream self abruptly became a golden retriever, but she later had difficulty trying to replicate this effect intentionally.

People do not usually realize the nature or extent of the dream control they practice because of being fooled by the illusions of dreams, both in sleep and in waking. In dreams, we usually remain unaware of our state and believe ourselves to be acting in the real world, or at least in something that exists independently of our minds. Our thoughts and subsequent actions therefore do not match our actual circumstances. We assume dream situations to be more out of control than they really are, since people, objects, and the environment exist independently of us in reality. Further, since we do not typically look to see how our thoughts do control our *perceptions* of external reality in waking—which they do because of the power of the interpretations we place on events—we do not look to see how they control what goes on in dreaming.

In waking, on the other hand, we often think dreams must be significant *to* the real world, because we cannot easily credit that we ourselves create such bizarre occurrences. If *we* do not create them, then some higher power or some "unconscious" part of the mind must create them for us. If such sources create dreams, it must be for one or more of several purposes: our physical, emotional, intellectual, or spiritual benefit. Otherwise, we would not have been given such a capacity, by God or evolution or both. So popular reasoning seems to run.

Yet if dream imagery shifts around in response to shifts of attention and changing thoughts and expectations as readily as the examples in this book suggest, how much room remains for the determinism required by traditional approaches? In one series of Lucidity Institute experiments, each time Ruth turned on her heel 180 degrees the new dream view seemed vague, only to fill in details before her eyes like a developing photograph. Upon completing a turn the original view would be restored, but never exactly the same as before. Attention made the new view develop just as lack of attention allowed the old one to mutate.

Even a seemingly insignificant act like making an offhand comment or staring into space in a dream, which one decides to do volitionally whether lucid or not, can potentially change a scenario's whole subsequent course. Unexpected effects can crop up at any time due to the tension between attention and instability. So when Janice exclaimed "Coach horses!" upon seeing some carriages in the distance in one lucid dream, her unintended wish was her command, for suddenly two black coach horses stood against a nearby wall. Dreams are in this way much more indeterminate than reality.

Taking Charge

People often learn, probably through trial and error or sheer repetition rather than reflectiveness, many kinds of direct intervention in their ordinary dreams that seem to be matters of tacit lucidity. These may include including flying, replaying scenes, willing changes, working "magic," creating happy endings, and so on. Thus dream control of even the most controversial kind, that of governing dream situations, characters, and scenes, occurs outside what would be considered lucid dreams in the strictest sense. Although even nonlucid dreams can include some degree of control, more control becomes possible after achieving lucidity because lucidity gives one a deeper understanding of dreams based on new, more perceptive observations. Extra options for manipulating imagery become available with a greater awareness of the principles by which dream imagery naturally develops and transmutes.

Becoming cognizant of the mechanisms that guide dream creation helps balance out the natural but erroneous belief in the dream's "reality." It also allows one to substitute conscious deliberation for automatism, to take more direct command over dream events. By taking into account the special characteristics of dreams and by controlling the dreaming *mind* rather than just the dream ego, people can learn to manipulate imagery more effectively than ordinarily possible. Lucidity and lucid experimentation bring about a more explicit awareness of the dimension of control, a greater understanding of the extent to which we *already* control our dreams.[19] With such an understanding comes the greater *flexibility* of control that would naturally result from an increased perception of what is actually happening. The dreamer has more choice as to how to utilize the control already implicitly employed. The question then changes from "How do I know when I should intervene in a dream?" to "How can I extend lucidity?"

We create our dreams, and our perceptions within them may usually be quite automatic, as in waking; but what we create is confused largely because *we* are confused. Increased lucidity and the increased control it enables can help one cut through the gnarly state of dreaming consciousness—to take charge of, rather than be deceived by, one's perceptions. Knowing that their own mental processes create the flow of dreams, lucid dreamers can learn to redirect those processes to suit their own purposes by intentionally making use of the same mental tricks that normally allow them to be deceived. Thus they can ad-lib an explanation for an anomaly rather than rationalize one, impose a story background on a situation rather than have a false memory of one, or make deliberate changes to various images rather than accepting changes from undirected instability. Why not use dream methods to solve dream problems? This is not to say that direct lucid dream control is always desirable or has no limits, but it would certainly qualify as a cognitive skill worth exploring.

"I Never Thought of That"

Both the specific aspects of control considered controversial and the negative loading of the term in general these days seem to be matters of cultural bias, not critical thinking. Both the "control-is-bad" and the "control-is-good" belief systems feature numerous logical flaws and a peculiar narrowing of perspective. In addition, dream control has many facets besides performing unusual feats, managing difficult characters and situations, and manipulating the dream environment, most of which are neither regarded as controversial among lucid dreamers nor even necessarily recognized as means of influencing dreams. Remembering dreams, mastering induction techniques, recovering waking intentions or other memories when asleep, and remaining emotionally balanced while lucid all constitute control. Control also includes preventing premature awakenings, recognizing and utilizing false awakenings, maintaining lucidity in the face of instability, extending lucidity in length and scope, learning flexibility in dream situations, and gaining command of one's thoughts and impulses. Only by experimenting in all these dimensions can one learn how far dream control can truly be taken.

EXPLORING EVERY AVENUE: DREAM CONTROL EXPERIMENTS

The three of us carried out innumerable experiments to find out the kinds of control possible for us in lucid dreams, learning a great deal about the nature of dream content along the way. This section will highlight some of our findings with regard to the dream self, the sensory aspects of dreams, dream places and objects, and dream characters. A concluding section will discuss the limitations of dream control that we came up against in our experimentation.

The Central Actor

All components of a dreamed experience—sensory impressions, actions performed, thoughts, feelings, etc.—tend to imply the presence of a body, since those elements derive from waking-world experiences that originally entered awareness through the physical body. So more often than not one eventually has an embodied dream ego through which to act in the imaginal world. But both dream world and dream ego are internally generated constructs that only reproduce realities. As a result, the dream body can display some unusual properties on close examination. For example, in one

Lucidity Institute experiment in which participants had to study their hands while lucid, most—including ourselves—noticed increasingly bizarre variations such as extra fingers appearing.[20]

The dream self responds readily to deliberate manipulations as well. We performed extensive distortions of the dream body, such as elongating our limbs, pressing one arm through the other, and even removing body parts. Such tricks took nothing more than a little concentration and the ability to get over any tendency to think of the dream body as something real; they did not hurt in the least. Some of our favorite experiments involved examining our reflections in dream mirrors and willing various changes. By controlling the reactions of her characters, Janice could make herself exceptionally attractive or even invisible, and she and Ruth had some success with transforming into animals and mythical beasts in their dreams as well.

The dream ego will by no means necessarily prove ordinary in it mental aspects any more than in its appearance. It is common to behave in a very uncharacteristic manner in dreams, as if keying into behavioral types beyond the ken of one's usual waking habits. Even when nonlucid or tacitly lucid, we often displayed a far freer attitude towards risk-taking, impropriety and immorality than that experienced within the strictures of waking reality. When lucid, of course, we could choose to enact any of a variety of emotional states, moods and behaviors for amusement, or to play the starring role in entertaining story dreams, even if it entailed taking on a different age or gender. This underscores the fact that the dream ego is really little more than another character in the dream.

To return to LaBerge's dictum, then, it is impossible in yet another sense to control oneself without controlling the dream, because the self through which one lives the dream is unquestionably part *of* the dream. The dream body is completely unreal, and even a person's self-conception while dreaming is often markedly different than in waking, influenced by the dream context and the general reduction in mental wherewithal that is characteristic of dreams. Consequently, any efforts to separate control of oneself—or of the projection that one takes for oneself—from control of the other characters and the environment will simply reinforce the illusion of the dream as somehow external to the dreamer. Ruth made exactly this confused misidentification of herself with her dream counterpart in one dream in which she stole some cake from a counter. At first she thought that if anyone accused her of theft she could claim that she had a right to any food she created, but then she considered that her dream ego did not create it, her sleeping mind did.

If the dream ego exists, bodily and mentally, only as part of the dream, then the self we all have to control must be the *dreaming self*.[21] To remain mindful of the dreaming self—that slugabed having the dream—instead of falsely identifying with the illusory character one has become, lucidity must be tantamount to understanding how one *is* generating and therefore controlling the dream. Taking an active stance in the dreaming process by deliberately extending that control serves as a reminder of who is creating the experience, and with the proper focus will tend to support the memory of one's real identity. If people care to discuss the possibility of integrating the self through dream lucidity at all, then the most pertinent form of integration may simply be building a bridge between the sleeping and the waking minds—that is, becoming lucid.

Overnight Sensations

Dreams only rarely manifest the complete range of sensory representation that people can, at least potentially, experience all at once in waking life. One thing that became abundantly clear in our lucid endeavors is that the direction of attention largely creates and dissolves the procession of illusory sensory information perceived in dreams. If we attended to one image, that image endured only until we turned our attention to something else. Given this basic tendency of the inconstant dream world to follow the lead of attention, one can control the sensory aspects of dreams simply by looking for them and, in fact, cannot avoid doing so.[22]

For one thing, concentrating on the sensory details of a dream almost invariably enhances them; visuals will come in sharper, colors grow brighter, and so on. Color, like any other sensory effect, can come and go depending upon the attention given to it, so the black and white dreams that some people claim as their normal style may simply result from not focusing sufficiently on color. All three of us managed to change the colors of dream objects by concentration, or added color to black and white imagery. We found it much more difficult to add light to a dark scene by such means, and dream light switches, of course, were seldom of any help.

Interestingly, though, manipulating the dream eyes by rubbing them, putting on imaginary glasses, and the like could improve the poor visuals that would generally accompany our sleep-onset lucid dreams. If it can be suggested away so easily, some of the darkness and lack of clarity that so often plagues lucid dreams may result from the fact that one can only pay attention to so much at a time rather than from any more specific limitation set by the brain or body. Certain aspects of dream vision may, however, be physiologically based, because if we intentionally held our dream eyes closed for long enough, visual imagery often obtruded eventually anyway.

The sounds in our lucid dreams were quite realistic, usually seeming fully directional in space despite being only in our heads and including wide ranges of pitch and volume. However, actions and their resulting sounds occasionally seemed asynchronous, and Ruth and Jay thought their dreams skipped a lot of incidental background noises; in Jay's case at least, this probably reflected his waking ability to tune out such distractions. Similarly, while Ruth could often add realistic scents to dream flowers and such by mental effort, Janice hardly ever noticed any odors in her dreams even when she tried, perhaps because her waking sense of smell seems to be duller than usual. All of us could, however, use concentration to enhance the flavor and texture of dream food to some extent, which was useful since dream food tends to be on the bland side.

While the sense of touch seemed fairly well-developed in our dreams, it did not always meet waking norms, it was particularly hard to reproduce the sensation of being wet, for instance. Perceived temperatures in our lucid dreams seldom approached the levels of heat or cold we would expect from the waking world.

Curiously, we varied markedly in our perception of dream pain. Janice and Jay seldom felt pain in their dreams, and when they did, the sensation did not rival in intensity or duration what anyone would endure in waking life under the same circumstances. Ruth, on the other hand, seemed far more subject to dream pain, and tended to avoid actions that might cause it. Although most people have a fairly automatic prejudice to direct attention towards pleasure and away from pain, we all did attempt to induce the sensation on numerous occasions for experimental purposes. Overall, deliberate efforts to injure ourselves in dreams seemed less likely to hurt than accidents, perhaps because our world models did not easily allow for intentional self-injury.

Simulating even unfamiliar movement like flying in dreams, on the other hand, usually presented few difficulties, one exception being the perennial problem of having a hard time moving early on in a sleep-onset lucid dream. In several instances we noted convincing visceral and vestibular sensations in our lucid dreams, like queasiness, balance or its absence, and pressures in the ears and head such as those produced by being under water or falling. Such subtle sensations probably reproduce best when the dreamer performs a familiar kinesthetic activity from waking, or at least something evoking a familiar activity. Conversely, the general absence of such details may account for much of the unreal character of many dreams. Overall, the kinds of sensory information which people commonly seek out actively in waking, such as major visual, kinesthetic and tactile cues, seem to be those most often noticed in dreams, probably exactly because dream creation requires the active participation of the dreamer. Perceptions which are normally received more as a matter of happenstance, such as odors and background noises, tend to drop out of the picture.

Land of Illusion: The Dream Environment

The features that distinguish the dream environment from the real world will no doubt seem familiar to most people who remember their dreams. Settings and objects alike can range from realistic to indistinct, from mundane to bizarre, even mixing these attributes within the same scene. Dream appliances of any kind seldom work properly, which is not surprising since they do not really exist. Worse still, because of dream instability, triggered by such factors as stray associations or the fluctuating electrical activity of the brain, one object or scene can unexpectedly metamorphose into another or disappear altogether. Unstable shifts are especially likely if the attention gets diverted, but even an *increase* in attention can set off transformations. The strangeness of dream objects tends to multiply with continued scrutiny; in one nonlucid dream a pile of dirt on Janice's windowsill seemed bigger every time she examined it, until it actually contained whole seashells and fossils and the woodwork featured ornate molded fish.

Memory seems to inform dream imagery in a somewhat unusual fashion. In our dreams a single location could combine the features of two known real places, or retrospectively look like someplace other than what we assumed it to be at the time. And though we usually did better in recreating the known than the unknown in dreams, a familiar scene might on close inspection fail to agree with our memory in many details. When dreaming, what initially appears familiar can become strange when stray associations connect with random factors that one feeds attention, since focusing attention on any divergences with reality will almost surely intensify them. Conversely, unfamiliar settings and objects may increasingly come to resemble familiar ones, due to thinking about the similarities or to sheer force of habit.

Being by nature strange, intangible and unstable, the dream world responds readily to alterations of any of the suggestion factors that shape it. Once we became familiar with effects such as those outlined above, we were able to utilize suggestions of various kinds to shape the dream environment as we chose. For example, when Ruth wanted to take a dream swim, she would enter the water fully dressed, knowing that her clothes would before long change into a swimsuit by the principle of association. When Janice wanted a bicycle in a lucid dream, she could simply expect to find one when she checked her dream basement or garage, and Ruth sometimes managed to generate appealing ocean or lake scenes by suggesting the idea to herself just before exiting dream buildings. Such tricks make deliberate use of a delay factor that often seems to affect attempts at influencing dream imagery. They also help sustain the illusion of having something "out there" to be found, and as such do not disrupt dreaming's normal reliance on waking-world habits of perception, so they have proven relatively successful in our experience.

However, since one's mental models derive their associative connections from the real world, the above techniques tend to replicate waking experience fairly closely and to rely a bit too heavily on having a favorable context. Using only association and expectation to control lucid dreams may lead, then, to the apparently common confusions, both large and small, between the dream ego and the dreamer and between the dream world and the real world. Such partial lucidity can end up placing limits on the kinds of control thought possible in a manner similar to nonlucidity, only expanding control to whatever extent one arbitrarily expects. This makes it important to learn techniques requiring more will and intentionality, in order to extend control beyond the limits of such perspectives.

The three of us learned, for instance, how to use one dream object as if it were something else and produce the intended results anyway, as when passing off a piece of paper as a backstage pass at a concert; to impose plot decisions like "I will find a key in my right pants pocket and it will open the third door on the left" on dream sets; to act as if missing objects were already present until they actually materialized in hand, even to the point of creating brand new, fully realized scenes out of blank phases; and, when the cards were in our favor, to transform one scene into another or conjure an item directly by an act of will. Changes effected primarily through sheer willpower tend to be the hardest to generate well. The dreamer may better understand a self-created image as merely thought-produced, and so it will tend to turn out more intangible than preexisting components that seem more "real."

Getting rid of dream images can be even easier than creating them, since ignoring something in a dream usually makes it disappear. Jay had some skill at willing dream objects to vanish.

As we have mentioned, jumping straight into dream walls and such can blank out the entire scene. When Janice did this, however, she almost always simply broke through into another scene, so different habits can be built up in this regard.

The flimsiness of dream sets makes it possible to push open locked doors, lift cars, knock down buildings, and the like with little effort. Janice and Ruth, perhaps following van Eeden's precedent,[23] did encounter difficulty breaking glass in their dreams, but Janice at least eventually overcame this limitation. Keeping in mind the unreality of the dream environment makes for some particularly entertaining activities, such as walking through walls, moving objects with the point of a finger, even cycling through different kinds of weather with a series of commands. Whatever can be pictured can almost always be done in a lucid dream, though it may take some practice.

The Life of the Mind: People and Animals in Dreams

Dream people and animals have essentially the same attributes as dream objects and scenes, and the quirky rules of dream memory and attention govern their dynamics in a similar fashion. They can certainly range into the fantastical; Janice has seen many dream animals and birds that would only be at home in the pages of a medieval bestiary. As for human characters, they often look convincingly lifelike but their features can become bizarre, especially when observed closely for too long.

One particularly unrealistic trait in our own dream characters was a certain resilience and rubbery plasticity of the flesh which could make them hard to damage in combat, but which allowed us to stretch and distort their features and limbs in curious ways. Perhaps trying to treat them as real and solid when they are actually nothing of the kind can create a consistency somewhere in between.

We have also come across characters who manifest only as voices or inchoate shapes, sometimes evolving into more tangible form during the course of the dream and sometimes not. And of course dream characters and creatures easily disappear or change from one image into another, sometimes even into inanimate objects.

Memory and imagination intertwine in the generation of dream characters. Familiar people appearing in dreams may not look or sound quite like themselves, yet still be identifiable by general similarities of behavior or perhaps by assumptions based on context. One might know that the character leading the class in a school dream, say, is supposed to be a specific teacher even though it barely resembles the person. Sometimes, too, the mind associatively blends known people with similar facial features or other traits, or even uses one person for another outright, as has happened with the images of two of Janice's quiet friends. While we might realize that something on this order had gone wrong if we happened to be lucid, we sometimes failed to spot such discrepancies or rationalized them away even then.

Unlike objects and scenes, dream characters have a dimension beyond their apparent physical properties that bears some discussion—that is, their mental properties such as temperament and intellect. Our characters could strike attitudes and show emotions quite vividly, although they generally did not seem to have much balance or range, and sometimes took a single personality trait and exaggerated it to the point of caricature. Furthermore, when pressed our characters typically displayed a decided lack of intelligence, often failing to answer questions at all rationally. For example, when Ruth told a dream character representing Jay, "This is a dream," he asked if she meant they were in a movie, and when she explained, "I am dreaming about you," he simply repeated her without any comprehension.

All three of us learned ways to get dream characters to say whatever we wanted, for instance by concentrating on the words until the character repeated them, as well as ways to make them *stop* talking. We could likewise use concentration and other techniques to change the physical appearance of characters, and bring inanimate objects to life by acting as if they were real. If we wanted to create dream characters from scratch, we could use expectation to find the sort of people usually associated with a particular context such as an office building, or sometimes even will them into existence. Ruth often called aloud for cats to come to her in her dreams then waited for them to arrive on the scene, while Janice could act as if a horse were present and mount and ride it invisibly until it eventually appeared. And of course we could ignore unwanted characters to make them disappear, as well as banish them more directly on occasion.

Thanks to the interpretive flexibility available with lucidity, we could impose chosen realities on dream people, making them respond in accordance with a carefully planned story idea or to the moment's whims. This required a quick creative reassessment of the characters, then keeping up the pretense by talking and acting with them accordingly. The average character is not difficult to influence in this way, right down to the subtleties of expression it will display in reaction to one's mental cues, although sometimes a little extra insistence is required. Occasionally, of course, we would come across exceptionally uncooperative individuals, some of whom met with untimely ends. On the whole, though, fashioning satisfying interactions with characters can be quite entertaining, and certainly formed the focus of Janice's lucid dream life.

The Sky's the Limit?

Whether or not one deems the complete control of dreams desirable, complete control will almost certainly not be possible due to a variety of limiting factors, some of which may indicate largely uncontrollable aspects of the dream state itself. Becoming lucid to begin with is no mean feat for most people. According to one account, while fifty-eight percent of the population have had at least one lucid dream in their lives, only twenty-one percent have one or more such dreams per month.[24] These rare dreams may also be disappointingly brief. We have heard anecdotal accounts of lucid dreams lasting an hour or more, but our own estimates rarely exceeded half an hour or possibly forty-five minutes at the extreme, and most individual incidents were much shorter. They were also frequently compromised by such inconveniences as poor visual and kinesthetic resolution, problematic phenomena which form part of a broader spectrum of inadequacies and inaccuracies inherent to dream perception, such as one taste or texture inappropriately substituting for another.

Although relative mental clarity is the hallmark of lucidity, rarely did the level of consciousness in our lucid dreams do more than approximate waking consciousness. Even after becoming lucid, we lacked our full abilities to think coherently, to sustain attention, to access memories, and to examine a variety of possible actions to the degree generally present in waking life. This situation negatively impacts the level of control possible. Further, since the dreamer has to maintain the imagery perceived in the dream even while trying to exert more direct control, the attention must be split between these two activities. Therefore, the quantity of even the limited amount of attention available for control is not high.

In our experience, with any shift of attention or lack of focus may come unforeseen changes: interruptions of scenes, alterations of objects and characters, and intrusions of unexpected, even bizarre imagery. Dreams follow the routes of one's mental processes almost unmitigated by cues from the external environment, and these dream mental processes are unstable, subject to whim and an ever-shifting labyrinth of associations. So, not surprisingly, dreams are themselves unstable, frequently altered in content or interrupted by stray ideas and other conflicting suggestion factors. Thoughts can meander associatively during daydreaming too, but will quickly get tugged back by perceptual ties to a reality that, fortunately, does not depend upon them for its stability.

We spoke in an earlier chapter of some common psychological impediments to control, such as impulsiveness, confining conventions carried over from waking, and convictions about what cannot or should not be done in lucid dreams, such as those derived from certain pervasive but restrictive theories regarding the nature of dreams. One particularly interesting psychological constraint that all three of us noticed was an instinct to avoid injury that activated whenever we attempted to perform in dreams what would have been hazardous actions in reality. When attempting to smash into solid masses at high speed, for example, not only might we stop ourselves at the last moment, we might hit without feeling any impact, or the dream itself might even seem to take preventive measures and steer us out of harm's way.[25] A lack of real experiences on which to model such dream activities might also have played a role in this phenomenon.

Dream control ability will also be limited by the level of talent attained. Not all people will be creative enough to visualize imaginative actions, exotic scenes and the like in convincing detail. Additionally, some effects require a rather subtle touch, deft strokes with the brush of attention that can take a while to master. But no matter how good one becomes, there will always be times when attempts at dream control will fail to work exactly as planned.

THE BALANCE OF POWER

We have not calculated our percentages of successes and failures with the various forms of dream control, if for no other reason than an incomplete database. Janice especially made no effort to record every single attempt and its outcome, since she had hundreds of lucid dreams annually during the time of our experiments. Such percentages would assumably be highly individual in any case, depending on subjective expectations, the quality of background information available, degree of practice, and other secondary factors. Even looking for such percentages in one's dreams could potentially change the level of control—or more specifically the control of control—experienced.

In any case, sometimes background factors will get the better of conscious direction regardless of all efforts to the contrary. Certain of the associations that propel dreams can be automatic or so weak as to seem random, making it easy to attribute the intransigence to outside oneself, or at least to outside one's conscious control. However, we have no reason to believe that any hindrances besetting dream control result from the resistance of an unconscious mind trying to recover the process of dream creation from the intrusion of the dreamer's willful lucid awareness. The truly uncontrolled aspects of dreams, once made distinct from the controlled aspects by an attempt to control everything, can still be explained by the same mechanism—i.e. suggestion—but with the initiating factor outside explicit awareness and the response simply reflexive. The obstructions usually encountered in controlling dreams seem quite specific and readily connect with the conditions of the state itself, such as instability and cognitive deficiencies, or with tacit suggestion factors easily accessible to consciousness, such as counterexpectations, associations and habitual reactions in conflict with the desired effect. In particular, lucid dreamers often do not really get over the idea of everything in the dream environment existing externally to themselves, and so end up at cross-purposes with the reality of their situation.

While in no lucid activity is control guaranteed or absolute, control can certainly be demonstrated time and time again in lucid incidents. Furthermore, the difficulties that sometimes occur do not *themselves* indicate that lucid dreaming and dream control should not be pursued, any more than the difficulties involved in performing any activity—golfing, acting, cooking, or whatever—indicate that it should not be practiced. In fact, given our observations concerning how dream content follows attention, every dreamer *must* be at least incidentally guiding all of his or her dreams every night, though within the bounds of the limitations pertaining to more direct control. The average nonlucid dreamer, hindered by a pronounced lack of memory from moment to moment, might even forget about having planted certain suggestions in the form of thoughts and interpretations, making his or her more direct control invisible.

Many aspects of dream control depend on such correlates of lucidity as clear thinking, access to memory, and sharp attention. Yet the normal condition of reduced awareness in the REM state can apparently be modified by lucidity only to a degree. The next chapter will take a closer look at the nature of dream mental processes and how these relate intimately to the process of dream generation.

Chapter 5

EMOTIONS, THOUGHTS AND MEMORIES IN DREAMS

The preceding chapter's review of our dream control experiments mentioned various ways to manipulate dream sensations, scenes, objects, and characters, including the dream self. Virtually all of these techniques involve, in one way or another, the control of emotion and thought. Further, attempting the techniques at all depends on having access to relevant memories, both from waking and from prior dreams.

This chapter will delve into the nature of dream emotions, thoughts and memories and show how lucidity commonly affects all three. It will also explore the extent to which dream thoughts and emotions can be controlled and memories accessed during lucid incidents, as well as discuss what our findings seem to imply about the dream generation process in general.

TIME OUT OF MIND: THE CHARACTERISTICS OF DREAM MENTATION

People can experience a range of thoughts and emotions in ordinary dreams fairly similar to that experienced in waking. Yet both may seem of a different quality when compared with emotions and thoughts in the outer world. Our mental attributes when dreaming would naturally deviate from the waking norm to much the same extent that dreams themselves differ from waking occurrences, since the strangeness of dream events would tend to provoke strange reactions.

Most of the time we uncritically assume our dream content to be real, a perceptual error that produces unpredictable and often disturbing results. In actuality, *only* the thoughts and emotions that make up the experience of dreaming can be called real. Along with a spotty, irregular access to the memories that would otherwise improve our perspective somewhat, they largely determine the flow of imagery and events that we usually focus upon both while having the dream and in later reflection about it. Understanding the characteristics of emotion, thought and memory in the dream state is thus essential to understanding the nature of dreaming.

Sturm und Dream

J. Allan Hobson, whose hypothesis of dream generation was introduced back in Chapter 3, reported that he and his associates found virtually no difference between men and women on measures of dream emotion. The investigators did, however, find that the proportions of various dream emotions reported by their subjects fell into a distinctive profile. Strong negative feelings such as anxiety and anger occurred more frequently overall than positive ones, although joy also placed strongly.[1] Such reactions might arise from how strange and frustrating, or perhaps wondrous, dream events can seem when approached with expectations borrowed from waking. Additionally, although dreamers commonly report a great deal of fear, surprise and so on, other negative affects such as guilt and shame appear to be markedly underrepresented in dream accounts.[2]

Hobson believes that dream emotions in general tend towards the excitatory and intense.[3] Indeed, recent research has revealed that some emotional centers of the brain become highly activated physiologically during dreaming, which would tend to foster emotional dream content.[4] We personally found, though, that our dream emotions might seem either unusually exaggerated *or* unusually understated. Both of these effects may relate to the fact that the physiological indicators of emotion are largely missing in dreams[5]—the sweats, flushes, palpitations, stomach clenches and so on that signal the strength of one's feelings in waking. The absence of such discomforts would make it easy either to feel oddly detached from dream events or to overreact to them without cost, or even both at once; Janice occasionally noted a discrepancy between a sense of inner calm and an outward agitation manifesting in her dream speech and behavior.

Understated and exaggerated emotions may also reflect an undercurrent of tacit lucidity running through dreams, of implicitly sensing that dream events do not really matter so one can just shrug them off or misbehave to excess if one wants. These unusual response patterns have themselves sometimes prompted us into lucidity.

The Sleep of Reason

The oddities of dream emotional response relate strongly to the nature of dream thought. Because the medium readily responds to thought without much time for reconsideration, people tend to behave impulsively when dreaming, and they legitimize their often reprehensible behavior with peculiar ease, which would account for the low occurrence of remorseful feelings reported. This rationalization tendency can extend to cover all manner of troubling discrepancies one might notice about the dream, letting the dreamer ignore or reinterpret any observations which would either disrupt the believed-in narrative or seem unsettling in normal circumstances. Of course, rationalizations also occur during *waking*; most of us make false assumptions from limited information and justify ourselves in the face of better judgment all too often. But waking rationalizations are usually more reasonable than, say, interpreting a high-resolution television as having come from outer space, like Jay did in one dream.

Much of the cognition in dreams seems irrational, muddled and convoluted by waking standards, since one is, after all, tired and asleep. Thought seems to become especially free-form in dreams that occur early in the night, and sometimes takes on an abstract or pictorial quality, as in one instance in which Jay saw images of worlds under construction while ruminating at bedtime about the creation of world *views*. Yet despite these vagaries, the ability for clear thinking exists in lucid dreams and even in many nonlucid ones. A dreamer can experience a sequence of thought every bit as rational as one during waking. In fact one study partly under the aegis of the Lucidity Institute found surprisingly little difference between subjects' accounts of dream and waking experiences on measures of most cognitive activities.[6]

This at least occasional clarity of thought opens the possibility that thinking in ordinary dreams sometimes seems "irrational" only because it tries as best it can to make sense of dream problems by ordinary means. Thoughts in nonlucid dreams are, from this perspective, often quite logical, but only in the setting of the dream. If Ruth sees a dream cat point a paw at its face and clearly say, "Face," why should she not interpret the talking animal as a genius cat? The validity of such dream-specific logic rests on automatically accepting the evidence of the senses in the dream. It ceases to make sense only *after* waking and comparing one's thoughts to waking memory, or after becoming lucid.

The Remembrance of Things Past

Dream thought processes become as divergent as they do largely because much of our memory of waking life, which normally provides a relatively consistent mental arena for our personal perspectives, becomes distorted and unreliable in the dream state. While we retain many learned skills that let us simulate activities convincingly in the dream world, we usually do not remember, when embroiled in a scenario, that we graduated from school years ago or that we never had any plans to take the trip for which we find ourselves preparing at the last minute. And while we usually recognize familiar objects, places and people in our dreams well enough, the altered or bizarre features and inaccurate details they take on may not register as odd at the time, and we may interact with them in uncharacteristic ways.

Further, we do not always remember dreams themselves easily from moment to moment as they progress. A dialogue with a dream character can quickly disappear from mind, and we can easily forget that the character looked like someone else a few minutes ago until we wake and recall both images. As a final extension of this host of memory deficits, most people scarcely remember their dreams at all without taking relatively great pains, though the ability does tend to improve with practice.

Whistling in the Dark: Thought, Emotion and Control

People generally do not, while awake or when dreaming, learn to adjust beyond a point to the special problems and characteristics of dreaming and dream mentation. The ability to learn about dreaming *while* dreaming is obviously attenuated, since dreamers usually remain unaware of their state. Moreover, memories of dreams are so impoverished, and the patterns of dreaming experiences so distinctively different from waking experiences, that even with their constant repetition from night to night it remains difficult to learn about dreams from personal experience without lucidity in dreaming and a fair amount of mental effort in waking.

Consequently, in ordinary dreaming our habitual, unquestioning belief in the "realities" we inhabit dictates our reactions—that is, our thoughts and emotions and the imagined "actions" we take based on such impressions—to the greatest extent. We become emotionally involved with fancies, exercise thought over nonsensicalities, vainly try to apply waking solutions to dream problems, and otherwise indulge in superfluous efforts as even the simplest of tasks becomes ridiculously complicated.

Since they do not accord with the facts of dreaming, our reactions do not always have the effects we anticipate, even when it comes to something as simple as trying to turn on a light. This difficulty in getting things to go right, coupled with the overall instability of dream mentation and imagery, lends to ordinary dreaming the general aspect of a lack of control, which in turn has apparently led to various theories explaining why dreams are or should be outside of one's control. However, using lucidity we find that dreams *are* directed by our awareness, including our thoughts and emotions. This happens in a manner that few real-life parallels prepare us to recognize easily, though even when awake our attitudes bias us so much that they often govern our perceptions of the world.

At root, becoming lucid involves recovering more of the waking-world memories that guide behavior and help define personality. Many dream "problems" may be solved when one realizes one is dreaming. The monster vanishes; the obsession with missing the train dissipates. Becoming lucid can bring emotional reactions more into line with the reality of the situation, and free thought from useless issues while widening its horizons and choices. So to the extent that people can learn to control or more appropriately direct their thoughts and emotions, they can also more directly control their dreams.

ALONG FOR THE RIDE: CONCEPTUAL OPTIONS FOR LUCID DREAMS

The core issue facing the dreamer after attaining lucidity must be the conceptualization of the dream, which will affect subsequent thought and emotion to a high degree. In ordinary dreams, this conceptualization is naive, because dreamers believe in the reality of what seems to be occurring. Since such a viewpoint dissolves with lucidity, what replaces it? The apparently simple concept of "realizing one is dreaming" has, it turns out, different meanings for different people.

Look, But Don't Touch

People take interest in lucid dreams for a variety of reasons. If they value dreams highly to begin with, and consider dreaming a psychological or spiritual process with which one should not interfere, they may attempt to maintain lucidity while otherwise trying not to change their dream content in any way. This type of conceptualization involves at least three major difficulties worth mentioning.

First, this standpoint assumes one *can* become lucid without changing the dream, as if the dream had an existence apart from one's awareness of it. We personally could largely set aside conscious control and let stray thoughts and habitual associations direct our lucid dreams to a greater degree, depending on whether or not we *wanted* to intervene more directly in a given situation, not because we had any moral objection to such intervention. Such a passive approach could even become a subtle form of control. When Ruth walked out to the back of her apartment building in one lucid dream, she recalled that she had wanted to find a garden there in her dreams during the previous spring and wondered if she would have better luck this time. Sure enough, that simple suggestion sufficed to create a nighttime scene of a park with trees and flowers.

In our experience the quality of awareness will alter dream content, even if only in slight or difficult-to-perceive ways. Awareness controls dream content because changing one's focus or interpretation changes the outcome of the dream. Since becoming lucid itself constitutes a change of focus and interpretation, lucidity will have to affect the dream's unfolding course. This often means dropping an unproductive activity for something more appealing. An initial dream situation will not typically reintrude after being abandoned for other activities unless the dreamer keeps thinking about it, although it would logically recur regardless if the dream actually had some point to make.

Second, in some situations a dream *cannot* unfold unless intentionally sustained with awareness. Becoming lucid could sometimes disrupt an ongoing narrative and break up a dream, forcing us to make a conscious effort to hold onto it. Further, expecting a dream event to play out in normal fashion on its own, or to have a plot without any direction from ourselves, often failed, presumably because dream imagery does not objectively exist and so depends on one's projecting and actively maintaining it. For instance, Janice found that if she made no effort at controlling the songs at dream concerts, the lyrics could turn into nonsense or the performers just fizzle and freeze. Similarly, the dream steeds she rode tended not to go anywhere without being steered. Such observations militate against the idea of any unconscious agency producing dreams.

Third, "going with the flow" or trying to "control oneself but not the dream" can mean settling for a partially lucid approach. For one thing, as we explained in the last chapter, controlling one's reactions without attempting to influence the other elements of the dream will affect those elements regardless, a fact any truly lucid dreamer needs to keep in mind. For another, serious immersion in what is really only another form of the naive role-playing that characterizes ordinary dreaming can lead to either forgetfulness of lucidity or only minimal lucidity, even if the role played gets shifted to unusual contexts, such as out-of-body travel or merging with "aspects" of oneself. Since lucidity always remains rather tenuous, almost any such distraction can lead to its attenuation or loss.

Moments of Truth: The Meditative Option

Another variety of lucid conceptualization could be called the meditative approach. Some dreamers maintain that their dream imagery can be suppressed partially or altogether by lucidly quieting their thoughts.[7] The three of us got mixed results in our own experimentation with this technique. It did appear to be possible to stop a dream in progress by such means, but if we did not just wake up or fall more deeply asleep, dream imagery tended to return in short order. The habit of dreaming at least *something* seems very strong.

We have heard of lucid dreamers who claim to be able to blend their own awareness with that of all the visible elements of a dream scene, slipping in and out of other perspectives with ease and directly perceiving how everything comes from their minds. While we consider this theoretically possible, given that everything in a dream *does* of course exist only in one's head, we have had only limited practice or success with the technique. When Ruth requested an experience of this sort from her dreaming mind one time, she felt herself lifted up into the air and began a pleasant, energetic flight. She struggled to become aware of the thoughts of all the characters of her dream world without success before giving up and landing.

Lucid Is as Lucid Does

The above considerations lead to the question of how lucidity, once attained, can best be sustained and extended without eradicating dream content. We believe that one can only do this effectively by conceiving dream content in a certain manner: by considering dreams as self-created, whether as entertaining artistic creations or as opportunities for experimentation. In other words, by taking responsibility for dream images and actively taking advantage of control techniques when desired, a dreamer can more easily maintain lucidity with fewer lapses. This is because any action based on lucidity will tend to reinforce it, while any less than clear-minded approach will tend to undermine it. Maintaining lucidity throughout an extended sequence requires continually reminding oneself of one's true circumstances and the consequences of one's choices of action, and attempts at dream control help in both regards.

THE HEART OF THE MATTER: LUCID DREAM EMOTION

Once the conceptualization of a dream has been altered with lucidity in whatever fashion, thoughts and emotions characteristic of *lucidity* will manifest. These can be quite different than the thoughts and emotions experienced in ordinary dreaming. We will begin by analyzing the changes lucidity's lens brings to the dream emotional spectrum.

"Don't Get All Excited"

We have already spoken, to some extent, of the typical emotional reactions to becoming lucid. Some people may simply be relieved or pleased to escape from the tedium of the ordinary dreaming perspective and its focus on unreal problems. Others, especially eager novices, become excited upon realizing they are dreaming, often to the point of inadvertently waking up. Still others develop excessive fear—negative excitement—at the onset of lucidity. Thinking themselves trapped in sleep or in the dream world, they do all they can *to* wake up.

Such effects restrict the emotional range of lucid dreaming. Although some adherents, such as Patricia Garfield, claim to reach dizzying heights of intensity in their lucid incidents while remaining solidly asleep,[8] we think it likely that most people who wish to remain both lucid and dreaming soon learn that the excitement must be counterbalanced, since it may otherwise overstimulate the brain and body into waking up, or at least distract one from lucidity.

On the other hand, the toning down of excitement at being lucid cannot be taken too far, either. Complete disinterest in lucidity will result in its fading or attenuation, since maintaining that level of awareness and responsibility will seem too much of a bother, especially once the practitioner gets on a declining curve of interest. If identifying a particular dream scene as such did not impress Jay, he would do nothing with his lucidity and soon lose it.

The common initial excitement may wear off for experienced lucid dreamers, as it does in other areas of human concern once experience increases. This does not mean that lucid dreams cannot still be stimulating or pleasurable, only that dreamers who get used to becoming lucid will probably realize that such dreams may be interesting or not, depending upon the content, its interpretation, or their own mood rather than upon the state itself. Becoming lucid can also put a damper on any ongoing dream activities, making one disappointed or dismayed that one is only dreaming. There is no one-to-one equation, then, between lucidity and excitement.

The Quest for Detachment

Beginners may tend upon becoming lucid to take disagreeable dream situations in hand in a brash or peremptory manner, which after more experience gives way to disinterest and the pursuit of other agenda. The achievement of an informed detachment from dream content would naturally follow from truly realizing its unreality, since it makes little sense to continue to care about nonexistent problems. Detachment has proved, for the three of us anyway, a more enduring and desirable effect of lucidity on the emotions than excitement.

Despite the general trend towards detachment, we did not come to lack *all* emotional response to our dream content, for several reasons. For one thing, there might be a delay before attaining detachment. All too often, emotions from the circumstances of what began as a nonlucid dream would carry over to the lucid portion. Also, we could lose lucidity temporarily and become emotionally engaged again before regaining lucid aplomb. In one dream in which Ruth had lost most of her lucidity, she became furious at the intransigence of one female character and smashed her fist into a couple of pastries before the realization that she was dreaming sank in again and she got control of herself.

Dream lucidity may be only intermittent or partial, then, while emotional detachment can be said, to a great extent, to vary in proportion with the degree of lucidity attained. This is because many emotional reactions derive from and are only appropriate for real experiences, and because emotions distort one's thinking heavily in any case. It said little for our critical reflection for us to get adversely affected by worrisome dialogue or overly involved in phony plot lines, as happened so often in semilucid incidents.

We could, however, remain relatively lucid while merely taking aesthetic delight in the creative aspects or sensory pleasures of dreams. Just as one may experience a full range of emotions when creating a painting or story, so one may when consciously crafting a lucid dream. Pleasant emotions may accompany the achievement of a desired effect, and irritations may ensue from the occasional recalcitrance of the medium. But any emotion experienced when fully lucid may have a different quality than when responding to realities, as in waking, or assumed realities, as in ordinary dreaming, since the interpretation of what is happening differs.

Particular images may still provoke strong reactions, negative or positive, even after a high level of lucidity has been maintained for awhile in a dream. Someone who loathes spiders, for instance, may well find them as distasteful in a dream as in reality. Lucidity will, however, tend to counter such emotionality and remind one that the experience will have no real effect. This helped Ruth overcome an habitual fear of heights as irrationally extended to dream imagery, though it did not mitigate her waking acrophobia.

Changes of Heart: Experimenting with Dream Emotion

As we have already demonstrated, controlling emotion can produce specific effects on dream imagery, like when overcoming fear negates a fearsome adversary. It might also prove interesting to try calling up a range of emotions in lucid dreams just for the sake of experiment. This makes a tricky proposition, however. If one retains full awareness of the unreality of the situation, one will not really feel the emotions, only act them out, as Jay found when he tried exaggeratedly laughing then taking on a downcast attitude in a lucid dream without feeling at all moved in either case.

If, on the other hand, one succeeds in generating the emotional responses, one may lose lucidity and forget the experiment, as almost happened to Janice one time. When someone showed her a red lobster in a dream, she decided to think of what might happen with different reactions on her part. When she imagined reacting wildly and hiding in a corner, even without actually acting it out, she started to feel upset and to identify with a new image of herself in the corner. Then she switched her perspective back to herself standing on the floor and imagined reacting disdainfully and kicking the lobster across the room. She felt perfectly cold, and walked away.

Throwing Caution to the Winds: Lucid Hyperemotionality

Sometimes people become *more* emotionally involved with what happens in their dreams when they become lucid. This may be either because they value and enjoy lucidity highly, or because they realize that they can now indulge their impulses towards sexuality, aggression or whatever else without consequence. Consider how some people prefer using automated teller machines instead of dealing with the living bank tellers they consider more troublesome, while others feel just the reverse. In a similar fashion, some people may prefer dream characters and situations to waking-world ones *because* the former are unreal—the same understanding that motivates others to disinterest. When dreamers become lucid, they know they can act with impunity, which easily disinhibits the playing out of emotions.

Lucid dreamers can also interact with images of relatives, friends, pets and locales in a pleasant if perhaps exaggerated and overly sentimental fashion. The extremes of emotion present in ordinary dreams may manifest in these interactions, followed after waking by embarrassment over such excesses or by lingering nostalgia over the dream, depending on the individual.

Many people have reported extremes of bliss and ecstasy in their lucid incidents.[9] Some may possibly have moved from dreaming into another state of consciousness, the bliss being all that remains after eliminating other objects of awareness. But the effect may as easily be due to the general exaggerating tendency of the dreaming mind linked with certain assumptions about lucidity as an altered state, and thus have more to do with such dreamers' belief systems and goals than with lucidity itself. In other words, the pleasure, though amplified by the attenuated focus of the dreaming mind, possibly stems from their having certain expectations of lucidity and then *interpreting* their dream content as something spiritual rather than from lucidity and the dream content per se. The emotion is, after all, their own and not embedded in their dream experiences.

To be lucid *about* dreaming, one must realize that although one's emotional reactions to dreaming may be real themselves, the images which inspire or arise in response to those reactions are not. So although the level of emotional involvement does not necessarily change with lucidity, the character of such involvement, and certainly the *objects* of emotion, usually do change because of the shift in perspective.

Ultimately, to remain lucid one must balance out one's emotional involvement with the content. When too little emotionally engaged, the dreamer stops promoting the dream, as when Janice became lucid while flying in an effort to avoid being late for school and then let the tension drain from her to the point of almost losing the scene. When too much engaged, the dreamer will lose lucidity. This would often happen when one of us got caught up in semilucid play-acting. A similar rule pertains for striking the proper balance with lucid dream thought, as the next section will discuss.

USING YOUR HEAD: THOUGHT IN LUCID DREAMS

Although beginners often have to puzzle their way through to the realization that they are dreaming, eventually growing lucid can become more of a quiet matter of reconceptualization not requiring much more thinking than one had already been doing in the dream. Still, the kinds of thought that may manifest during the subsequent course of the dream remain of some interest, since they so greatly determine its outcome. Lucid dreamers have to learn to monitor and control their thoughts, not merely for the purpose of managing characters, scenes and so on, but in order to maintain lucidity and its mental enhancements. This, as we will show, is no easy task.

Points for Participation

Once a person becomes lucid, he or she must choose between the various activities and modes of involvement possible in dreams, such as pleasure-seeking or storytelling. No matter what the choice, to remain lucid one must remain thoughtful and critical, aware of how one is influencing the scenario. This can involve taking on a stance similar to what social scientists call "participant observation": engaging in activities while keeping an analytical eye on the details of how those activities work.

It takes skill to observe the workings of the dream and participate in the plot simultaneously, though. Overdoing the first can lead to disruption of imagery; overdoing the second, to forgetting oneself and losing lucidity—"going native," as the anthropologists would say. Jay grappled with this dilemma in one dream in which he became aware that he was creating one scene after another to illustrate a long-winded narrative. As he created in his mind the great concrete steps up to the doors of a public building in Washington, D.C. and watched them fade in from nowhere, he realized that now that he was more aware of how he was producing the scenes they seemed less convincing and more illusory. He continued the story without lucidity.

Keeping the unreality of the dream in the back of one's mind while still maintaining the ongoing situation lets one have fun in the creative or poetic ideas. Although not every thought will translate into an image, like any kind of thinking fantasizing may end up affecting the dream in progress by causing scene shifts and the like. In one dream in which Ruth looked into a water dome with a scene inside of a quaint and beautiful castle on a hill, she wondered if there could be tiny people living in that scene unaware that she held their world in her hands. Then she saw that the building on the hill up ahead of her now looked like a castle itself.

Even though we were not particularly vivid fantasizers, the three of us occasionally mistakenly judged ourselves as having waking fantasies when actually dreaming, because the imagery so completely depended on our thoughts. Janice also had numerous lucid dreams in which she controlled virtually everything the characters said and did by deliberate fantasizing. These totally thought-dependent dreams probably tended to occur in light sleep.

At Your Wit's End: Lapses of Lucidity

The quality of thought generally improves with lucidity, becoming more similar to waking thought in such dimensions as reasoning ability and decision-making capacity. This helps maintain the critical awareness necessary to attend to and evaluate the effects noticed in dreams. Still, the unclear thinking that characterizes ordinary dreaming easily reasserts itself. Fancies and irrationalities, as well as niceties only pertinent in waking circumstances, creep into thought fairly often during lucid dreaming, creating the tangle called semilucidity. Such flaws in logic might be caught and recognized in time, if they did not cause our lucidity to lapse entirely, but they might not be recognized as such until after waking, if even then.

Just as in nonlucid instances, we could when lucid blithely ignore or rationalize away anything unusual in the dream, such as friends or teachers looking exactly the same age as when we knew them years ago. These problems too might either be corrected eventually or allowed to pass unnoticed until after we woke.

Many unwanted intrusions on dream thought took the form of impulses towards specific behaviors. Whatever we thought about, we often came to believe or act out in our dreams, even completely bizarre impulses like Ruth's peculiar notion to fly like a moth into someone's mouth. Janice's lucid dreams occurring early in the night seemed especially prone to this effect; she could easily become fixated on running around wild and doing mischief like scaring people by jumping in front of cars pretending to be a ghost.

Thinking Caps

The level of mental clarity in a dream would be equivalent to its level of lucidity, in the general sense of the word. Yet a lack of clear thinking and an exaggeration of emotionality prevail in ordinary dreaming as well as in many lucid dreams, which themselves occur rather seldom overall. Therefore one can confidently consider dream thoughts and emotions intrinsically more likely to be muddled and disproportionate than those during waking. However, while dream emotions and thoughts generally *are* less reasonable than those in waking, the fact that we all *may* think clearly and calmly when nonlucid and *may* when lucid make our perspectives better accord with the truth brings up the question of why we do not commonly do so. The clouding effect on our thoughts and emotions has become relative, so what factors determine the extent of its presence?

Certain physiological variables such as depth of sleep and time spent asleep appear to have an impact on the matter, given that people seem more likely to be impulsive and irrational in lucid dreams occurring early in the sleep cycle. These factors do not explain the whole situation, though. Since dreamers often recover a fair amount of emotional detachment and rational thinking after realizing they are dreaming, as well as consider new courses of action, the nature of our thoughts and emotions must depend to a great extent upon our *beliefs* concerning what seems to be happening to us. If we believe dreams real, then we fear threatening figures, worry over ineffective actions or malfunctioning objects, and overlook absurdities. If we believe lucid dreams should be pleasurable or spiritual, we may grow ecstatic or have "meaningful visions" after becoming lucid, with no mental balance at all.

Striking content, too, can reduce lucidity by inspiring a strong attraction or repulsion that gets the better of one's judgment.

This leads back to a consideration of the state of memory during dreaming. Some dream happenings and our beliefs about them can be so bizarre that we could only accept them as possible if we have forgotten the nature of reality. Most of us are not, after all, typically menaced by monsters or able to fly in the real world. The more ordinary scenarios in which we get enmeshed also depend on how little we may remember of our current lives, or we would not so often find ourselves interacting with people and places from earlier periods. Even after becoming lucid, what happens to be remembered of the implications of lucidity will differ from dream to dream; Janice and Ruth have sometimes regressively suspected that other people would see them flitting around during an OBE, for instance. So although the lucidity of dream emotions and thoughts will vary along with sleep physiology, one's beliefs, and one's dream content, level of lucidity also correlates strongly with the degree of access, or more specifically *lack* of access, to orienting memories.

FOR THE RECORD: LUCIDITY AND MEMORY

Scientists now consider memory to comprise several discrete systems, each with its particular neurological underpinnings.[11] A person with a head injury that has caused amnesia about recent events may have a perfectly intact ability to memorize telephone numbers, for example. Without going into detail about the formal distinctions and interrelations between these processes, we will discuss in this section how lucidity affects several aspects of memory, so many of which function so poorly in ordinary dreaming.

Memorable Scenes

The operation of memory improves distinctly in conjunction with becoming lucid. Characteristically, we started recognizing the divergences with reality and the unstable discrepancies from moment to moment that we would otherwise overlook. We could also repeat information about the dream to ourselves and commit many details to memory for later recording.

Certain details, particularly lexical ones, posed a problem in this regard, though. We found it difficult to retain passages read or speeches heard in dreams, and the tunes and lyrics of songs generated in dreams might be nearly impossible to memorize, to Janice's perpetual regret. She noticed a similar if less pronounced effect when trying to remember waking-world music heard for the first time. Memory does in large measure depend on association and repetition, so while someone might not be able to retrieve the lyrics of a new song just played on the radio, he or she might well recognize the number upon hearing it a second time. Such repetition will not typically occur with dream material; a spontaneous dream song is hard to place in an associational context and will never be heard again.

Music aside, lucid dreams usually seem much easier to remember than most ordinary dreams. This may be due to some slight shift in brain chemistry that accompanies lucidity, or to the increased critical attention given to dreams once the dreamer becomes lucid. In other words, being lucid may allow one to notice more about the dream and to make better sense of it—to process it—which would result in better memory.

We could relatively easily remember a lucid dream even after continuing to sleep for some hours before waking enough to record it, though some details might be lost. Janice found it helpful to take notes on the content while still dreaming. Even though the actual notes could not, of course, be retrieved, the action of "writing" them helped fix the information in her mind. Nevertheless, it *is* possible to forget lucid incidents, as we mentioned earlier in the book.

The Best-Laid Plans: Memory and Experiments

Some people feel sure that they have full access to their waking memories when lucid, but this cannot always be true. As a case in point, although we could on many occasions remember a waking intent to execute a particular experiment, the memory of the planned format might be imperfect. Success rates of even remembering an intention at all seem to vary widely from dreamer to dreamer, or from time to time for the same dreamer. Other experimenters have noted these problems as well.[12]

Interestingly enough, performing an experiment in a lucid dream occasionally preceded our explicitly remembering the idea for it. This underscores the fact that the memory depended upon to execute experiments, and even to become lucid intentionally, remains largely *waking* memory, since the real mental effort occurs during waking programming for the activity. Waking thoughts and intentions create and support dream lucidity to such a great extent that we cannot discuss the mental attributes of lucid dreams without at least mentioning this interconnection.

In any case, one can easily devise and perform lucid experiments to test dream memory itself. The exact extent to which dream memory falls short of waking memory may be difficult to establish, though. Waking memory has a distinct advantage, since during waking people have recourse to a variety of contextual cues and memoranda to assist them. Most of us would not escape distraction or recall the day's projects successfully without a proliferation of reminders: alarm clocks, notes, irate bosses, etc. Furthermore, since one has to sustain the dream while attempting a memory exercise, one cannot give as much attention to the task of remembering as would be possible when awake. Too much thinking could destroy the scene and bring the dreamer too close to waking for a fair comparison.

Assessing the differences between dream and waking memory on the basis of deliberate-recall experiments is also problematic because memory in lucid dreams does not necessarily equate with dream memory in general. We attempted a range of experiments to test the accessibility of various kinds of memories during dreaming, and found our memories generally more accurate with lucidity than without it, though far from perfect. Although we did not typically perform memory exercises in nonlucid dreams to compare with lucid efforts, our thoughts and actions when nonlucid displayed well enough how poorly we remembered waking life. In ordinary dreams we accepted highly improbable scenarios having nothing to do with our everyday lives as believable simply because we were involved in them, which would make us disinclined to remember our real circumstances even if we could.

Sometimes, too, a nonlucid context would in fact spark a recall attempt that illuminated our memory deficits in stark relief. In one nonlucid classroom dream, a fellow student asked Janice what she had done during the weekend, and she remembered an earlier nonlucid scene about getting papers back from the bank, not a real event. In another case the locker combination she thought she remembered turned out, on waking reflection, to be her current account number with a book club. Jay could not even remember where he lived in one nonlucid dream, telling someone he lived in Buffalo, New York when he actually resided in Pennsylvania and had only ever been to Buffalo once.

Chapter and Verse: Rote Memory

In Lewis Carroll's classic tale of Wonderland, the dreaming Alice found it impossible to remember the multiplication table, geographical data, or familiar poems properly, let alone her identity. Unlike Alice, in our lucid experiments we recalled facts of common knowledge, such as capital cities, with ease. Nor did we have much difficulty reciting rhymes we had learned by rote in the past, except for an occasional lapse when it came to song lyrics. Jay repeated Carroll's own complex nonsense poem "Jabberwocky" successfully, while Ruth and Janice rattled off "Twinkle, Twinkle, Little Star" and "Humpty Dumpty" respectively without a hitch. Getting our voices to work properly and maintaining the dream at the same time as concentrating on a recitation proved harder than remembering the material, since trying hard to remember things can make dream visuals disappear.

The three of us each had rather different results when attempting to repeat basic mathematical formulas or to do arithmetic in our lucid dreams. Janice started having trouble with the 4 X table by the time she got to 4 X 3; when she got to 4 X 6 the scene went gray and she woke. Jay had to pause and think at least twice while saying the squares up to 12 X 12, though he made no mistakes. Ruth had the most success, probably thanks to being a schoolteacher. She made it to 4 X 9 without hesitation and even worked out two-digit addition problems.

The Lucidity Institute once sponsored an experiment that required trying to remember several items in one's lucid dreams: the current date, one's sleeping place, and the day's entry from an assigned list of common words. Janice, Ruth and the other participants almost always succeeded in retrieving all the required information correctly while dreaming.[13] The ease with which the material came to them varied from trial to trial, however. Janice had to dredge up the answers in one case, and in another she came up with the *previous* day's word, "wind," by a false association to the fact that she happened to be creating a breeze at the time by flying in her dream. Also, the participants may have been less adept at recalling the dates and sleeping places had they not memorized and rehearsed both.

Facts and "Facts"

Even without prior memorization, in our respective lucid dreams all three of us could remember basic facts about our waking lives. We could state our names, addresses, employment, ages and other miscellaneous personal data fairly well, as opposed to the situation in Jay's nonlucid "Buffalo" dream above. Sometimes, though, we ended up reciting outdated information, as Janice did with an old address and telephone number because she happened to be at the former house in the dream. She often got the date wrong by many years in her lucid dreams. This again shows that lucidity does not automatically equal perfect memory.

Janice had a hard time forcing herself to think straight for articulating the information during one of the Lucidity Institute trials. Her mind tried to think "July" for the month and she had to insist to herself, "You know perfectly well it's October."[14] Even in waking her immediate mental response to asking herself a question might be completely random, though she would find it easier to focus her thoughts to get the correct answer when awake than when dreaming. So sometimes our lucid memory recitals of whatever kind swerved into nonsense or went unfinished, since concentration can be difficult to maintain and since dreams easily follow impulses.

A popular notion of dreaming maintains that, whether because the "unconscious" forgets nothing or because the brain processes information in REM sleep, one has greater access to memories in dreaming than in waking.[15] The very rarity of any high degree of lucidity in dreams flatly contradicts this assumption. Forgotten memories of varying degrees of remoteness do apparently spring up in dreams from time to time when nudged by association, as indeed they do in waking. But neither Janice nor Ruth, when performing another part of the Lucidity Institute experiment mentioned above, could deliberately coax their dreaming minds into retrieving facts they had forgotten in waking by any means tried: asking dream characters, looking up the information in dream books, or striving to remember it. Neither could the vast majority of the other participants.[16]

Unrehearsed Memory: The Importance of Context

Context has a pronounced effect on the memories that spring to mind in both lucid and nonlucid dreams. Facts relevant to the circumstances of the dream can often be recalled, whether they come from waking or from other dreams. Janice made use of two unforgotten childhood lessons in one dream in which she used a wet washcloth and crushed charcoal to filter toxic fumes, and Ruth simply had to try to help an apparently injured dream horse after remembering the hurt horse that had featured in another recent lucid dream.

One of the most striking findings in all our lucid experimentation bears on this issue of context. Despite the usual memory improvements that accompany lucidity, while lucidly dreaming we had great trouble remembering recent events in our waking lives, even though the information returned immediately upon awakening. We could recall that we graduated from school some time ago, got married, and so on, and even remember current waking preoccupations, but we would encounter considerable mental opposition when it came to pinpointing specifics like what we did yesterday in reality.

In one lucid dream, when Jay tried to remember what had happened to him the day before he could only think that he had been reading a certain magazine and had been talking to his mother. When he woke he remembered that the week's issue had not come in the mail as expected so he had bought and read another magazine instead, and, further, that he had been talking with his mother in a previous dream scene, not in reality.

This particular aspect of memory did not show much improvement when lucid compared to the nonlucid status quo. Janice tried to remember the previous day's events in one nonlucid dream, but ended up recalling a nonlucid dream from the previous day. On another nonlucid occasion, she simply drew a blank. Even in one lucid attempt she could not, despite trying for a long time, remember anything she had done the day before, though she felt that she had meant to write to Ruth. She recalled some earlier dreams of the morning, and knew that they had been dreams, but no details of her real day, despite the fact that memorable things had indeed occurred, such as an "unforgettable" meal at a gourmet restaurant.

In another lucid dream Janice tried to remember what had happened a *week* before in reality, but could think of nothing. She could only infer that she had probably done some work on this book, even though she had in fact hosted a New Year's Eve party. In only one experiment trial did she get any better results, probably because it took place in the same setting as the remembered event, making for less contextual displacement than usual. This happened to be the apartment where she lived at the time, which would naturally provide certain cues that might help trigger memories of the preceding day. Recalling her experiment intentions during this OBE dream, she asked herself what movie she had seen last night. At first she thought of the last movie she had seen in a theater, then corrected herself; she had seen a specific videotape, and had walked to the video store to pick it up and then to a relative's house.

Stuff and Nonsense: Confusions of Memory

Both Janice and Ruth considered their lucidity higher on average in dreams they entered consciously than in dreams with a dreams in which they do realize it, but falsely assume themselves constrained by certain conventions. One's thought processes may be clearer in the second type of dream, but lucidity gets compromised because its implications are not followed through.

On the other hand, a tacitly lucid dream can still be relatively low on the lucidity scale in other ways. If dreamers tackle dream problems competently but believe in the reality of those problems, they remained inappropriately engaged with content it might be better to ignore. So while level of lucidity is best measured by the appropriateness of one's thoughts, emotions and behaviors to the fact that one is dreaming, these three measures can vary independently of one another, which again goes to show the striking variability of the perceptual faculty called lucidity.

A TALE TOLD BY AN IDIOT: MENTATION AND DREAM GENERATION

This chapter has discussed dream mental processes in so much detail because the nature of those processes can illuminate the nature of dream creation itself. With neither external sensory information nor recent waking memories to guide us, we all naturally become disoriented in dreaming sleep. The lack of easy access to orienting memories severely constrains attention in ordinary dreams, usually to the immediate content of the dreams themselves. Such a "dream-specific" perceptual bias causes dream-specific thoughts and emotions—thoughts and emotions driven by and only relevant to the context provided by the temporary dream situation—as well as further inhibiting access to contradictory memories.

This present-tense, limited focus could in fact help account for the exaggerations of emotion and shortcomings of thought so common to ordinary dreams, in much the same way as any limited focus in waking tightens one's mood and restricts the type of thoughts and memories likely to come to mind. An intense argument, a state of depression, or a good football game can easily narrow the attention to the point of making us forget or dismiss any ideas that run counter to our present assumptions, although we may well entertain those same ideas in other, less constraining circumstances.

Even false memories and rationalizations reflect the habitual tendency for the mind, whether dreaming or awake, to be insufficiently critical and overly impressed by the "truth" of whatever passes before its notice. Indeed all of the difficulties with emotions, thoughts and memories that this book has discussed, while certainly more extreme in dreams, also constitute common issues in ordinary waking perception. The fact that such difficulties seem to lie at the heart of the dream-generation process underscores the perceptual nature of dreaming.

As an aside, because of the tendency to be overimpressed by what goes on in a dream, lucid or otherwise, dreamers sometimes have the delusional feeling that they are experiencing something deeply meaningful or that a great truth has been revealed to them. One famous example is an incident attributed to William James himself, who reputedly once woke up convinced he had discovered the secret of life in a dream then later discovered that what he had actually recorded was: "Higamus Hogamus, women are monogamous / Hogamus Higamus, men are polygamous."[18] Unfortunately, such conviction—or for that matter *any* strong sensation, emotion, thought, or "memory" in dreams—tends to make some people believe, even long after they awaken, that something important must really have occurred. As a result, if the content no longer seems to make much sense they may look for meanings somehow apparent to the dreaming mind, but not yet available to them in waking, when the dreaming mind and the waking mind are really the same thing in different circumstances.

A worthwhile insight may come along now and again in dreams, and an emotion or thought may indeed be profound or intellectual from the relative standpoint of a *dreaming* perspective, given the overall attenuation of our mental abilities in sleep. The image of the bearded northern god Thor in his flying chariot pulled by goats may possibly have influenced the later tradition of Santa Claus in his reindeer sled, as Janice speculated in one nonlucid school dream. But more often than not such convictions do not stand up to the light of day and more critical waking assessment.

The historical record will not bear out that certain prominent Afro-Americans grew up in Ireland's County Mayo, nor that the writer Doris Lessing got her start with a controversial biography of Marilyn Monroe, for all the persuasiveness of Janice's and Jay's respective dreams to that effect.

In any event, if we receive no conflicting sensory data, do not remember the recent past, and believe in the proof of our senses, a dream *is* our reality. Problems arising to thought get rationalized away, and the dream progresses accordingly. At every step irrationalities, rationalizations or false memories block our potential rememberings. If for some reason these mental crutches should fail us and we were to realize the strangeness of our behavior and the faultiness of our memories without becoming lucid, we would end up extremely bewildered. This did indeed happen to Ruth in one very upsetting dream.

Although it prevents such bewilderment, the usual obfuscation surrounding dreaming may be not so much an embedded defense mechanism to preserve sleep, as some psychoanalysts have maintained,[19] as a natural, human reaction. We assume we know what we are doing in the real world; we believe ourselves in the real world when dreaming; therefore we assume we must *still* know what we are doing—even though we may be muddling through a convoluted and highly improbable dream scenario. A lack of dependable sensory cues starts it off, loss of orienting memories and reality-checking abilities results, and clouded thinking and poor memory keep the process going.

The psychological factors behind the lack of clear mentation in dreams, and its physiological basis as well, bear further examination. According to the suggestion theory, these pervasive factors would tend inspire similar images and problems in many dreamers, which in turn would tend to be rationalized away in ordinary dreams. The next chapter will examine such common dream situations and show how from a certain perspective they all reflect the basic characteristics of the dreaming process.

Chapter 6

THE ORIGINS OF COMMON DREAMS

Dreams can be so intriguing that, no matter how strange or nonsensical their content, people will often conclude they must somehow have meant something. Yet according to the theory we have been presenting in this book, dreaming may simply result from the mind attending to and transforming various suggestion factors during that state of attenuated awareness called sleep. If this is indeed the case, then the general characteristics of sleep should operate on similar mindsets to produce similar experiences. The sleeping body and brain function in an entirely different physiological and psychological climate than that of the waking norm, one marked by minimal sensory information, changes in the status of bodily systems, and limited access to memories. These common conditions, in turn, should readily evoke common human needs, desires or fears.

In this chapter we will reexamine some key properties of dreams—instability, bizarreness, and critical thinking and memory flaws—in the light of recent physiological evidence, as well as for the clues they provide about the perceptual nature of dreaming. Some of the problem areas encountered in trying to control lucid dreams make better sense from this combined perspective. Even many of the classic themes associated with dreaming, from flying to being disoriented at school, may have humble origins in sleep physiology and ordinary habits of perception, and hence not necessarily be of any great psychological importance.

STRANGER THAN FICTION: PERCEPTION AND THE UNREAL

The dream milieu has several curious properties that distinguish it from the arena of everyday life. Perhaps the most obvious difference between the waking and dreaming worlds lies in the variable but ever-present instability of dreams. Objects, characters, and even whole scenes can alter from one look to the next; big leaps in time and space can occur with the speed of thought. Thus the same special effects enabled by the shift in perspective called lucidity—dream elements appearing, changing and disappearing in response to thought—also occur frequently *without* lucidity because of dreaming's innate mutability.

This section will discuss how common perceptual habits may interact with the indeterminacy inherent to dreams to create the unstable and bizarre features that lend dreaming its distinctive surreal ambience. First, though, we will have to offer a quick look at the neurological substrata of perception.

Cracking the Code: Neurophysiology and Perception

The internal activity of the sleeping brain has prompted some important considerations about its possible influence on dream content. According to the activation-synthesis hypothesis promoted by sleep physiologists J. Allan Hobson and Robert McCarley, dreaming depends on erratic electrical signals in the brain's own sensory and motor neural networks. Higher processing centers also located in the cortex, or upper part of the brain, try to take this information as input and organize it into something remotely sensible.[1] This hypothesis presupposes a direct correlation between pseudo sense perceptions in dreams and activity in the corresponding neural systems pertaining to the physical senses.[2] Such correlations do not prove that activity in the sensory systems during dreaming invariably affects the higher areas and not the other way around, since when lucid one can deliberately produce a wide variety of dream sensations. Still, if dreamers consistently fail to simulate certain senses as often or as convincingly as others, this may indicate that the brain structures underlying the underrepresented sensory modalities naturally undergo less activation in dream sleep.

To make a start towards understanding how quantifiable aspects of REM physiology might tie in with content, McCarley and his colleague Edward Hoffman formally analyzed the descriptions of

104 dreams recorded by a group of laboratory subjects.[3] Visual, auditory, and kinesthetic descriptions predominated in these accounts. Temperature, touch, smell, and taste were underrepresented, while accounts of sexual and pain sensations were nonexistent. This profile clearly falls subject to individual variability, and does not make clear to what extent a deficit in *reporting* a particular sensation really implies a deficit in *experiencing* it. As an obvious example, many people enjoy sexual pleasure in dreams and might be inhibited about recording that fact in a laboratory report.

More importantly, the senses apparently best represented in dreams are those most frequently employed by the mind's world-modeling function, that digest of past perception used for orientation in both waking and dream experience. In the real world, visual, auditory, tactile and kinesthetic stimuli are the primary means of perceptual orientation for humans. According to the suggestion theory of dream generation, this bias should also influence dreaming, and certainly dream reporting.

Such excellent sensory simulations as dreams sometimes contain, which we all think we observe but actually project from our own mental maps, hint at how much of our supposed perception of outer reality may be all in our heads. Any data we take in through the senses comes to us only through the intermediary of neurological impulses that must be coordinated and translated into meaningful symbols along the way. For all the complex functioning of retinal cells and the visual areas of the cortex in response to light, for instance, it takes a further complex process to organize that data into useful, recognizable patterns, though we do not normally make a distinction between reality and the way we have personally mapped it.[4]

Since so much of perception occurs within the brain's structuring mechanisms anyway, any internal activity we may read when disconnected from the world will easily seem real too. So if the visual system is stimulated by pulses from the brainstem in much the same manner as it would by true visual sensations, as Hobson suggests,[5] it will essentially "see" images. Whatever threads of data it may gather during sleep, the same modeling process that stitches together ordinary perception also weaves the web of imaginings that manifests as a dream.

The Winds of Change: Attention and Instability

The above model accounts for dream instability as largely the result of REM brain activity being too chaotic for the synthesizing dreamer to keep up with.[6] Furthermore, a given cluster of signal-generating neurons can only stay on so long until another takes its place and generates a new set of images.[7] Perhaps, too, the integrity of such codes decays with varying degrees of rapidity, leading to all manner of bizarre distortions since the signals will no longer quite match anything in the identification system trying to read them.

Neurology aside, however, we personally would stress the importance of attention in this equation. While neurologically based dream instabilities may grab the attention at times, the inconstancy of attention itself creates further instabilities, since we have so often observed changes of focus causing shifts of imagery. Take the mind off anything in a dream for long, and that thing will surely change around or vanish.

Exerting too little attention fails to provide sufficient structure to dream content and so encourages instability. In lucid dreams, maintaining the proper degree of attention will usually hold things more steady, at least for a while, and the dreamer can guide the direction of an unstable change rather than leaving the result entirely to chance or association. Redirected attention can even overcome seemingly intractable elements of possible neurological origin. Janice has used singing, for instance, as a refocusing device to divert herself from negatively loaded dream imagery, to make a pressing mob of characters disappear, and so on.

Much more often, though, dream awareness remains too absorbed in what it assumes to be going on around it to rescue itself, as well as highly distractible. This condition need not result solely from being tired, as one might at first think. Even when an individual is awake and alert the attention cannot easily occupy itself with unchanging stimuli, but tends to habituate or become "bored" quickly, and so considerable shifting of attention easily becomes a perceptual habit. Carried over to dreaming, this constant shifting of focus would assure that the imagery would also change or seem to move. Of course, too much attention for too long can promote imagery shifts as readily as too little attention.

According to the suggestion theory, we dreamers commonly try to behave as if we were awake, inappropriately applying the habits of perception learned in waking to our dreams. If we create dreams by imposing real-world patterns in this way, why do dreams not more closely resemble waking? Because our perceptions of the real world depend for their accuracy on the stable nature of that world; we continually monitor a relatively consistent external environment to regulate them. Dreaming, on the other hand, lacks that crucial external stabilization. In dreams, the world-modeling function would have to use stored sensory data, presumably as encoded by particular patterns of neural activity, to produce a dreamscape off which the mind can cue instead. This would provide the customary sense of self as separate from the environment, but allow attention to wander to extremes.

The misapplication of the monitoring habit would create endless associative digressions, since changeable, moment-to-moment situations have become our only input. Dreams thus seem discontinuous by waking standards, although they may not really be much more unstable than our thought processes, which jump around in either state. Habitual perceptual patterns, some quite fitful themselves, interplay with the instability of various other factors. Were the mind not responding to fluctuations in physiology, emotional states and its own thoughts, it presumably *would* create dream imagery more like waking experience.

Curiouser and Curiouser: Generating Dream Bizarreness

In waking we learn to depend upon the consistency of physical reality. In fact, sometimes expectations from established models override perception completely, as when Janice adds what should be a striking new element to the home decor only to find that Jay obliviously fails to notice it without her pointing it out. At other times our attention lights on any incongruity we notice until we can reconcile it with our ideas of what should be present, as per existing models. So it may take people a moment to figure out that Jay, whom they can sense looks different *somehow*, has cut his hair or shaved off his moustache.

The same technique of applying greater attention, used automatically in dreams, often fails to have the same effect of reconciling inconsistencies, and could help explain the frequency of anomalous and bizarre images in dreams. Such distortions of reality are possible simply because dreams are not real, and they reveal our limited ability to visualize complex and coherent realities in our minds alone. Oddball perceptions cannot easily be corrected, since our habit, borrowed from waking, is to look for new information from a steady reality, which does not exist in dreaming. Instead of rectifying small discrepancies, then, this mechanism can *magnify* them into large, bizarre features by means of the attention focused on them.

For example, when early lucid dream explorer Hervey de Saint-Denys remarked in a certain dream that he had been served a dish as hard as shoe leather, it was immediately replaced on his plate by a piece of shoe leather.[8] The brain's efforts to distinguish internally generated sensory perceptions from thoughts would understandably remain imperfect, since both come from within, and therefore any thoughts related to interpreting a dream image should readily affect it. The habits of perception underlying this distortion mechanism may be so automatic as to go unnoticed without lucidity. *With* lucidity and thought control, dream bizarreness can actually be avoided to a fair extent if desired, simply by not investing it with such extra attention.

Why do people not become lucid more often, if their own dream mentation usually creates large numbers of patently bizarre features? Because, like the tired husband who does not notice the wife's new decorative touches, as dreamers we also reflexively tend to smooth over divergences with normality, when we think about them at all with our limited, sleeping awareness. We ignore them, rationalize them away, or change what we experience to agree, at least in part, with what we expect. For instance, Janice once caught herself in the act of jumping out a dream window and decided that since she was memories affects even lucid dreamers and serves to entrap them in their self-spun narratives until waking clears away the cobwebs.

At one point Jay posited state-specific processing to explain the difficulty recalling certain things pertaining to the real world while dreaming—separate memory systems for the dreaming and the waking minds. This explanation became too hard to defend, however. Successive dreams can switch scenarios abruptly, with new sets of incomplete or false memories in each instance. Furthermore, dream content clearly draws upon waking memories of past experiences and preoccupations, even if it mixes things up in curious ways. So what really is going on?

Random Access Memories?

In normal experience we automatically believe in the reality of almost everything we see before us and consider whatever has hold of our attention important, so naturally we usually do the same while dreaming. Taking the immediate situation in a dream as real and meaningful may in effect block memories that conflict with these assumptions, or at least reduce the likelihood of critically reassessing the situation, so that we continue to remain naively ensnared in a given scenario. Many memories, even if accessible, will not be relevant to the scenario at hand and hence will not likely come to mind anyway.

Think of how easily, when tightly focused on a demanding task that requires staying late at work, one can forget or dismiss other obligations such as the special dinner planned by a spouse. In a parallel but more extreme manner, while dreaming we get taken in by the seeming "evidence of the senses" without any contradictory information to counter our assumptions—and no one to ring us with a reminder. We take it for granted that we are at work, at school, in a hotel, at the seashore, or wherever else our thoughts place us, and our associative concatenations can run amok.

In reality we can count upon a supply of continuous data to contradict any false impressions we might receive and set our perceptions straight. But in dreams we rely completely on mental maps with all the flexibility and fallibility of thought—not actually perceiving anything, but spinning illusions. To sustain these illusions, if we should manage to notice or remember anything discrepant, we will most likely come up with a retrospectively ludicrous rationalization to account for it. So when Ruth rode in a dream van that passed harmlessly through a building despite her fears, she blithely attributed the "miracle" to the presence of some magical Afghanistani companions.

Since we normally rely on what we remember, we do not think to discredit the false memories that crop up like weeds while our real ones lie dormant. If Janice dreams about school and by some chance remembers that she already graduated, to reconcile the conflicting thought with the evidence before her she will concoct some rationale for her behavior. She may decide that she had to repeat a grade because of some legality or wanted to further her education. If she sees what looks like a former pet in a dream, then recalls that it died long ago, she may "remember" that someone gave her an identical pet in consolation, that the animal miraculously revived after dying, or that it sometimes comes back to visit her as a ghost. She would probably not reach such fanciful conclusions under similar circumstances in waking, where she would know that none of these things could or did happen. False memories and rationalizations thus go hand in hand with the critical thinking and memory problems besetting dreamers.

Dream memory blocks do not occur solely as the result of believing dream situations to be real, however. Although memory for the actual circumstances of our own lives did improve after becoming lucid—that is, deciding that a scenario could not be real and discarding any farfetched notions—we continued to have a great deal of trouble retrieving recent waking memories. When very recent material did turn up in our dreams, it might well be in the form of gratuitous images, not thoughts, as in the case of the dried birds that Janice dreamed about nonlucidly after having seen some toy birds in a mail-order catalog.

In her early study of the written accounts of several lucid dreamers, Celia Green similarly noted that "there appears to be a positive resistance to accurate memories of the most immediate and specific concrete details of the subject's life."[9] Such retrieval difficulties may occur because short-term memory depends to a great extent on contextual cues from the environment. Since we all lose our sensory orientation to the waking world while sleeping, even when we know a dream context is not real we still respond as if it were and reflexively cue from it as we would if awake, but there may well be nothing in the scene to remind us of recent waking events.

Still, people can travel from one city to another in waking without becoming befuddled and forgetting everything they did yesterday. So besides the above factors, to a large degree the abnormal mentation in dreams may be caused by the dream state itself, since it features a completely different biochemistry than waking. According to Hobson, certain brainstem neurons producing compounds necessary for critical attentional and memory tasks take a breather during REM sleep and reactivate upon awakening. Moreover, the frontal area of the cortex, associated with directed thought, judgment, and working memory, becomes less active during REM.[10] Without the neurological support needed for clear thinking and proper access to recent waking memories, we could all the more easily accept any time in the past as current, any location as our present home, and so on.

Moreover, when people do remember things pertaining to another physical context in waking, they often use mental images, which might be hard to do if that capacity is already taken up with a dream scene. In other words, the creation of the dream may fill up a kind of visual short-term memory buffer in the brain that blocks access to genuine recent memory but does not typically get processed into more permanent storage itself.[11] As an analogy, while typing a paragraph on her computer Janice may have a divergent idea and switch into a new document. She will no longer see the first document on the screen and, caught up in her new focus, will forget most of the details of its contents. Something similar may happen when we switch from thinking in the waking world to creating a dream scenario. Giving less attention to the scenario at hand should per this analogy increase memory retrievability, though Janice found this hard to confirm in the only lucid experiment devoted to the question.

"Just Forget About It": Dream Amnesia

The possibility that dream experience is not normally processed into a higher frame of reference as it occurs, that is, analyzed and stored in the way of waking experience, would help account for the striking failure most people have in remembering their dreams. Although lucidity seems to compensate to some extent, while dreaming we may not usually bother to put forth or be able to put forth the level of attention required to remember much of what happens. Thinking over what *can* be recalled upon awakening from a dream would consign the scraps remaining in working memory to more permanent storage after the fact,[12] when one's brain chemistry has shifted to allow efficient processing again. In the terms of the computer analogy, anything Janice writes in the second, "dream" document will be lost when she switches back to the main, "waking" one unless she has the presence of mind to save the stray file to disk or to clip part of the text and bring it back to the main document with her.

Alternatively, we may tend to forget dreams in part because waking up is so discontinuous with the preceding action, making poor recall as much a matter of dissociation as of poor memory. Indeed, occasionally a forgotten dream will return in a flash after some chance reminder later on, showing that it did somehow register, at least for a while. Also, with practice it becomes easier and easier to remember dreams, so they cannot be so removed from awareness as all that.

It would, however, prove maladaptive to transfer ordinary dreams *as they occur* directly into memory, because they are erroneously taken as real. They must be reinterpreted first, making a psychologically sound case for simply forgetting them. If bits of them do chance to linger or return after waking, once classified as imaginary by the waking mind the material will not alter any records of the past or models of the world. Lucidity would tend to remove this obstacle by allowing a correct interpretation during the dream itself.

Familiar Faces

Most of us seldom make the leap to lucidity, however, and because of the critical thinking and memory deficits in dreams, we tend to tolerate peculiarities, however absurd the story or situation presented. Therefore, role-playing plays at least as great a part in ordinary dreaming as it does in lucid dreaming. A lucid dreamer might act a part or go along with a scenario for fun, but when nonlucid our tenuous mental status lets us get caught up in all manner of strange entanglements.

Further, underneath the veneer of the unfamiliar in dreams lies the familiar. This may be another reason why strange dream events often do not surprise us much, since they largely arise from our own expectations and internalized models, including models of the imaginary as presented in works of fiction. While we may have problems with certain aspects of explicit recall, tacit memories of the structuring principles of various events and interactions seem to be out in abundance. No matter how weird, then, dreams could *seem* familiar and sensible.

This substructure of the familiar upon which even the oddest dreams are built impressed the occult philosopher P. D. Ouspensky, who emphasized motor memory as a primary factor motivating the incidental images in dreams. Ouspensky observed that familiar routes become impressed in memory and reproduce themselves in dreams, in general feeling if not necessarily in exact detail. "The 'road' you see in dreams," he wrote, "may not resemble outwardly the road you actually know and remember when awake, but it will produce the same impressions as the road you know and are familiar with, and will give you the same sensations."[13] Janice often noticed not only fictive dream streets, but also rooms and other locales having the "feel" of and readily converting into familiar ones on their own or with minimum effort.

This effect emphasizes the fact that, since we have minimal sensory cues while asleep, we must rely for the construction of the dream environment on mental records, including those of recurrent experiences and long-term memories of various kinds. Thus the frequent occurrence in dreams of familiar people as well as places.

Only a low percentage of the dreams of 1650 subjects analyzed by researchers Calvin Hall, Robert Van de Castle and Frederick Snyder contained fantastic elements, while nearly all dreams featured at least one character familiar to the dreamer.[14] Of course, a dream character may only *suggest* a particular person without really bearing him or her much resemblance, a detail which might not be noted in a recorded account. Treating the character accordingly anyway can enhance the resemblance, showing the shaping power of memory at work.

Keep That in Mind

In addition to familiar perceptions, current waking preoccupations often linger in the mind during sleep, then help shape dream content. For instance, when Jay fell asleep on the couch in the evening after reading Hobson's *The Dreaming Brain*, he dreamed about continuing to read from the book. Such persistence of memory allows some individuals to program in advance for specific dream content. Janice can still remember successfully concentrating upon dinosaurs before sleep to produce images of the awesome creatures in one childhood nap.

However, the thoughts we have *while dreaming* largely determine dream content, whether they cover the same matters as our waking musings or not. Because dreams are indeterminate and usually follow our thoughts and expectations, anything that we anticipate happening often does. So when Jay and his family stopped at a run-down hotel in a nonlucid dream of his, he feared the accommodations would be terrible, and sure enough the whole wing they walked through got progressively worse until nothing remained but broken doorways and missing walls. In dreams, we can live through our greatest hopes as well as our worst fears, typically without even realizing how we have set ourselves up.

Indeterminacy characterizes not only dream imagery, then, but dream narrative itself. Dream plots can change direction from one scene to another without any coherence, and according to some research rarely have a consistent narrative structure from beginning to end.[15] One association simply follows another, which follows another in an infinite digression. Such fragmentation and lack of thematic continuity go hand in hand with rambling, go-with-the-flow thinking, itself abetted by the usual lack of clear memory from moment to moment while dreaming.

This would also explain why so many dreams remain incomplete, ending before any story comes to a resolution. As with lying, once we start to confabulate, we must continue to confabulate in an attempt to reach a satisfactory conclusion, until very complex scenarios get constructed. More often than not, however, we wake up before reaching a conclusion.

By that point, thanks to the memory problems that plague dreams we often remember chiefly the last part of the story. We may have forgotten so much of it that we will not be able to see where the confabulations started, and we may even falsely reconstruct the actual sequence of dream events or unknowingly invent a few. Because of the digressive nature of dreaming, what we do remember may well be at the greatest contrast to reality, and far away from the original suggestion factors which started the process. Still, a bit of reasoning may be able to tease some of these out, as the next sections will demonstrate.

BRAIN MATTERS: PHYSIOLOGY AND CONTROL

Several aspects of dreams often prove especially contrary for the lucid dreamer attempting to control them, including visual resolution and lighting level, bodily movement, and reading text. This section will show how the problems that arise in these and other areas can be traced both to specific neurophysiological causes and to misapplication of effort on the part of the dreamer, erroneously trying to treat the dream environment as if it existed independently of the mind.

You Can't Win 'Em All

Instability and inaccuracy have a way of sabotaging even the most lucid of dream endeavors. Getting anything done in a straightforward manner in a dream can be difficult indeed, since dream elements so readily appear, alter or disappear from moment to moment. Random intrusions make for a perceptible disjunction between the scenario assumed or imposed by the dreamer and the actual imagery produced, with a constant tension between the two sources of suggestion.

Further, because the mind alone really produces the effects in dreams, the dream ego's direct efforts and actions will often fail: it cannot move, cannot see, cannot hear or smell or taste, cannot manipulate objects properly, and so on. Some of the factors whose combination creates expected images may be absent. A great deal of frustration and anxiety in dreams may thus result not as a reflection of any waking psychological distress, but from trying to think and behave logically in an unstable environment where nothing reliably works.

The dreamer typically resorts to rationalization to account for the various malfunctions and instabilities experienced while dreaming. Yet why extend the rationalization tendency into waking and assume that such dream problems must somehow be meaningful? Dream telephone failure, for example—a very common vexation—may have more to do with difficulty simulating the operation of an electrical device that normally works independently of one's thoughts than it does with some symbolic inability to "get through to someone" in waking. Similar simple explanations presumably exist for all the difficulties the dream ego will commonly face.

Cast Into the Inner Darkness

Consider how false awakening and OBE-type lucid dreams occasionally start out dark or even completely imageless. Seeing this lack of resolution as somehow symbolic—of being unable to shed light on a situation, say—would overlook more empirical explanations. For one thing, the dreamer may have been concentrating heavily on kinesthetic rather than visual sensations to begin the experience. For another, given that it usually *is* dark when people sleep, if they sleep lightly enough to detect this or even just remember when they went to bed, their bedroom scenes will likely be dark, while their random scenes may have more freedom from this restriction, as was the case for Janice. Additionally, given that if one stays asleep long enough the lighting usually increases, the brain may have to reach a certain level of activation to generate normal dream vision, perhaps moving from NREM to REM sleep.

Many lucid dreamers report generally finding it impossible to enhance the lighting level in a room immediately by means of dream lamps.[16] These frustratingly stay unlit, flicker, or come on only dimly—an effect Keith Hearne called the "light-switch" phenomenon.[17] Lamps, like all electrical devices, commonly fail to work properly in dreams because, after all, they are not actually wired to the household current, being mere simulations of physical objects. Sometimes, though, a bit of focused attention and will can help them function more normally.

Stephen LaBerge set out to test this factor using *NightLight* subscribers as his subjects.[18] Once lucid, the volunteers tried to turn a dream light on and off mechanically and also to will it on and off. With either approach, about half of the attempts succeeded in making lamps go on, so the "light-switch" phenomenon did not always prevail. Even more attempts succeeded in making the lamps go off, perhaps because doing so restored the original ambience of the dream held in the back of the dreamer's mind, or because it is easier to ignore than to stimulate whatever brain activity may be necessary for the illusion of light. In fact, of those who managed to turn on a fixture, not all experienced a change in the actual *illumination*, a distinction which the experiment instructions did not make. Ruth noticed that there was never any real illumination of the room, only the brief illusion of a light going on. At any rate, the reported results, and a few of our independent dream experiences, suggest that lighting level is not entirely impervious to change, but there is nevertheless a general difficulty with increasing it which may indicate that the potential intensity of this quantity tends to be governed by the state itself.

To turn to another visual resolution issue, the sudden, temporary fading of an ongoing scene that interrupts so many lucid dreams does not always result from attempting some disruptive maneuver or failing to promote the dream actively, some observed face of pretend adversity. Interacting with other characters in a dream scenario in that manner would almost require occasional efforts at control, of one's thoughts at the very least, to remain mindful of lucidity and not automatically respond as one would to a reality. The distinction between reacting to dreamed events as if they were real and *pretending* to be reacting as if they were real for the plot's sake is a subtle but crucial one. When lucid enough Janice would try to be careful about the way she conceptualized her assumptions, thinking for instance that when she made a lot of noise other characters could be *presumed* to have heard her rather than that they did hear her.

Some dreamers may prefer to divorce themselves more thoroughly from the circumstances of the dream and not participate so directly in the action. Stephen LaBerge asserted in his popular introduction to lucid dreaming that he never becomes lucid in dreams that he simply observes and that "participation seems a virtual requirement for lucid dreaming."[10] Yet we personally found that the amount of "physical" involvement with the dream on the part of the dream ego made little difference in terms of becoming lucid or maintaining lucidity. We could be just as lucid when disembodied or quietly standing around watching and mulling over a scene as when engaged with an activity—perhaps more so—although without at least some attention focused on it the scene could disappear.

Variations in activities and modes of involvement depend upon the inclination of thought after attaining lucidity. The choices seem to be highly capricious, and inclinations may change from time to time during the course of the dream if it goes on long enough. One might interrupt a story briefly for an experiment, say, or jump between active role-playing and being a disembodied observer to the dream, sometimes by deliberate choice, sometimes not. It becomes quite a challenge to stay lucid through such changeability.

Wishful Thinking: Dreams and Fantasies

We found that we could take time out to daydream and fantasize within lucid dreams, even sometimes come up with preliminary nonlucid stretch. After all, they brought more of their faculties along from the start—more of their waking personas, memories and critical wherewithal. False awakening or OBE-type dreams usually had the greatest mnemonic advantage when it came to remembering intentions for lucid activities.

There was an interesting twist to this matter of false awakenings, though. Even when we seemed quite lucid, an inaccurate false awakening setting would usually make us assume ourselves asleep in a former house or other incorrect location because of the misleading context cues. This suggests that lucid dreamers do not always remember that they went to bed not long ago so much as infer it from the realization that they must be dreaming, and that the specifics easily disappear along with everything else about the recent past.

Other memory confusions can muddy the lucidity of dreams as well. Even when lucid we sometimes recalled dated material as current, as with the local shop Janice misremembered as a shoe store although it had long since been replaced by something else. We also identified incidents from earlier dreams as valid events, as in the case of Jay's talking with his mother recounted above. Or we concocted completely false memories about events in our lives to advance the dream in the dearth of conflicting real ones, often until waking dispelled such notions. Ruth believed in one incident that she had recently visited Janice in England rather than Pennsylvania, and wondered why she could not recall what the English countryside looked like. In this the dream state bears a curious resemblance to the kind of amnesia caused by damage to the frontal lobes of the brain, a condition similarly characterized by false memories, confabulation, poor deliberate retrieval of information, and a tendency to be unaware of one's memory problems.[17]

An interesting complication is that increased lucidity sometimes *decreases* control ability. With greater access to memories one may remember more interfering factors, such as the confining laws of interacting with the waking world or one's own insecurities about control. Tacitly lucid instances in which dreamers exert direct control over situations without literally realizing they are dreaming may therefore exhibit more lucid behavior than some semilucid obviously in the real world her stunt proved she must sometimes do that kind of thing even in reality. Quite often, we comprehend certain dream features as bizarre only *after* waking and gaining back our real-world perspective. Only in a dream would Janice use burning matches to affix stamps to envelopes, though it seemed natural enough at the time.

Our *concurrent* reactions to dream bizarreness vary widely, depending upon what we manage to think about strange incidents as they occur. If we can remember enough of waking concerns, a situation which would be startling in waking, such as a lion prowling on one's street, will also be startling in a dream. If, on the other hand, we do not worry about such imagery, we can ignore even the most potentially frightening scenario.

Uncritical acceptance of certain dream images may reflect a lack of clear thinking, if for instance we do not recognize the lion as a threat and remark, "The neighbors have let that lion of theirs out again." A blasé attitude may also indicate tacit lucidity, if we discard the possibility of a threat and think, "A lion? I can handle lions." Strong emotional reactions more appropriate to waking, like "Oh my God, it's a lion!" would fall somewhere in between. All possible reactions to strange imagery, when considered together, thus display a range of "lucidity" even within the so-called nonlucidity of ordinary dreams.

A HEAD IN THE CLOUDS: DREAMTIME THOUGHTS AND REMEMBRANCES

Differences in the ways that our mental abilities function in the waking and dreaming states significantly shape dreams and account for much of their strangeness. Although rationality levels usually drop during dreaming, the phenomenon of lucidity demonstrates that this does not have to be the case in order for a dream to go on. Another prominent characteristic of dream consciousness, however, is much more critical to the process of dream creation: the peculiar state of dream memory. While some memory components, such as associations and habits, make up many of the constituent threads of dream experience, a lack of connection with other orienting causes that we discussed previously. Sometimes blank spots—which almost always had a neutral color tone ranging from white and gray to brown and black—occurred even when we remained fully engaged with a scenario. This type may tie in with a phenomenon documented by sleep researchers: the alternation within a REM episode between active *phasic* periods and more quiescent *tonic* periods.

In phasic REM, correlated in laboratory studies with vivid dreaming, the eyes jerk about and muscles in the limbs, face and middle ears twitch. The more relaxed tonic REM, on the other hand, correlates with more thoughtlike mentation.[19] If periodic bursts of eye movement normally excite the visual system and help produce dream imagery,[20] this might explain why Janice found that waiting for a minute or so, without making much effort to persist with the scenario, could nevertheless restore lost lucid dream visuals, and why deliberately rolling her eyes sometimes brought them back even faster, though they might be sketchy at first.

Perhaps, too, from time to time one simply senses one's real closed eyelids, darkening the scene by suggestion. This would probably occur most often during light sleep. Some blank spots may even be an artifact of lucidity pushing the mind closer to wakefulness. On the other hand, since a dream perception exists only as long as it gets attended to, and since people do not customarily *look* for light in order to perceive it in waking, dream lighting should be experienced as unstable, readily ceasing when the dreamer pays more heed to something else.

Presumably, comparable blank spots of whatever origin occurring in nonlucid dreams would usually be elided by the mind, which would afterwards recall only a scene change. Janice did on one occasion remember an imageless interlude of thinking and imagining between nonlucid dream scenes when she woke shortly afterwards, which she had not registered at all while dreaming. Although we personally never noticed any blind spells in our nonlucid dreams, Ouspensky did report having nonlucid nightmares of blindness, which he eventually concluded had resulted from sensing his shut eyes.[21]

"School Nights" and Other Miscues

Memory problems inform a distinct class of standard dream plots. Consider school dreams, for instance: plaguing dramas of trouble remembering one's class schedule, locker location and combination, or test material. Interpreters might take such dreams as indicating fears of failure of various kinds. However, school obviously made a big impression on all our lives for many years, creating a deep rut in the path of our long-term recollections into which dream ruminations could easily slip.

Perhaps the difficulty accessing *recent* memory in the dream state evokes that time when memory constituted a major concern, no matter how well we performed scholastically. Once regressed, we cannot remember our classroom, locker number or exam answer because there is no such thing *to* remember. We have simply cued off the school scene reflexively, assuming that we belong there, so when we do not know the required information we conclude we must have forgotten it or never learned it. Incidentally, the fact that people do not typically come up with any *real* factual information of the kind sought during school dreams indicates again that we do not automatically gain access to forgotten memories from bygone eras when dreaming.

The same combination of miscuing and lack of memory may also create another common school dream theme, that of falling behind on course reading, homework or projects. Naturally we cannot remember having done any schoolwork, because we really have *not* done any, so if we accept the idea of being in school then of course we must be behind due to absence or negligence.

In later life, we may find ourselves unprepared to give a speech or presentation in a dream because we truly did not prepare one. Similarly, if we come across a dream library book or videotape, we cannot remember checking it out so it must be long overdue. Or if we find that we have a pet or plant we cannot remember owning, we must have forgotten to feed or water it, as invariably seemed to happen with the mysterious tropical fish Janice used to find in her dreams. This dream pattern does not, then, have to be a metaphor for some unresolved issue facing the dreamer in the real world. The

"It's an Omen": Religious and Folk Belief

Another common approach has taken dreams as messages from some external spiritual agent, whether from God or any number of gods, angels, or even devils. The ancient civilizations of Mesopotamia, Egypt, China, Greece, and Rome accorded dreams the status of oracles, and their kings, priests and prophets especially practiced dream incubation as a method to receive oneiric revelations on particular issues. The Bible includes numerous accounts of divinely inspired dreams, such as in the story of Jacob's ladder, although medieval European Christians came to associate dreaming with witchcraft and thought dreams of violence and sexuality inspired by temptations from demons.[4] Certain people in Western society today still regard at least some of their dreams as coming from God or actually involving encounters with divine beings.[5]

Coexistent with this religious view of dreams, another perspective has taken dreams as divinatory vehicles of less clearly defined origin. In nearly all times and places, dreams seem to have had a place in folklore as omens predicting future happenings. To decipher such messages, specific images were assigned specific symbolic meanings, some fairly obvious, others varying widely from culture to culture because of unique linguistic associations. So, for instance, in ancient China a dream of a heavily laden orchard logically signified that the person's line would be fruitful, while in ancient Egypt to expose the bottom in a dream meant that the dreamer would be orphaned—not as arbitrary a connection as it looks, since the Egyptian language used the same word for both "buttocks" and "orphan."[6]

Such folk interpretations remain quite common, and abound in the numerous books available on dream meanings. Many are so generalized as to be reminiscent of fortune cookies, such as assertions of good luck to come, while others can be detailed and specific to the point of absurdity. This example from a popular symbol dictionary must originally have been one person's bizarre montage, since the chances of anyone replicating it are nil:

Hobson's Choice: Movement as Motivator

Since the visual component of dreams disappears so easily in blank spots, this otherwise prominent sensory element may often be one of the higher levels of elaboration on whatever internal stimuli provoke dreaming.[22] The sense of having a movable body, however, is the most persistent perception in blank phases and therefore possibly a more primary component. According to the activation-synthesis hypothesis, in fact, the complex excitation patterns of the brainstem neurons that generate sequences of coordinated movement compel the dream ego's motions and hence the course of the dream. "The conscious correlation of the brain's motor commands," writes Hobson, "form an important part of dream-action construction . . . . In REM sleep, these motor-command sequences stimulate the perception of dream acts."[23]

Undeniably, whatever motor neurons remain "up and running" during sleep send out real movement commands, which must be inhibited by another set of impulses to prevent actual movement during the intense neural activation characteristic of REM.[24] We have occasionally awakened with the real body briefly acting out what began as deliberate or involuntary dream motions, usually in light sleep. We have also seen motor effects in action while in hypnagogic sleep, similarly resulting in actual movements of the physical body since the muscles, though relaxed, are not actually immobilized at that phase. For instance, Ruth had a hypnagogic experience of cutting a triangle out of paper and found her thumb and forefinger moving back and forth as if she really had scissors in her hand, the motion persisting even after the visuals faded.

We do not, however, commonly experience during dreaming what Hobson called a "sense of compelled or involuntary motor activity," which he took as evidence for underlying movement commands from the brainstem propelling the dream ego around.[25] We *could* feel pushed along in such a manner when we deliberately stopped directing our movements in lucid dreams and ended up floating along willy-nilly or gently propelled in one direction—which, incidentally, some would interpret as giving up control to the "spiritual" or "unconscious." Ruth experienced uncontrolled, usually high-speed dream movement from time to time; she had one case in which she felt her body involuntarily moved backwards along a sidewalk for a time, as an example. However, our dream movements have so much more often been purposive that in our view, brainstem activation may account for occasional instances of uncontrolled movement but perhaps usually only underlies dream activity to an extent without completely determining it.

Hobson acknowledges that dream movement is not necessarily entirely automatic, since the motor cortex, center of voluntary movement, also remains functional during dreaming.[26] Hence it seems obvious that not all dream motion occurs via the mind trying to make sense of the brainstem's patterned motor signals. Laboratory equipment has verified this by showing electrical activity in the relevant muscles when a trained lucid subject makes deliberate movements with the dream body. For instance, Stephen LaBerge could spell out his initials in Morse code while lucid by clenching his dream fists, the impulses in his real hands being sufficient to register on an electromyograph (EMG) device.[27]

In lucid dreams one can definitely stop moving or take other volitional actions apart from the dream flow, as Janice discovered when she decided to brake her dream bicycle while zipping downhill and received quite a jolt when it stopped dead. Moreover, since intentionally moving around in imageless zones or at the start of OBEs will eventually bring on imagery, it may make no difference to the synthesizing brain whether the motor impulses it incorporates into its constructions go off on their own or arise from volitional dream actions.

Although the prevalence of the kinesthetic element in dreams may be due to the high level of activation of the motor-pattern generator during REM, some alternative explanations suggest themselves. Exaggeration of movement may as likely result from the overall impulsiveness of dream behavior, coupled with the fact that the excessive but illusory motion can only wear out the dream body by expectation. Ruth and Jay could run and fly inexhaustibly in their lucid dreams, and while Janice typically could not, she certainly put on incredible bursts of speed. Since exaggerated activities in dreams expend little if any real energy, and exact no social cost, little exists to constrain them—though excitement will sometimes increase heart rate, blood pressure and other stress-activated systems to the point of waking the individual.

Also, seeming movement may be as much a matter of focus as any other component of dream experience. Janice began to notice at a point that she covered more ground at a stride when walking at a normal pace in her lucid dreams than she could do in reality. Remembering an old trick, she looked at the corner ahead of her in one lucid dream and wished to be beside it; after a brief wavering effect to the visuals, she was there. Every subsequent time she tried this trick in the dream, she ended up inadvertently lifting off the ground and floating to the desired point instead. Still, both effects show leg motions such as those stored in motor memory to be quite superfluous when it comes to moving the dream body.

Even more tellingly, we succeeded on occasion in moving the dream scene without moving the dream body at all. Jay once rotated his vision of a dream hallway around while simply hovering in the air, and Janice found she could make the scenery outside a dream window roll backwards and forwards as it would appear from the point of view of flying over it while merely sitting still looking out at it. This suggests that movement may be overrepresented in dream accounts at least in part because one might naturally assume that normal movement occurred when actually the dream ego's perspective merely changed in response to changes in attention.

Reading Into It

The problems many people report with reading in dreams might also be illuminated by considering the neurological and perceptual deficits inherent to dreaming. Dream print may be indecipherable, or if it can be read the words may prove nonsensical or shift between glances. The late astrophysicist and author Carl Sagan, who found dream text impossible to register, attributed this difficulty to impairment during sleep of the left cerebral hemisphere, which contains centers for verbal ability and analytic recollection.[28]

Janice occasionally noticed a kind of verbal disability in her dreams, in that she would have trouble remembering names or would misidentify people and things, as when she saw a big house under construction and impulsively exclaimed, "Westminster Palace!" although there was no resemblance. In one case the sentence she wanted to say came out as nonsense with unintended noun substitutions, reminiscent of Alice's distorted verses in Wonderland. Yet, people usually seem to speak and understand speech in dreams well enough, so their verbal ability cannot be all that impaired. In fact LaBerge found evidence of left hemisphere *activation* accompanying the onset of lucidity,[29] though lucidity does not make it any easier to read dream print.

More simply, attempts to decode dream text should prove problematic because of the false assumption that the written words exist at all. We dreamers try to perceive what we in fact project, that is, generate from our own knowledge sieved through learned patterns of verbal construction. Real words may similarly be nearly illegible or even seem to "change" when, inaccurately filling in information from an inner model, we misread something at first in the outer world. But in such cases we will eventually lock onto the right interpretation because the words actually exist. Not so in dreams, where modeling alone generates the text.

Moreover, the dreaming mind's simulation of any item is potentially inaccurate and bizarre, and it cannot sustain stable imagery of any kind for more than a short period of time. Text, as a particularly detailed and specific image, should therefore be particularly hard to simulate.[30] Difficulties with dream reading will sometimes translate into images of poor quality print or bad handwriting as a kind of rationalization.

Janice and Ruth also had trouble with the verbal task of attempting to write words, particularly at length. Their dream fingers might skip letters or make other ones than those intended, and the letters tended to alter once written. Jay speculated that such dream "dyslexia" might result from impeded fine motor control due to lack of proper feedback from the hands rather than from any left-hemisphere impairment, since drawing complex pictures in dreams, a comparable manual activity involving the *right* hemisphere, can also present problems. Yet Janice and Ruth had no difficulty cutting out shapes in dreams, another spatial, largely right-brain task requiring fine motor control. So if changes in brain-region activation do have some bearing on the skills possible in dreams, it would seem to be a rather more complex matter than simple hemispheric dominance.[31]

Perhaps the reading and writing problem indicates a more tenuous *communication* between the two hemispheres of the brain in dreaming than in waking, the pattern recognition of print being more of a right-brain function, sequential interpretation of it a left. In any case, instability interfering with letters, words and lines staying put, plus trouble with detailed visualization, could account for the bulk of the problems with reading, writing and drawing in dreams, *and*, one might add, with no symbolic implication of any waking communication problem.

Out of the Mouths of Dream Characters

Speaking of communication problems, quite often the speech of dream characters, while conforming to standard rules of grammar and roughly forming a conversation, will make little actual sense. At times character talk may even be an unintelligible jumble, perhaps gibberish overheard from the dreaming brain. For example, one female character whom Ruth queried about dreams came out with a senseless word salad, and a male character a moment later said he dreamed "European dreams."

Paul Tholey maintains that the commentary of characters merely *seems* like nonsense to the inexperienced, when in fact it takes the form of coded messages. "Most of these figures," he asserts, "play word games involving hidden or multiple meanings which the dream-ego can not initially understand. Thus, it is not surprising that the dream-ego considers the other dream figures [sic] speech to be pure nonsense—although it can later often be shown to have a logical meaning."[32]

More likely, the Babel effect comes from the dreamer anticipating the kind of reasonable response usual in waking, without realizing how his or her own attention must interact with the imagined conversation for it to have a semblance of intelligibility. In our experience, rational conversations with characters usually do not last long, because their speech becomes incoherent or ceases when one stops paying attention to it or even pays too close attention to it. Switching focus, whether by listening intently to the words or by attending to other thoughts entirely, seems to inhibit generating the speech. Any "hidden meanings" to the resulting mishmash will merely be imposed on the text in later consideration.

In support of this interpretation of the phenomenon, our dream characters did not, overall, exhibit more than a borrowed awareness. In one case Janice kept thinking of things she would like to script a dream man to say then deciding she would rather have his speech be spontaneous. He all the while kept making as if to speak then hesitating during her moments of indecision, with the result that the poor man never got to say anything. Also—again due to the limitations of attention—we found it almost impossible to maintain two sensible monologues at once, that of the dream ego and that of a dream character. This too suggests that both word streams come from a single source.

MUCH ADO ABOUT NOTHING: DREAM MOTIFS UNMASKED

Many of the classic images and themes that intrigue dream interpreters, and which almost everyone has experienced at one time or another, can be divested of symbolic significance by a more closely reasoned approach to why such elements might turn up frequently in dreams.[33] This section will consider a number of such motifs and how they might be inspired not by perceptions relevant to the dreamer's waking life, but by such suggestion factors as sleep physiology, bodily sensations, memory problems, and the effects of attention, all tapping into typical aspects of human psychology.

Falling For It

Since bodily feelings—or the lack thereof—can sometimes affect dream content, perhaps specific sensations common to sleepers can elicit specific common imagery. As a case in point, one of the standard reality tests employed by lucid dreamers hinges on the dream body's ability to float. Weightlessness in dreams probably results from the sleeping brain receiving minimal input from the physical body, including no pressure on the soles of the feet to indicate that they rest on the ground.[34] Given the age-old human fascination with flight, partially recognizing this *absence* of sensation may lead to pleasant dreams of flying, or, if it causes panic, to dreams of falling. Kinesthetic images of flights or falls do not, then, have to evolve from respective waking feelings of elation or despair about life situations.

Some researchers suspect a correlation between dream falling and sleep-related disruption of the vestibular system, the inner ear structures that control balance.[35] The brain might get confused by the flood of dream motor impulses suggesting motion when it simultaneously detects the real body lying still. In a similar vein, Hobson maintains that the galvanic muscle jerks at sleep onset that occasionally jolt people awake come from the motor system remaining active after higher brain systems have shifted gears for sleep. Sometimes such a twitch is accompanied by a sensation of falling, a dream fragment probably suggested by the momentary motor impulse[36]—and a less than pleasant literalization of "falling asleep." Janice has had sleep-onset dreamlets about trying to stop objects or herself from falling, resulting in her real arms or legs jerking and so waking her. She has also observed sleep-onset "falls" that seem to tie to startlement at the sudden absence of bodily perception, or even to the beginnings of conflicting dream-body perception.

Think too of the recurrent dream disaster of *teeth* falling out or breaking, traditionally interpretable as representing losing face or stature in some way. On the other hand, all of us share a degree of dentistry alarm, memories of childhood or adult tooth loss, and a strong cultural emphasis on the importance of a good smile. Any of these factors could well influence our dreams from time to time. And maybe that particular set of anxieties can sometimes be evoked by purely physical stimuli, such as the absence of the sensation we would normally get when our teeth solidly touch together, or perhaps bruxism, the common but harmful habit of grinding the teeth in sleep.

Paying too much attention to dream teeth could also cause a certain amount of instability and exaggerate any known flaws. Attention certainly seems to create other dream "health problems" by playing on our fears. Any minor condition a person has been monitoring in waking can magnify into a serious disability when viewed through the distorting lens of dream perception. For instance, in one nonlucid dream Jay noticed a dramatic bump below his right thumb, apparently in reflection of a small bump he had had below his *left* thumb temporarily in reality.

Embarrassing Moments

Some of the most embarrassing dream incidents may devolve from simple physical sensations or discomforts playing on one's conditioned inhibitions. Dreaming of being naked or incompletely dressed in public, for instance, may not pertain to any waking-life insecurity, as those partial to symbolism might conclude. Since the three of us often found our dream selves in an approximation of whatever we wore to bed, dream states of undress may merely reflect a habit of sleeping in the nude or lightly clad, or else result from not sensing one's bed covers or from being cold, as Ouspensky pointed out long ago.[37]

The dream ego may be unperturbed at being in dishabille in certain instances, or only vaguely concerned, as when a nonlucid Jay found himself in pajamas and thought he should start dressing better for work. It may even feel inclined to disrobe, an activity sometimes hampered by an unusual difficulty in removing the unwanted clothing. This may reflect a conflict with waking-life behavioral rules, or just the ordinary problems attendant on trying to use the dream body like a real one.

Running up against our universal training not to relieve ourselves while asleep might figure in the unpleasant occurrence of dreams about hard-to-find, crowded bathrooms and toilets too strange or too dirty to use. Such dreams could easily be prompted by a real need to urinate rather than, say, some waking complex. Toilets also overflow frequently, malfunctioning just like other dream appliances, so this does not have to indicate difficulty flushing out negativity.

Jay used to have similar dreams about worthless shower installations when it was nearly time to get up and get ready for work, on one occasion finding himself trying to take a shower in a bedroom where neither the window blinds nor the door would stay closed. The frequent lack of privacy during dream bathroom or shower quests may result from our fears about such intrusions serving to produce them, or even from the fact that solitude seldom lasts long in dreams even under less compromising circumstances. Characters tend to appear whenever the dream ego stays alone and still, perhaps because activity in the brain will always suggest activity going on around one.

Romantic assignations in dreams also often lack privacy, presumably for the same reasons. The frequency of sexual encounters in dreams may relate not only to our culture's engrossment with sex, but to the fact that both males and females normally experience genital engorgement during REM sleep. Sexual arousal may be a consistent feature of the dreaming body because the hypothalamus, the part of the brain which regulates sex hormone release, also regulates dream sleep[38]—a core of verity to Freudian theory, less the negative psychoanalytical connotations. In any case, the turgidity might tend to suggest sexual content—although, interestingly, there appears to be no automatic correlation between erotic content and wet dreams.[39]

In addition, the typical dream tendency to act on impulses with little reflection and without real consequences would likewise encourage dreams of sex, including variants one might avoid in waking or liaisons with normally prohibited partners. Impulsiveness could also evoke the instinctual "fight or flight" response and promote violence and other excessive or immature behavior not necessarily typical of the waking personality. Janice has amazed herself with the fluent and uncharacteristic cursing she can muster in dreams. Such behavior may not, then, really indicate any serious latent deviance, however surprised one may feel about it after waking up.

fact that dreams *can* center around unresolved issues of the past or present may be because the very ambiguity of the dream environment suggests such issues to the dreaming mind.

The preoccupation with time and fretfulness at being late endemic to the modern world inform some dream scenarios dependent on miscuing and memory problems. Whether we have a real memory about needing to go somewhere in the waking world or only a stray thought about taking a wholly fictive trip, we assume in the dream that we *are* supposed to be going there imminently and thus must be running late—fittingly enough, since the time available in a dream is indeed limited. Janice was forever being surprised by "dream vacations" for which she had to prepare at the last minute. If we suddenly "remember" about going on such a trip, we must not have packed for it or picked up our tickets, since we cannot remember doing so. Then, in accordance with our anxious expectation, we will probably even miss or experience delays on the public transportation, a scenario which does not have to be a metaphor for missing some real opportunity.

Out of the Loop: Traps of Attention

The perceptual habits we build up in waking do not always serve us well in dreams. Since we do not normally put forth any mental effort to keep the physical world in line with our expectations, while dreaming we will tend to extend this habit. Consequently, we easily fail to find something we know we saw just a few minutes ago or which we only passively expect to locate in its normal context. The missing element becomes the mainspring of a dream plot if we focus on trying to figure out what happened to it and how to get it back, but it has no necessary ties to any personal qualities we may need to seek within ourselves. Hence too the penchant of dream buildings and streets to rearrange themselves until everything gets stranger and stranger and *we* become hopelessly lost, not as a reflection of any waking predicament but because we do not realize that we may have to *make* them configure normally.

A trick of attention likewise creates the common theme of

wandering endlessly through rooms in a house or otherwise looping through part of a dream over and over. Fixation on a dream task, from avoiding enemies to climbing up and down staircases to opening doors to searching for particular characters, serves to perpetuate it, rather than signifying being stuck in some inescapable waking dilemma. The fun variant of discovering intriguing new rooms or secret passages in one's home would similarly seem to arise from the fascination lavished on the exploration rather than heralding some untapped potential.

Occasionally a given element catches the attention enough to recur in various dreams throughout the night, since recall of striking scenes will tend to influence later ones. This effect can also occur when the dreamer is unwell or ill at ease and single-mindedly preoccupied with his or her malaise, such as the night Janice had an awful cold and invariably dreamed of London Underground stops every time she managed to nod off. Unusual dream motifs that recur repeatedly over time for individual dreamers, such as horseback riding in Janice's case, typically connect with their individual interests and preoccupations and may be seen as part of their personal styles of dreaming rather than as especially important personal symbols.

Your Own Worst Enemy: Creating Nightmares

Nightmares have exerted a grim hold on the human imagination for ages. Yet these dark and troubling episodes do not necessarily point to serious conflicts or phobias within the dreamer, nor even to overwhelming waking troubles of an external nature like income tax crises. They may more often result from confusion over what is happening *in the dream*, from mistaking wild and frightening dream events for realities.

Also, since thoughts and feelings help generate dream imagery, an anxious thought, whether carried into sleep or provoked by the dream scenario, can manifest as a threatening character. This objectified fear often cannot be evaded or destroyed, not because we lack the ability to deal with some real problem, but because as long as we sustain the anxiety during the dream, it will continue to project in some form. Even in lucid dreams, where one does not fear the threatening characters, they still tend to persist from the unwonted attention given to them.

Some nightmarish elements may relate to certain side effects of sleeping. Consider the classic nightmare sequence in which the victim cannot run to escape the pursuer. Such immobility, for all its fright value, could arise from nothing more than detecting a specific bodily sensation endemic to sleep: the inhibition of motor impulses that keeps us safely in bed during REM. One would be most likely to notice this paralysis during a full-fledged dream either when in some especially awkward position in bed, or when intently focused on trying to move—such as when fleeing in panic. Hence it may have nothing whatsoever to do with feelings of helplessness regarding a waking-world crisis, as an interpreter might suppose.

For some people, sleep position seems to affect the likelihood both of having nightmares and of having lucid dreams. Ruth has most commonly had bad dreams when lying on her back, probably for some physiological reason such as greater difficulty breathing or greater impedance of circulation in that position. Janice found as a teenager that sleeping on her left side prevented the weird sleep-onset hallucinations that she found so disturbing when sleeping on her back, though she later switched to the latter position when she wished to encourage such experiences and to train herself to dream lucidly. Interestingly, the Lucidity Institute reported the results of an experiment suggesting that sleeping on the back or right side correlated with an increased likelihood of having lucid dreams, possibly because of differences in the hemispheric activation associated with particular positions.[40] This finding needs more thorough investigation, however.

The thrashing, screaming "night terrors" which so many children experience are not nightmares per se but panic attacks that accompany incomplete awakenings from NREM sleep.[41] The motor system activates while much of the rest of the brain remains hallucinatory for a while, such that concerned parents have a hard time soothing the hysterical victims. Jay, who suffered from such incidents as a small boy, has speculated that he might have panicked at becoming partially lucid in the midst of deep sleep, something not easily classifiable by his young, sleeping mind. We will have more to report on the strange world of sleep-border phenomena in the final chapter of the book.

TAKING THE GENERAL VIEW

This chapter has discussed the probable impact of a number of neurological and somatic suggestion factors in the creation of common dreams. Yet such factors can be ignored or habituated and so may only occasionally intrude on awareness enough to elicit specific dream content, though they may often influence such content. Whatever its physiological underpinnings, dreaming is a complex psychological process involving the play of attention, as mediated by personal and generic habits of perception, against a variety of possible suggestion factors within a field of remembered and imagined sense impressions. Since dreams largely remain in the control of one's thoughts, emotions and perceptual biases, their contents must be as numerous and diverse as the possible combinations of such thoughts, emotions and biases. This diversity falls largely outside the realm of *common* dreams, except when shared personal or cultural affectations provoke common imagery, as in the case of the wish-fulfillment dreams of American males about becoming sports stars.

The sheer variety and arbitrariness of personal or cultural suggestion factors puts most such additional "common" dreams largely beyond the range of this book—except insofar as the whole book can be considered an argument about this very point. Since it posits dreams as created by the dreamer from moment to moment, the suggestion theory does not predict the *specific* details of dreams, and in fact states that no theory could. Any more deterministic schemes which try to encompass the great diversity of dream possibilities within a limited sphere of interpretation would, from our perspective, be unlikely to be true. We will critique such schemes in greater detail in the next chapter. Nevertheless, the effects of dream thoughts, feelings and perceptual habits differ from those experienced in waking in a *generalized* manner, and in turn alter one's dreams in what is usually a general rather than a more specific manner, which we have sought to describe.

In outlining his own dream theory, David Foulkes similarly stressed the importance of studying the commonalities of dream *form* instead of concentrating on dream content, something which is too obviously unpredictable in nature. He pointed out that dreams almost invariably meet certain formal criteria: they involve a sense of participating in perceptually convincing dramatized events, some but not all of which will echo past waking experiences.[42] While we can certainly think of exceptions to these rules, we share Foulkes' view that dreaming can better be approached as a process, a way of organizing consciousness and its contents, than as the forced product of either an unconscious agency or a particular physiological state.

Hobson, too, has emphasized the universal form of dreams over their individual content. Regardless of the exact status of activation-synthesis in describing the creation of images, Hobson has made a good argument that many of the defining characteristics of dreams identify dreaming as essentially an organic mental syndrome similar to other such syndromes, like alcohol-induced delirium or Alzheimer's disease. The shared features of such syndromes strikingly include, in his words: "disorientation; distractibility; spotty memory and confabulations; visuomotor hallucinations and delusions; and a lack of insight that appears to be related to a loss of self-consciousness."[43] We will discuss these characteristics and their importance to dream creation in greater detail in Chapter 8, when we consider their underlying biochemistry.

To recap our own perspective, dream generation is an active, creative process in which, far from having a narrative imposed by any outside source, a dreamer personally composes a plot as he or she goes along. The mind spins out its skein of memories, interests, concerns, impulses, and motivations, colored by certain aspects of physiology such as limited sensory input and partial amnesia, then takes up these threads to weave a story. It does this by calling upon the interlaced patterns of habits and assumptions that structure experience, thereby fashioning an imaginal milieu in which the constant shuttling interplay of suggestion and interpretation causes the fabric of action and reaction to unfold. And this craft of imposing order on disorder, more so than any obscure symbolizing, is what gives dreams their meaning.

Chapter 7

DREAM INTERPRETATION

What is in a dream? Many varieties of dream interpretation exist, promoting diverse, often conflicting views about what dreams may mean. The conflicts between different interpretive approaches derive, in large measure, from differences between the various models of dream creation, and the accuracy of any such approach ultimately depends on the accuracy of the particular creation model underlying it. If any model can be proven more feasible than the others, then dream explorers of all persuasions should be able to navigate between opposing claims to arrive at a better understanding of what, if anything, dreams signify.

Here again the phenomena associated with lucid dreaming have considerable importance. If the suggestion theory of dream generation, as developed based on observations of controlled lucid dreams, is relatively accurate, it should sharpen anyone's interpretive abilities. This theory does, however, cast a strikingly different interpretive light on dreaming than do any more common perspectives, and in its own way illuminates a much wider range of dreams than those perspectives typically explain.

In the discussion to follow we will review the most pervasive conceptions of dream origins in order to contrast them with our understanding of the suggestion theory and its implications for dream meanings. We will then offer comment on several ways in which interpreters traditionally attempt to derive meaning from dreams, as well as suggest ways in which lucidity can play a part in developing a new interpretive method.

LAST YEAR'S MODEL: THE PREVAILING THEORIES OF DREAM CREATION

Just about everyone must have wondered what some striking dream or other might have meant, and probably without having to look too far to find someone eager explain or interpret it. We will not go into detailed descriptions of the varieties of interpretive systems here; they are too numerous, and comprehensive accounts exist elsewhere.[1] We will, however, classify the major models of dream generation upon which the different interpretive approaches are based, since a consideration of those models pertains to our argument. Where, then, do dreams come from?

Other Worlds: Shamanistic and Occultist Thought

From long ago, there have been people throughout the world who have explained the convincing nature of dreams by believing dreams real in some sense, whether as journeys to alternate realities or as interactions with spiritual realms such as the abode of the dead. Thus the Temiar of West Malaysia, among many other native cultures, reportedly view dreams as the literal experiences of the soul or part of the soul freed from the body during sleep.[2] Such nocturnal excursions can result, per this philosophy, in various mishaps due to the ill will of malevolent entities or sorcerers, necessitating calling upon the local shaman to search the dream world and retrieve the lost soul. Shamans themselves classically receive their calling through initiatory dreams or vision quests in which they come under the tutelage of supernatural beings.[3]

This essentially occultist approach to the inexplicable but profoundly affecting persists in today's society, as numerous reports of literally interpreted shared dreams, out-of-body flights, ghost hauntings, UFO abductions, channeling, and various "mystical experiences" attest. Not only is seeing still believing for some people, others become believers after only *hearing* about such strange and exciting possibilities. While there may yet turn out to be some truth to such claims, the suggestion theory, of course, emphasizes the role of human suggestibility in creating experiences in keeping with one's convictions, and encourages taking a critical stance towards dreams by viewing them as self-shaped illusions.

> To see a horse in human flesh, descending . . . through the air, and as it nears your house is metamorphosed into a man, and he throws something at you which seems to be rubber but turns into great bees, denotes miscarriage of hopes and useless endeavors to regain lost valuables.[7]

Whether or not dreams ever involve contact with the divine we cannot say. Although our theory would not disallow the possibility of suggestions coming from a higher source, we do know that encounters can be simulated and "messages" readily concocted from existing beliefs. And while even ordinary human percipience *might* be able to shape some dreams that parallel future happenings, most dreams probably do not. Any correspondences that come about may more often do so through coincidence or self-fulfilling prophecy—intentionally or unintentionally *making* expected events happen. We also oppose the notion that one image would invariably have the same meaning for all dreamers, even within a given cultural group, due to the diversity of causes that could suggest a specific image into turning up in a given dream.

Letters from the Unconscious: Psychoanalytic Constructs

The potential psychological dimensions of dreams have not been lost on people from other times and cultures. Some American Indian tribes, for instance, purportedly considered dreams the expression of desires and conflicts that need addressing.[8] The idea of dreaming as a psychologically revealing medium received considerable attention in nineteenth century thought, culminating, in the early years of the twentieth century, in the fledgling science of psychoanalysis.

Psychoanalysis proposed the idea of an unconscious mind generating dream imagery—an *internal* agent discrete from ordinary awareness. Many people welcomed such models, in part, because they explained dreams as products of the human mind alone. This at least took a positive step away from the superstitions that so often surrounded considerations of dream phenomena. However, different approaches to dream analysis developed based on differing opinions of how this hidden unconscious worked, opinions which themselves depended on a limited understanding of neurological functioning and on highly speculative theories of human psychology.

In his 1900 book *The Interpretation of Dreams*, Viennese psychoanalyst Sigmund Freud described dream creation as the camouflaged action of repressed feelings and motivations unacceptable to the civilized ego, such as incestuous urges.[9] According to his psychodynamic model of the brain, such impulses had to go somewhere, dreams in sleep being a safe outlet. Although he thought all dreams the vehicles of impulses, Freud took less interest in dreams with obvious deviant content than in dreams with benign imagery that he thought "disguised" deviant content in symbolic form. By thus asserting that only he knew their "true" meanings, he gave himself a license to impose whatever interpretations he wanted on his patients' dreams.

Many aspects of Freud's approach to dream interpretation remain popular, in part because of their sensationalistic nature. He was as fixated on the sociopathic and sexual aspects of dreams as any medieval theologian, and such topics have a perennial lurid appeal. However, his theory, much like the external-agent models, ascribed specific meanings to specific dream images; a snake would virtually always symbolize the male genitalia, as an obvious example. Such biases make Freudian dream theory at best transitional between folkloric and scientific.

Carl Jung, attracted by Freud's work, exchanged hundreds of letters with him from his native Switzerland until they terminated their six-year correspondence due to increasing differences of opinion.[10] Jung took especial interest in "archetypal" imagery, dream and mythic images held in common between peoples and cultures. These he explained as arising from the "collective unconscious," an objective, archaic dimension of psyche shared by all mankind.[11] According to his theory, the mind sought wholeness, with dreams as a regulatory mechanism which compensated people for the narrowness of their individual experiences by presenting alternative behaviors and points of view, thus helping them to achieve balance. Integrating with various instinctual and archetypal patterns of behavior and perception aided this individuation process.

Jung's approach, although heavily influenced by Freud's, was more positive in aspect than Freudian theory, and in some ways an elaboration of earlier mystico-religious views. It became the progenitor of the most pervasive current therapeutic approaches to dream interpretation, because his ideas were widely incorporated into many interpretive systems and popular beliefs about dreams. These ideas include the notions that the unconscious mind knows more in many ways than the conscious mind; that dreams present communications from the unconscious in symbolic or metaphorical language; that dreams articulate things unperceived by the dreamer; that the same image can mean different things in different circumstances; and that dreams should be collected, decoded and examined in series.[12]

Succeeding generations of theorists, of various scholarly persuasions, have continued to disagree to a great extent about the nature and meaning of dreams. In the 1950s, Calvin Hall wrote that dreams embodied thoughts revolving around major life conflicts.[13] In the 1960s, Fritz Perls promoted the idea of dream images as the projections of unincorporated parts of the dreamer's personality.[14] Montague Ullman's contemporary approach has promoted dream discussion in a group context, which allows the dreamer to sort through a variety of perspectives before settling on whatever interpretation feels right.[15] The diversity of such psychoanalytic systems underscores the fact that most remain matters of opinion, since the basic dream-generation model underlying them all has no firm grounding in scientific fact.

As we proposed earlier, psychoanalytic paradigms depending on an "unconscious mind" may, in fact, be anthropomorphising a rather machinelike part of the brain's functioning by ascribing sentience and intentionality where none exist. We see no reason to credit the concept of dreaming as a mechanism by which an unconscious mind expresses repressed desires or profound insights by juggling symbols around. The habit and practice of reality-modeling by the mind provides a simpler explanation for the apparent meaningfulness of dreams. Because it relies on the same mechanisms involved in waking human perception, the suggestion theory explains the characteristics of ordinary dreaming—including the expression of desires and insights from time to time—in a more parsimonious manner. It accounts for all of the effects seen in lucid dreaming as well. The idea of dreams as created by the unconscious can thus pretty well be cut from dream theory as having unnecessary concomitants.

Let's Be Reasonable: Scientific Perspectives

The suggestion theory does not stand alone in its critique of the dream-creation models discussed thus far. Other, more scientific dream-generation models proposed over the years have ignored, sidestepped, and sometimes even debunked the idea of dreams being interpretable in either the occultist, folk belief, or psychoanalytic senses. These would include theories based on sensory, cognitive and physiological observations, such as the fact that both animals and human infants dream, yet could hardly benefit from being awash in repressed urges or significance-laden symbols while asleep. Again, we will not attempt to review all such models in detail here, as authoritative reviews exist elsewhere.[16] Their proposers have primarily belonged to the mainstream scientific community, and many have understood that the issue of *how* dreams are generated has everything to do with the question of *whether* they qualify as meaningful at all. Only by approaching the subject in a more scientific manner can anyone adequately address and, hopefully, resolve these issues.

Astute observers of dreams have long had some grasp of the role of suggestion in producing dream content. The seventh century Chinese, for instance, recognized that dreams could elaborate upon external stimuli.[17] In the late seventeenth century the empiricist philosopher John Locke proposed that all dreams result from sensory determinants.[18] Because such incorporations can easily be investigated under controlled conditions, they formed an important part of early scientific dream research. Alfred Maury, the Marquis de Saint-Denys, and many other enthusiasts experimented along these lines.[19]

While few would take Locke's extreme position, some more modern researchers have persisted with such inquiries. Others have studied the effects of waking thoughts, emotions and memories on dream content via experiments with presleep suggestion, such as by introducing controlled sources of "day residues" in the form of disturbing films shown to subjects.[20] Mentation *during* sleep, however, may have a greater impact on dream construction, and forms the basis of David Foulkes' cognitive approach to dreaming, which describes dream experience as the involuntary conscious interpretation of diffusely activated memory units in the brain.[21] Foulkes' model repudiates conventional notions of dream interpretability; in his words, it "denies the encoding either of particular wishes or fantasies which need 'release,' or of particular messages or gems of wisdom which . . . can help us set our lives aright."[22]

Other scientific work on dreams has focused on determining their physiological foundations. Certain nineteenth century theorists, for instance, thought that dream images might originate through some form of internal stimulation of the visual system, perhaps of the retina itself.[23] Later research demonstrated that activation of the visual system did play a major part in dreaming, but with quite a different source—the rapid eye movements of REM sleep, first noted by sleep physiologists Eugene Aserinsky and Nathaniel Kleitman.[24]

In the late 1970s J. Allan Hobson and Robert McCarley integrated decades of findings in the field of neuroscience and asserted that dreaming has an entirely physiological basis: the random stimulation of the brain's sensory and motor systems by activation signals originating in the brainstem. Their activation-synthesis hypothesis explains dreaming as the brain's "best guess" as to what is happening to it during this barrage, the imposition of meaning on purely neurological events.[25]

The suggestion theory has obvious similarities to the activation-synthesis hypothesis and to other scientific theories of dreaming. Rather than overextrapolating from certain classes of suggestion factors in the manner of earlier models, though, ours maintains that *any* suggestion factor entering awareness during sleep, not brainstem signals alone, or physical sensations alone, or thoughts, emotions, memories, intuitions, or sexual impulses alone, can initiate dream images. Hence we can defend ourselves against the charge of reductionism so often levied against proponents of scientific models of dream creation.

Sacred Bull

In contradicting the idea that the unconscious or a wise inner self formulates dreams, researchers like Hobson and McCarley have had to face considerable opposition from those who believe dreams meaningful in what has now become an orthodox or traditional sense among interpretive specialists—that is, people with a vested interest in dream interpretation. Psychoanalytic theorists have proved hostile to more scientific approaches from the beginning. Hobson himself has this to say about the Freudian effect on dream science:

> *The Interpretation of Dreams* was antiscientific because Freud so forcefully dismissed all previous writers that he actually aborted an emerging experimental tradition. . . . [Even] within the field of modern sleep research, the tenacity of psychoanalytic views remains impressively obstructive to integrative theorizing.[26]

A number of conservative researchers and, we can only hope, at least some of the general public have remained skeptical of the ideologies of the psychoanalysts, with their unproven and sometimes uncritical assumptions. Still, various dream interpretation proponents continue to promote versions of the strangely fascinating and appealingly overelaborated theories introduced by Freud and Jung. Many psychoanalytic treatments of dream interpretation have reached sizable popular markets in the form of New Age and self-help literature, and within the dream community virtually anyone can set up shop as a "dreamworker," guiding groups of people interested in using dreams as oracles for personal development.[27] Nor is it difficult to find literature and workshops by individuals with folkloric or occultist interests in dreams, such as psychics and out-of-body enthusiasts.[28] Those people working within the most popular approaches to dream interpretation get involved precisely because they are *already* convinced that dreams convey uniquely important meanings, and usually for no more creditable reason than because dreams seem so compelling, since no one has yet indisputably substantiated the accuracy of any theory.

Contemporary occult, folk and psychoanalytic interpreters, if only because of their vocal testimonies and easy answers to difficult questions, commonly pass as experts on dreaming, despite their notable biases. According to the suggestion theory, such people will not only tend to *find* a certain number of dreams fitting their theories—since diverse factors influence dream content—but will actually tend to *produce* compatible dreams in themselves and others. This would help clarify why such a variety of beliefs has had such wide appeal; the theories seem to explain people's dream experiences when in fact they often create them, or cause analysts to select out and emphasize those which match their own interpretive slants.[29] The ordinary lack of lucidity *about* dream phenomena can account for the peculiar history of ideas about dream generation and the stubborn appeal of many widely accepted "explanations" of dreaming.

OUT OF YOUR HEAD: DREAMING'S PERCEPTUAL ORIGINS

According to the suggestion theory, dreaming results when the mind tries to operate without the stabilizing effects of consistent external sensory input and ends up projecting an hallucinatory habitat from its own thoughts and memories instead. This perceptual version of events also has its historical antecedents, going back at least as far as the Classical period and the reflections of Aristotle and Cicero.[30] The nineteenth century philosopher Arthur Shopenhauer also proposed something similar.[31] Such earlier thinkers, however, seemed to see dream creation as essentially a reflexive matter, missing the equally important role of flexible conscious processing of the products of the otherwise automated human perceptual system.

The suggestion theory's interpretive implications impact heavily on traditional approaches in such sensitive areas as the nature of dream perception, the meaning of imagery, the importance of impulses, the development of common dreaming patterns, and the relevance of dream behavior to waking life. This section will examine these five topics in some detail, and we will continue to return to them throughout the chapter.

Creating New Worlds from Old

The most basic tenet of the suggestion theory asserts that while the dream *state* may be determined by physiology, dream *content* is determined from moment to moment by awareness interpreting and coordinating various suggestion factors through the world-modeling function. It follows that dreams make convincing sensory experiences not because they must represent literal or metaphorical reality, but because they employ the same capabilities the mind uses to create the perception of reality to begin with. As Foulkes has remarked, "To the degree that dreaming employs systems whose major function is the apprehension of what the world is like, then any activity in those systems is likely to be treated as if it reflected world events."[32]

In other words, far from being messages from an intelligent external or internal source pertinent to the real world, dreams can be said to result from a certain form of confused perception that mistakes reflexively generated constructs for realities. By this reasoning, incidental images in dreams neither directly depict realities nor stand for other concepts in the manner of literary symbols emplaced by an author's intelligent intent. Instead they objectify, and develop as the result of habitual associations between, the *ideas* or *models* of real things only. Dreams may sometimes substitute one image for another, but only because certain similarities between images act as suggestion factors, not because the substitutions must mean anything.

This does not imply simply that "sometimes a cigar is just a cigar," as Freud apocryphally conceded, but that a dream cigar is neither literally nor even figuratively a real cigar, let alone a phallic symbol. It is only a mental image. The surrealist René Magritte may have come closer to the truth when he created *La trahison des images (The Treason of the Pictures)*, a realistic painting of a pipe with the large caption, "Ceci n'est pas une pipe" ("This is not a pipe").[33] We think he was not only tweaking Freud, but being lucid about his painting. However convincing, it remained a picture, not a pipe.

Intelligence or Intelligibility?

Taking the preceding argument a bit further, we would say that dreams can be intelligible not because they come from a discrete part of the psyche responsible for their creation and having its own itinerary for the benefit of the self, but because they reflect the habitual imposition of meaning by learned reality-modeling processes. They seem meaningful because they depend upon the mind's established network of associations, which it uses to *determine* meaning. As a corollary to this idea, associations in dreams do not automatically have great meaning just because they occur in dreams. In our view, they come from no "deep" source in the mind but from the same parts of the mind operative during waking, simply in a different conscious state.

The seeming intelligence of dreams, then, may boil down to intelligibility, which is not the same thing at all. Intelligibility can arise from either intelligence *or* habit. Just as we all learn to read, advancing from identifying individual letters to complete words to whole sentences until we can skim complex paragraphs without thinking about how the process works, so we can spin dreams in a manner under our own control without also being aware of the underlying process. Some may object that we do not *learn* to dream the way we learn to read, and so the analogy does not hold, but in fact the dreams of children do show a gradually developing complexity in keeping with the growth of their waking cognitive abilities.[34] Learning to perceive reality through ever more sophisticated models in waking is therefore all that it takes to "learn" how to dream.

Although dreams can illustrate the patterns of association playing within a person's mind, such associations in effect remain dependent on awareness. That is, while the lack of a consistent external world may sometimes force the mind to work in an associative or even random mode, it does not abolish awareness as the primary director of dream imagery. Associative and random factors do create certain instabilities, and they sometimes influence the imagery more than one's thoughts do. Still, dreams chiefly follow the lead of the notoriously unstable attention in flitting from one thing to another; and all imagery, no matter how unexpectedly it appears, must receive attention in order to remain and be fitted into the developing narrative context. Dreams may also seem intelligent, then, because besides relying on a foundation of meaningfully linked associations, they also respond to how we direct our awareness, which *is* intelligent.

The Senseless Storyteller

Dreams are not preprogrammed, it follows, but the nearly instantaneous, impromptu creations of the dreamer. This becomes clear when it is remembered that lucid dreamers, and by implication all dreamers, affect the flow of a dream by how they choose to interpret events in progress. We may decide the meaning of an ambiguous image almost automatically, depending on our state of mind and the overall dream context, but we nevertheless decide it, since we *could* as easily interpret it some other way and get a completely different result. So when the lone figure on the dream street corner ahead turns out to be the mugger, police officer or whatever we expected it to be, this does not confirm our suspicions, as it would in waking, but *reflect* them, since our thoughts and expectations interacted with the imagery to shape it. Furthermore, any stray thought, emotion or sensation can influence dream content. Dreams may often feature impulsive, violent and sexual content, then, not because they necessarily express repressed desires, but because they respond directly to momentary impulses of various kinds which can quickly play out in imagery.

A person usually has many associations for a concept, so a certain image may suggest any number of other images to follow it during the ongoing interpretive process that *is* dreaming. This would account for the endlessly creative nature of dreaming, but make the redundant, waking interpretation of specific images without any particular purpose in perhaps most instances, since many other images could as easily have come up at any given point. When awake, if Jay hears the name "Walt" and picture of Mickey Mouse pops into his head, it does not mean he has a deep, unconscious wish to visit Disneyland; and in dreams, there is no reason to believe that images signify hidden tendencies or feelings of particular significance any more than stray thoughts and associations normally do during waking. Especially insofar as dreaming involves a particularly fuddled variety of thinking, dream images should have no more importance as psychiatric source material than the images of waking thought or imagination.

A Lot in Common

Of course, people may find dreams meaningful anyway, just as they may find a work of literature applicable to their lives without it being written especially for them because it relies on certain tried-and-true patterns. As a creative process, dreaming may have no predetermined content, but commonalities of perception shared by human beings, as well as the habitual perceptual styles of individuals, would tend to create common or repeated images that suggest certain meanings to the waking mind. The last chapter demonstrated how classic dream images and motifs could arise from typical preoccupations and mindsets that would color the way the human mind tries to make sense of the unique aspects of dreaming experience: the instability and strangeness of imagery, the loss of most orienting memories and sensations, the concomitants of sleep physiology, and so on. Similarly, "archetypal" imagery does not have to emerge from a magical collective unconscious; archetypal interactions, when not simply suggested by familiarity with Jungian theory, may be no more than universal psychological patterns dramatized in dreams.[35]

Individuals will find more personal "meanings" in their dreams because such constructs reflect their own thoughts, hopes, and fears, or some specific and very personal expectations and desires. People can also interpret a dream as relevant to their lives either from sheer suggestibility or from the fact that human beings are such complicated—and inconsistent—creatures that just about *any* observation may apply to them in some manner. Read an unsuspecting person the horoscope for a random astrological sign as if it were his or her own, and it will quite likely still seem to fit. Since most of us become very suggestible in certain situations, and the suspension of critical thought makes us especially so, we should be very wary of similarly trusting a dream interpretation just because it "fits." Dream interpretations may well apply in certain contexts, but if we approach them in a state of nonreflective trust we will tend to misuse *any* observations by thinking of them as portents or signs rather than as possibilities.

The Dream-Specific Nature of Dreaming

The final postulate of the interpretive approach implied by the suggestion theory states that the diverse roles we play in dream narratives do not exist to compensate us for our limited experiences. Since most people forget the vast majority of their dreams anyway, one wonders how much good such a compensatory mechanism could do. Instead the altered personalities that so often characterize dreaming seem to derive from our forgetfulness of who we are when we cue from diverse dream situations.

Dreams remain far from unfailingly applicable to real concerns, feelings and conflicts, since what we think, feel, and believe *while dreaming* guides dream images, and these mental processes do not always parallel those of our waking lives. The applicability of a given dream would seem to depend, to a large extent, on the degree to which the underlying awareness reflects the waking personality.

Yet what we consider and do while dreaming frequently applies only to the specific, often highly unusual circumstances of the dream itself. Both lucid and nonlucid dreamers alike can behave in ways at great contrast to any typical waking thought or action.

We personally do not claim that dream content, including apparently divergent content, *never* stems from pertinent sources such as psychological problems or insights about the real world; even these should be able to function as suggestion factors. But we do maintain that it does not necessarily, and probably does not usually, do so. The majority of suggestion factors do not relate to anything important, making it hard to discriminate what in the resulting froth of dreamfluff *may* be important.

Many enthusiasts have selected out and overemphasized fantastic accounts of correlations between dreaming and reality, such as objectifications of psychological issues, creative solutions to waking problems, or seeming psychic predictions, as proof that *all* dreams must have such relevance, and regardless of the real use a correlation might have to the dreamer. While we do not mean to belittle whatever capacities people may possess to receive intuitions, in their dreams or otherwise, in our experience dreams are not dominated by intuitive capacities, and these have nothing to do with the process of dream creation. Most dreams do not appear to cue from such factors, being propelled instead by dream-specific thoughts, assumptions, motivations, and actions. One usually responds to *dreams* in dreams, not directly to one's waking concerns.

This would explain why so many "important" dream messages would be so obscure as to need interpretation at all. It must almost always require a stretch to make dreams fit waking realities. Standard interpretive approaches to dreams seem to arise from the human interpretive impulse—the tendency to try to make sense of *any* data available by making it fit within a familiar framework and glossing ambiguous stimuli with highly specific, slanted perceptions.[36] Dream interpretation can be considered an attempt to continue the dreaming process *while awake*, pursued because of the nagging incompleteness and obscurity of many dreams, which themselves amount to the mind's ongoing interpretations—however incorrect—of what is happening to it during sleep.

A CASE OF MISTAKEN IDENTITY: THE DREAM-SPECIFIC PERSONALITY

The subject of personality in dreams warrants further discussion in a section of its own. Not only is dreaming naturally creative and impulsive, but a dreamer often acts in ways inconsistent with his or her inclinations and behavior patterns in the waking world. Indeed, some of the worst nightmares feature *oneself* in the part of the monster. Such dreams can seem quite foreign to any of us when we wake, so we may feel inclined to attribute their creation to some mysterious activity beyond our control. However, a more provocative explanation for such anomalous behavior would be that dreamers, both lucidly and otherwise, commonly take advantage of the fact that nothing is real in their dreams.

Whose Dream Is This, Anyway?

The three of us found it useful to conceptualize any persona through which we experienced a dream as a *dream-specific personality* (DSP). This personality would sometimes be essentially the same as the normal waking self, sometimes far from it, depending on the novelty of the scenario and, presumably, on neurophysiological factors that affect memory and quality of thought.

A dream-specific personality of ours would often display an uncharacteristic naiveté or emotionality. It could be oddly childlike, subject to fancies we would not consider seriously in waking, such as a fear of being assaulted by ghosts or vampires. On the other hand, a DSP could display tacit lucidity. We sometimes seemed to know that we had dream situations under our control, though not necessarily why. We could feel at home in the dream world, accepting the unusual and taking unusual liberties. Just as some people may be polite in public but swear at or malign others in private—as long as they think they cannot be heard—so people may, without considering why, behave poorly or strangely in dreams by waking standards, since dreams are the most private of experiences.

By way of example, Janice, although respectful and studious in her school days, later usually had school dreams in which she acted up in class and did not much care how she performed. This attitude seems to have reflected not a new-found delinquency but a kind of tacit lucidity, an implicit knowledge that nothing she did within the dream scenario would much matter. Similarly, in her dreams Ruth has sometimes engaged in social activities she would feel no inclination to get involved with in waking. Her uncharacteristic behavior might even become a lucidity cue, as it did one time when she realized she must dreaming because she wanted to get up on stage and sing.

Although the DSP in charge could vary markedly from dream to dream, it tended towards the uninhibited. A DSP version of ourselves would commonly not only act out impulses without restraint, but take its exaggerated emotions and behavior for granted within the dream state, probably because of lack of access to the waking memories which would provide a more cautionary frame of reference. Making the concept more general, then, a dreamer's DSP might think nothing of aggressively hurting or killing fellow characters, having any type of sex with any partner, violating various laws of physics and society without a care, and so on. It might be fair to say that each DSP has its own, relatively undeveloped world model, sometimes prescribing acceptable experiences and behaviors for it that the waking self would consider unusual or aberrant.

A DSP's world view can expand to include the certainty that nothing around itself really exists: the DSP can become lucid. With lucidity on their side, self-reflective dreamers realize *why* they can "get away with murder" and so on—because they are only dreaming. This does not mean that the dream self will always snap into alignment with the waking personality. When lucid the three of us appreciated that impulses in the dream world could be disinhibited without consequence, and so experimented with attitudes that we would not use in waking or found clever ways to work our will on various dream elements.

These lucid attempts at intentionally dream-specific behavior did not always work out as planned, though. Occasionally, a waking standard of behavior would interfere with the dream-specific one. This might show in the adverse responses of other characters or of the dream environment to our actions. However, the same escapade that met with some psychological resistance on one occasion might be pulled off with no such difficulty on another, again underscoring the inconsistency of dream personality.

Memory and the DSP

Whether or not a dreamer has ever technically been lucid, he or she can have a certain number of tacitly lucid dreams. A tacitly lucid DSP may exhibit special skills relevant only to the dream world, like knowing how to fly or how to change endings and manipulate imagery to make satisfying stories. Such a DSP can learn its control abilities afresh on the spot, as in one case where Jay slowly discovered that he had extra powers like the ability to float through the air. Sometimes, though, the DSP may tap into memories of previous performances which occurred in similar dreams or which form part of lucid habit, as when Jay became lucid one time because he noticed that he was descending a staircase by skimming his feet over the edges of the steps and remembered that he had done so in past dreams.

In our experience, whereas the lucid DSP often remembers its earlier exploits quite clearly, the tacitly lucid DSP usually seems to recall general, repeated *patterns* of dream-specific behavior, like the bare fact that it can jump out windows unscathed, rather than specific *instances*. The poor quality of the memories available during most dreams would allow for such abilities, if one cannot remember factual experiences to contradict one's "powers."

It is not likely that a DSP can access memories from lost dreams that the waking mind never reviewed, since the brain by and large cannot store information in any enduring form while dreaming.[37] However, we occasionally saw certain dream contexts evoke, by association, memories of relevant prior dream events we had once recalled on awakening then forgotten about at some point. For instance, one time Janice entered one of her lucid serial sites and unexpectedly found two of her nieces working at the reception desk, a surprise which reminded her that she had found them there the last time she had visited the site, as she soon confirmed in her written records.

In other cases—and much more often—we felt convinced while dreaming that we had dreamed about the present scenario or some element in it before, but once awake we could neither recollect nor find reference to any such earlier version. In these instances we may possibly have accessed memories of genuine dreams somehow stored mentally though never remembered nor preserved in accounts, but such dream "déjà-vu" much more likely comes from the rationalizing tendency of the dreaming mind, with its penchant for fabricating false memories.

A Certain Slant of I

The variable range of memories—waking, dream or false—available in a given dream can activate a range of potential dream personas. Given all the subtle variations we have observed, we do not claim that the DSP takes up a discrete portion of the mind, like the unconscious or deeper self. Nor can it be a stable entity like an alternate personality, since selective memories shift its perspective from dream to dream. We claim that what we term a dream-specific personality is the dreamer's *temporary persona* in a specific dream situation, with only partial memories on which to base its self-conception.

People constantly manifest situation-specific behaviors in their day-to-day affairs. Everyone can act one way at home, another at a sporting event or concert, yet another at work. Likewise, given the usual lack of proper contextual memories, often coupled with a low level of awareness that dreaming is "not for keeps" mixed up with the assumption that the dream *is* reality, a person will act in a manner applicable only to a given dream. This makes a DSP comparable to a temporary social persona rather than to any specific part of the mind as such.

The Powers That Be?

What of the fellow personalities we all come across in our dreams? As a corollary of the idea that dream characters personify parts of the psyche, some interested parties impute great importance to them, even to the point of reverential regard. Paul Tholey, who values lucid dreaming as a tool for self-discovery, goes so far as to suggest that dream characters can have independent awareness. "They behave as if they possessed their own perceptual perspectives, cognitive abilities . . . and even their own motivations," he observes. "We concluded from this that we must treat dream figures as if they were real 'beings.'"[38]

In Tholey's view, incidents in which the characters know themselves to be in a dream involve a higher level of lucidity than usual and enable insightful inner-personal communication.[39] The characters can, some would say, inform people of things they need to know about themselves—hidden aspects of personality, buried or unacknowledged negativity, forgotten memories, repressed childhood traumas, and the like. We would say rather that with such psychoanalytic concepts and concerns on the dreamer's mind, his or her dream characters may well start spouting related "communications" with no guaranteed truth or value. For a while after she read about such claims, Janice's dream people occasionally took on self-important postures, telling her she was supposed to learn things from her dreams, but their supposed intentions were usually quite lost on her.

Our own dream characters did not seem particularly privy to lost memories. They on rare occasions appeared to remember or embody facts that we could not, but these facts were either forgotten details of earlier, recorded dreams, as in the incident with Janice's nieces recounted above, or else were readily accessible to us while awake and only forgotten *during* a given dream. For instance, in one dream where Janice could not remember the name of a certain actor, a character came by with a pointy snout on his face, an obvious hint regarding the name she wanted, "Michael J. *Fox*." But when asked, characters proved unable to dredge up information completely lost to our waking minds, instead giving wholly erroneous guesses. This does not bode well for any "insights" they might appear to offer.

Echoes in the Mind: The Interpretation of Dream Characters

At base, characters probably appear in dreams because we have grown habituated to being around people and have compelling social needs. From memory, assisted by the associative context of a given scene, we can fashion constructs representing people whose features we know—family, friends, acquaintances, celebrities—or invent composites reflecting our generic conceptions of cultural types such as cowboys or muggers. They will seem as real as everything else in the dream, if we do not question that reality. Just as we usually listen to musical tones without thinking about how they were really made by a musician playing an instrument, we normally react to characters as if they existed independently of the invisible generative process that produces them—a process that would appear, on the whole, to be a reflexive aspect of world modeling.

This does not mean that dream characters have no relevance to personal psychology. The wide range of associations and expectations that motivate them must be unique to each individual. Characters may even sometimes reflect aspects of our personalities, in the sense of depicting behaviors and tendencies that we ourselves display. But this is not the same as saying they directly symbolize those aspects. The distinction makes a world of difference when it comes to deciding the significance of one's lucid interactions with them. Not only will those interactions have no magical repercussions on the psyche—as made clear in Chapter 4's critique of the LaBergian perspective—but because we can choose to react in a variety of ways to a given character, the resulting exchange may give no indication of how we would normally feel about the particular affect represented.

It may be that any part of our mental functioning that somehow seems foreign to us could devolve onto a character distinct from the dream ego. In deference to the therapists, it does seem as though people sometimes project varying viewpoints regarding matters about which they have mixed feelings onto separate characters. For instance, the Marquis de Saint-Denys reported the case of a friend of his whose conflicting ideas about getting married were personified in two dream characters debating the issue with him.[40] However, this phenomenon need not *always* implicate significant indecision so much as imagination overdramatizing a stray thought or emotion into perceptible form.

Characters can also reflect concerns about what *other* people might possibly think and feel regarding our behavior. Such internalizations may result in the appearance of annoying censors criticizing certain dream actions, like the characters who mocked Jay one time for always trying to jump through ceilings in his dreams. But this does not reveal whether or not one *personally* feels any real conflict over those actions, many of which would only occur in dreams anyway.

The hyperbolizing tendency of dreams makes the psychological relevance of characters problematic in another way as well. A dream encounter with someone may drastically overemphasize a small aspect of any actual relationship with the person. An admired teacher may become an illicit lover, or a concerned parent may dog one's every step and scold like a harridan. While some analysts might light on such incidents as signs of one's "true" or "suppressed" feelings about the person, they seem at least as likely to be due to the constriction of focus that prevails in dreaming, much as when too much attention to the bizarre details in a familiar scene ends up multiplying them. Here again, the concept of a dream-specific personality shaping dreams in unusual but not necessarily relevant ways may provide a welcome alternative to traditional notions.

THE CHALLENGE TO DREAM INTERPRETATION

If commonplace mental habits and a dream-specific personality—not a wise unconscious—give shape to dreams, what remains for ordinary interpretive methods to analyze? Dreams may not spring from an inner core of the self deliberately trying to communicate some vital message, yet may still prove meaningful in some instances. But while stating that dreaming *may* allow for certain interpretive possibilities, the suggestion theory as presented in this book places heavy qualifications on *when* and *why* such possibilities hold true. This section will look at some of the criteria people use in selecting dreams to analyze and several of the ways in which they hope to benefit by doing so, discussing which of the basic premises seem to remain valid and which become suspect in the light of our own perspective.

How Does That Strike You?

The psychotherapeutic tradition maintains that dream symbols, properly interpreted, can lead to a wealth of personal insights. Of all the many possible dreams to consider, people will in all probability feel impelled to interpret those which seem most vivid or striking to them in *waking*, whether or not anything about them seemed particularly striking *during* dreaming itself. This fact alone means that the waking mind singles out dreams that it assumes have some important relation to its waking-world concerns; it does not typically start by examining dreams as a whole and impartially, but only through the bias of its own interests. So, for example, people influenced by psychoanalytic thought may focus on their strangest and most puzzling images on the Freudian supposition that bizarre features disguise unconscious wishes.

Dream imagery lends itself to such selectivity by its very incompleteness and ambiguity. Since the waking mind always reads something *into* imagery to get something *out* of it—at the least, imposing its assumption that the imagery must mean something pertinent to waking—its bias will distort and perhaps determine any potential interpretation. Often enough people might do themselves a favor by *not* presupposing that striking images mean anything and getting themselves concerned to no good purpose. As Hobson has pointed out, because bizarreness is simply an inherent characteristic of dreaming, attempting any serious analysis of strange imagery on an overdetermined basis may be "not only gratuitous but even possibly hazardous."[41]

Some dreamers may instead pay special heed to images and

scenarios that evoke strong emotions as the hallmarks of meaningful dreams. Again, they will be judging mainly by their waking reactions, which may or may not involve the same feelings experienced while dreaming. One might, for instance, worry that an unsettling dream about a figure from the past implicates some terrible, repressed childhood incident, or believe that a dream providing a positive rush heralds an inner breakthrough.

Unfortunately, people may not be approaching the matter in a sensible manner, if they impute meaning to a dream or indeed to a waking experience only on the basis of the strength of the feelings it inspires, and not by any logic or perception they can demonstrate. A strong emotional reaction to a dream *might* indicate that it has some significance, but not if the content in question is merely dream-specific, like flying or finding inappropriate places to urinate, or due to a temporary fixation like reading a fantasy novel or watching a horror movie. A dream may be meaningful or not, depending largely on the suggestion factors involved. Therefore it seems best to eliminate conditioned reactions, any temporary mental diet, biases of the DSP, and other less than meaningful suggestion factors from the equation before measuring imagery for significance.

Repeat That, Please

Suppose people look to *repetition* of elements or patterns in their dreams to narrow the field of inquiry? While repetition would seem to indicate some sort of resonance in the personality, its overall significance remains questionable, and it certainly does not offer proof for an "unconscious mind" struggling to draw attention to something. Recurrent images and themes may simply indicate a unique dreaming *style*, and may be due to habit alone, to strong memories of prior dreams constantly being recalled, or to a fixation caused by taking certain other interpretive approaches too seriously.

Janice had an impressive but gratuitous repeating character in some of her lucid dreams which appeared to have been lifted straight off the cover of a fantasy novel. This character initially caused her some alarm about "archetypal imagery" and "unintegrated aspects of self" since it had such a classically sinister appearance. Eventually, though, she decided that the unsettling image only kept turning up all the time because she kept worrying that it would. Once she started imposing less portentous interpretations on it, with various accompanying changes in its demeanor, the image lost its power over her imagination. Hence we cannot credit the notion that recurrent images must have something important to convey.

"I Had a Hunch": Dreams, Feelings and Intuitions

What do people seek to gain by interpreting their dreams? Some enthusiasts suggest that dreams can respond to subtleties of thought and emotion normally masked during waking by attention to events in the real world, and thus present the dreamer with unarticulated perceptions not previously brought into full awareness.[42] These supposedly include discomfiting feelings like seething rage or romantic crushes that one has trouble admitting to in waking—though they may be obvious to everyone else—but needs to acknowledge for positive growth.[43] According to this view a dream could also, say, dramatize a half-noted problem with one's car that needs attending or amplify an intuition about an associate's secret motivations, helping one to perceive it.

The notion of "true" feelings being revealed in dreams is, we fear, more a source of confusion than an aid to personal development, since it is too easily taken as invariably the case. And while hunches or neglected observations could conceivably function as suggestion factors, we personally have seldom seen any indication of it in our own dreams, and have in fact received numerous outright erroneous "insights" in this fashion. If certain thoughts and emotions could be masked in waking by external concerns, they could also be masked in dreaming by dream concerns. People become so wrapped up in nonissues while dreaming that the time and effort involved in trying to unravel any meanings from dreams could perhaps be better applied to developing their waking powers of perception.

Still, dreams put us all into unusual situations, whereby we can see how we might react to unexpected circumstances. While this shows what we are *capable* of being like rather than what we secretly *are* like, it may illustrate unclarified thoughts, emotions and motivations—or unrecognized possibilities. We can be fools or scoundrels or unlikely heroes in the theater of our dreams. Some lucid and tacitly lucid incidents, for instance, demonstrate how the dreamer might behave if endowed with magic power, which should be of interest to an analyst. So even if dreams do not intentionally instruct, there is no reason we cannot take lessons from them, albeit under advisement.

Afraid of Your Own Shadow

Some analysts, following Freud's lead, maintain that dreams can reveal insidious desires or fears so disturbing that only the unconscious mind registers them, such as death wishes.[44] While we personally find that formulation suspiciously convenient for the analyst, we *have* observed dreams responding directly to impulses that the waking self would better control, so we agree that they *may* potentially illustrate hidden tendencies of the self. The problem is that dreams exaggerate wildly, and in depicting an unchecked impulse can blow some minor negative tendency out of all proportion to its true place in a person's psychological makeup. Even if one *should* happen to have violent or antisocial inclinations in waking at times, moral and legal principles usually suffice to overrule them for most people; only acting on them uncontrollably would constitute an affliction.

Our lucid observations also suggest that insignificant thoughts and emotions that people would normally justly dismiss or consider only in a nonserious way in waking can play out in vivid action sequences in their dreams. Thus disturbing dream sequences, however affecting, may come down to only loose association rather than to any deep-seated complex. If someone dreams of performing an action he or she "would never dream of doing," like committing murder or incest, it does *not* necessarily mean the individual harbors any perverse hidden inclination toward such behavior. The stray thought of the deed may simply have passed through his or her mind and taken on a life of its own, then been rationalized as appropriate behavior, or recognized as harmless in the case of a lucid dream. Such behaviors and rationalizations would in effect set up a temporary DSP with little or no bearing on reality.

If a dream-specific personality can run the show as long as dreaming continues, then how a person behaves during dreams may simply not apply beyond a point to his or her waking self. Most people's waking perceptions grow flexible from observing others, participating in social interactions, and, nowadays, from watching all manner of entertainments through which they can become caught up in the motivations of diverse characters. As a result, just like an actor, one can cast oneself in an engaging dream role and follow standard narrative plot structures without being in any way prone in real life to the actions, feelings and beliefs appropriate to the part. Genteel lucid dreamer Mary Arnold-Forster, as a case in point, reported a dream in which she was reading a book about a recalcitrant murderer, and the next moment found herself playing the part herself, justifying her lack of contrition over the death of another.[45] This role-playing propensity severely limits the relevance of dreams to waking personality.

Besides, the "negative" acts one conceives in dreams are often physically impossible otherwise. An attitude or mode of behavior of any importance manifesting in a dream will in all probability occur at least occasionally in waking as well. For all these reasons, then, one should not assume that the unusual activities of a DSP, for all that they might challenge one's self-conception, reflect legitimate though "repressed" aspects of personality. The potential for pointless psychological damage would seem to outweigh any possible advantage of such an assumption, since, tragically, people can *give* themselves problems by worrying about what dreadful things their dreams "reveal" to be wrong with them.

Metaphorically Speaking

In yet another application of dream interpretation popular in contemporary therapeutic thinking, people try to see dreams as metaphors for circumstances in their real lives, often quite successfully.[46] For instance, the novelist Amy Tan had a dream about flying with twenty-five-cent wings she had rented. Suddenly realizing the impossibility of it all, she started to fall. When she remembered she had just *been* flying, she began to fly again. After flying and falling several times in succession this way, she finally decided that her own *confidence* had been what allowed her to fly. She applied this insight to her life and realized that she denied herself many things because she lacked the requisite confidence, feeling dependent on the props, the twenty-five-cent wings.[47]

Tan's dream made an entirely valid, even literary-sounding metaphor for certain mental processes, and she usefully applied it to an aspect of her life. Yet in our view her whole dream situation and its resolution were dream-specific, and only *applicable* to real-life concerns, not symbolizing them directly and intentionally. In other words, dreaming is not automatically symbolic of waking thought, but it involves a kind of thinking that is occasionally symbolic in quality, perhaps most often by accident at that.

An easily read dream "metaphor" could occasionally match a real-life problem because both play out a commonplace structural pattern from human psychology, as in Tan's case. After all, the same mind fashions one's dreams as fashions one's life. Metaphoric imagery could also arise because one has been thinking about a certain problem so much that it gets dramatized in a dream, perhaps under the shaping influence of an associated idiom in the language. For instance, one person we know who was worrying about a lapse of faith dreamed of a car rolling backwards down a hill, the mind pictorializing the associated term "backsliding." Neither explanation for dream metaphors implies any intentionality on the part of an "unconscious" or "higher" self to direct one's attention to the pictured problem, let alone to propose a solution to it.

Nevertheless, since the dreaming process sometimes recasts thoughts and emotions into concrete form, it can make a useful descriptive tool. The concrete can be easier to focus on and therefore to understand than more abstract thoughts or emotions. If dreaming results from the mind transforming thoughts, emotions, and other suggestions into more tangible images and events, small wonder that dream images sometimes make valid metaphors, since objectifying a thought or emotion into an image could be considered the definition of a metaphor. Translating dream images into metaphors for life situations thus may have some value as a starting point for analysis and discussion, as long as one avoids naive literalizations such as taking the images as actual "parts of oneself" or as intentional "messages."

LUCIDITY AND THE QUEST FOR MEANING

The dreamer may recognize a dream as relevant to his or her life after eliminating questionable possibilities using the above qualifications. This point, at least, does not conflict with the methods of more sophisticated interpretation approaches today, which emphasize that people must find the relevance of their own dreams, since only *they* know their unique associations to any given image.[48] It supplies a rationale for such an approach while avoiding the suggestive influence of overly specific interpretive techniques—those that proffer cheap or "fortune-cookie" meanings for dreams.

The suggestion theory could be considered an aid to interpreters, since it separates what may be important in dream content from what may be merely state-dependent, dream-specific, or suggested by external authorities. However, the basic approach to dream creation this book presents may be much more broadly relevant and useful than the typical perspectives of interpreters. While robbing validity from some perspectives, it gives it back to others, chiefly of the more generalized, scientific varieties. It maintains that although all dreams are in one way or another controlled by the dreamer, because of their perceptual nature they do not always tell much about the waking personality or other individual waking-world concerns. This section, then, will offer a few suggestions as to what people might try to get out of their dreams instead of the usual supposed "meanings," based on what we have learned from our own lucid experiences.

Wider Patterns: The Perceptual vs. the Personal

Dreams display general human psychological traits in abundance, often even more vividly than in waking. These include the imposition of existing internal patterns on what we all see, the play of associations and rationalizations on our thinking, how easily we deceive ourselves, and how expectation and selective attention prefigure situations. By observing these processes at work in dreams, at one remove from the ordinary lives to which we may be too close for objectivity, we can learn a great deal concerning the workings of perception. What we can glean from dreams about how humans perceive the world has potentially much greater value and utility than would a few personal characteristics or foibles we probably already know.

The diagnostic approach considering dreams pertinent to the psychology of the individual took root in the Freudian preoccupation with abnormal psychology, nurtured by the habit of seeing dreams as outlets for antisocial desires because of their exaggerations and bizarre details. This is not to say dreams have no applicability whatsoever on the personal level, as has hopefully become clear by this point. Such applicability usually becomes apparent after the fact, when people wake and reexamine dream content, but it occasionally does so even during the dream, as happens in some lucid dreams.

The ability to find useful meaning in dream material largely depends, though, on how self-aware a person already is. "Unless you know as much as possible about what [dream] patterns mean in terms of your life," warns one advocate, "you may as well pick an interpretation off a list with a pin, or decide to believe it is all the work of a ghost, a god, or a demon."[49] Ironically, then, anyone who is self-aware enough to understand the relevance of a dream to his or her personal psychology hardly needs to bother interpreting it, since this often only restates the obvious.

Interpretations Interpreted

For those who still feel a need to look for personal meanings in their dreams, we have a few recommendations. In our view, dreams are controlled and dream content determined not so much by personality, as in psychodynamic theories, as by the commonalities of human perception. This in turn makes *individual* perceptual styles more important than the specific dream images they underlie. Therefore, dreamers might be better off examining the way they interact with their dream content in terms of their own waking perceptual habits.

If, for instance, certain people have a high number of anxiety-ridden dreams not obviously prompted by a waking-world crisis, they may simply tend to interpret unusual situations, whether in dreams or otherwise, in a suspicious and fearful manner. If patients in therapy tend to have dreams reflecting the assumptions of their therapists—having "Jungian dreams" while in Jungian analysis or "Freudian dreams" in Freudian analysis—this may indicate a preoccupation with therapy, not that the patients' dreams have become more meaningful. Perhaps some people even train themselves to have a greater than normal proportion of symbolic content by thinking of dreams in symbolic terms. As a friend of ours has remarked, instead of looking at one's dreams to understand one's life, it may make more sense to look at one's life to understand one's dreams.

In any case, because of the variety of suggestion factors involved, analyzing a dream in any meaningful way requires flexibility of interpretation. We advise against accepting any interpretation imposed by an external authority or even assuming that a dream has a fixed meaning. In fact one might more profitably look not at the imagery and its dubious significance, but at the attitudes embodied in one's personal reactions *to* the dream. Reactions to dream material and to ideas about dreams can reveal many of one's biases of thought. By this means, incidentally, interpretation schemes *themselves* become interpretable. People who believe, say, that dream characters must represent aspects of their personalities have as inflexible a stance as people who think dreams totally irrelevant.

Making Head or Tail of It: The Creation of Meaning

People may also benefit by studying the associative and other mental processes that produce dream imagery. The thoughts and emotions that dreams call up while in progress continuously structure and impose meaning on the whole experience, making a narrative unfold. Thus the same dream may look quite different in a typical account describing its surface action than in a description from the perspective of the dreamer's thought processes; and the latter might reveal how those processes respond to and influence images.

For example, after having written up a standard account of a lucid dream during which she had kept careful tabs on her thoughts and feelings, Janice wrote another version for Jay to demonstrate her way of assessing imagery to fit it into her narrative plans. This second version, which approximated her thought processes, revealed that she had facetiously interpreted a character as a Wise Child archetype, which almost certainly influenced the way the boy then sagely offered her a gift with a symbolic resonance. Such factors were not obvious in the first account, which left out most of her concurrent impressions.

All in a Night's Dreamwork: Interpreting Lucid Dreams

Lucid dreams can readily be analyzed in terms of perceptual styles, since psychologically revealing attitudes toward dreams, lucidity and control manifest in lucid dream content. Upon a time Jay had a habit of popping off dream characters' heads, for instance, which could be taken as emphasizing that he knew they did not really have minds of their own. Lucid dreamers have the advantage of being able to "interpret" their dreams *while* still dreaming by controlling their reactions to imagery, changing interpretive approaches as it suits their purposes. Lucidity and control thus come within the bounds of a new interpretive method rather than obstructing interpretability and existing in opposition to any "natural" process of dreaming, as many therapists seem to think. More standard styles of interpretation can themselves create a far greater distortion of the original content of dreams and the dynamics of their creation than anything typically induced by lucidity or dream control and their supposed sublimation of the unconscious.

Lucidity does pose certain problems for the traditional interpreter, though. One's behavior during lucid dreams will often be even *less* relevant to waking psychology than one's behavior in nonlucid dreams, because in nonlucid instances people can and often do believe themselves to be acting in reality, with all its moral strictures. Rather than being an intrusion of the censorious waking ego, suppressing the dream ego's impulsive urges and obviating a chance to learn from them, lucidity probably more often encourages the dreamer to *express* such urges, since he or she will recognize the situation as merely a dream.[50] Only with a fairly high level of lucidity will the dreamer decide not to *bother* indulging impulses for the same reason.

Moreover, the truly lucid dreamer knows an antisocial dream action from an experiment in dream control, whereas a person assessing such an action externally from a recorded account might not. And if a lucid dreamer can stop a nightmare in progress, deliberately adopt alternative dream personas, and otherwise alter the content of dreams through control of his or her thoughts and emotions, the analysts may well feel their interpretive authority compromised. Thus, the criticism that lucidity interferes with the interpretability of dreams has some validity, but only because the facts of lucidity puncture the inflated claims of many interpretive approaches by qualifying them almost to the point of inapplicability.

Multiple Personalities?

The lessons of lucidity have important implications for anyone interested in human psychology. Dreams analyzed from our perspective do not indicate the missing pieces of some larger personality in need of integration or acceptance, a construct that theorists may have posited largely *because* of the diverse actions and attitudes of the dream self. Instead dreams yield the message that personality may simply be situation-dependent. The substitution of fictive perceptions for important terms of reference while dreaming renders human awareness dream-specific. This recurrent dissociation would seem to reflect only naive and usually unavoidable self-deception, not a lack of integration. This in turn means that dreams of even the most bizarre variety are usually natural and harmless, and not indicative of inadequate self-development or a need for therapy.

The suggestion theory requires no deterministic schemes, such as Freud's "id-ego-superego," Perls' various "aspects of self," or Jung's "shadow," "animus/anima" and so on to explain the inconsistencies of behavior noted in dreams and waking alike. Instead it states that, for most of us at least, the "self" is neither unintegrated nor hierarchical but *itself* inconsistent and dependent on situational cues, on the balance of brain chemistry, and on access to orienting memories. Even the psychiatric condition known as multiple personality disorder (MPD) or dissociative identity disorder might simply be a more extreme form of the dissociation we all normally experience. This view accords well with scientific research into organic brain disorders such as Alzheimer's disease and their dramatic, often devastating effects on personality and behavior.[51]

PSYCHOANALYSIS IN DENIAL

In the preceding section we sketched out several ways to interpret dreams, ways that we think improve considerably on conventional methods. However, working with dreams even in the manner we have described necessitates caution, whether one interprets them after waking or within the dream state itself. All sorts of studies *other* than dream interpretation yield information about personality, and since it can be difficult to discern what specific dreams may be relevant in a mass of irrelevant ones, it may be better not to try. As one contemporary psychologist has written, "Despite the symbolism and fascinating condensation of ideas to be found in dreams, there is no evidence that a more useful understanding of personality can be gained from them than can be divined from the realities of waking behavior."[52]

People will much more likely find clues to their real psychological problems in the external world rather than in the dream world. Though of course certain social and organic afflictions may require counseling or medical treatment, many others come down to basic human failings and misperceptions which do not require psychoanalysis to understand so much as a little honesty. Attempting dream interpretation to figure out such a problem may be more complicated than the problem itself, a mere diversion in the quest for an answer.

The traditional role of the analyst in the therapeutic setting has not progressed very far from that of the primitive shaman searching the dream world for lost souls, if he or she only approaches the client's psychological healing through the magic of interpretive doctrine. An understanding of dream-specific behavior and of the arbitrary nature and sheer improbability of many interpretive schemes may help people feel more inclined to discuss *all* the dreams they remember, and not just the ones which seem agreeable or exciting to a certain audience. There is a real need for such an understanding in therapeutic situations, where even the merest of dreams may be interpreted as full of portents, leading the client to hold back on, or in some cases even to play up, anything the analyst might take overseriously. In today's society, where media coverage and the talk-show culture make it seem fashionable to be unbalanced in some way, the self-preoccupation encouraged by many therapeutic systems can be worse than any small "neuroses" or facile revelations uncovered through dream interpretation.

We do not maintain that therapy focused on dreams can never prove effectual. Supportive dream-sharing between therapist and patient, between dreamworker and dream group, or between friend and friend can establish strong social bonds. Even a solo dream interpretation can make for an enjoyable literary exercise. Like attention to *any* subject, these activities may yield usable results, if not necessarily for the reasons commonly believed. The clinical success of a given therapeutic system may attest more to the flexibility of the mind than to the validity of the system—in other words, to the power of suggestion. In many instances, then, people would probably do well to reconceptualize their interpretive endeavors as stimulating social and artistic outlets rather than as anything more profound.

In the final analysis, since the psychoanalytic models of dream creation largely conflict with the discoveries of modern neuroscience, they can safely be considered obsolete.[53] It is to be hoped that the psychiatric professions will not indefinitely continue to overlook or dismiss more scientific findings pertaining to dreams, nor to try to identify the components of the Freudian psyche in the architecture of the human brain. Such approaches only feed the suggestibility so often at the heart of people's problems. Modern researchers have discovered and explained so much about sleep and dreaming that we will attempt to integrate our own alternative explanation for dream creation with their work in the next chapter.

Chapter 8

THE FUNCTIONS OF SLEEP AND DREAMING

People sleep, on average, about a third of every day—or at least wish they did. Of that time, they spend about two hours in rapid-eye-movement (REM) sleep, the periodic phase that correlates with the most intense dreaming.[1] So human beings typically spend a total of nearly *six years* dreaming in an average life span of seventy years.[2] This abundance of dream time, along with the striking and sometimes remarkable content of dream experiences, leads many people, including many sleep and dream researchers, to believe that dreaming must perform some essential function. What that function might *be* remains unclear, however, although a number of theories exist.

Any theory purporting to explain all dream phenomena must account for the distinctive, observable characteristics of lucid dreams to be truly inclusive. These characteristics—such as the tendency of imagery to come and go in conjunction with changes in attention and the ability to control content by controlling one's thoughts and expectations—illuminate the way dreams work, which in turn reflects back on their function. We believe, therefore, that lucid dreamers such as ourselves can usefully contribute to the technical dialogue regarding the purpose of dreaming.

We have already addressed the implications of lucidity for the most popular, though not the most scientifically creditable, theories concerning the purpose of dreaming: the psychoanalytic models. This chapter will highlight some of the more important findings of sleep research, including those pertaining to the neurological and biochemical components of sleep, as well as consider the natural history of sleep and dreaming. This will set the stage for discussing several popular physiological models of dreaming and explaining what the general indeterminacy of dream content means when it comes to choosing a reasonable perspective regarding dreaming.

THE BRAIN TRUST: DISCOVERIES OF SLEEP RESEARCH

Before discussing those theories of the function of REM sleep and dreaming still seriously considered by mainstream scientists, we need to present several important facts uncovered in recent decades. While *dreaming* remains somewhat mysterious, researchers have discovered a fair amount about the nature and usefulness of *sleep*. Since dreaming is one aspect of sleep, any approach to dreaming should have a firm grounding in sleep research so as not to contradict what science already understands. Despite its passive appearance, a great deal of internal activity goes on during sleep, most of which has been discovered only through laboratory studies.

The Stages of Sleep

Sleep, according to a standardized scheme, consists of four distinct stages that succeed one another in a repeating cycle. The first occurrence of Stage 1, at sleep onset, coincides with drowsy ruminations and loosely structured dream fragments. Stage 2 usually evidences thoughtlike mentation but can, especially for light sleepers and near the end of the night, include dreaming.[3] Stages 3 and 4 both represent types of deep sleep. All these different phases can be distinguished from one another by distinctive patterns of electrical activity in the brain.

Normally, the brain winds down through to Stage 4 then back up again to Stage 1, which this time becomes a REM period, with the characteristic darting eye movements that so struck researchers they came to call all the other stages of sleep non-REM or NREM.[4] The periodicity of this interval varies between species. In humans, the whole cycle lasts ninety to a hundred minutes and repeats throughout the night. Each time the relative proportion devoted to deep sleep decreases while that given over to Stage 2 and REM increases.[5]

This explains why Janice could upon a time spend two or three hours waking from and returning to lucid dreams using various protodream and reentry techniques, since her sleep, during an extended period in bed after her having fully rested, could be virtually all dream sleep. Moreover, not everyone follows the idealized scheme; children, as well as adults taking naps, often have sleep-onset REM,[6] which would be favorable to lucidity. Since Janice had very irregular sleeping habits, sleep-onset REM may well have been possible for her.

In any case, the brainstem controls the order and timing of the phases of sleep. It also governs the overall alertness level of waking, as well as many basic autonomic functions such as breathing and heart rate. The periodic release of certain nervous-system chemicals called neurotransmitters mediates these functional variations. Hence the cyclical patterns of sleep and waking have both electrical and chemical controls, although those determining factors themselves largely depend on one's personal choices to go to sleep or to stay awake.[7]

A Peace of Your Mind? Sleep and Its Purposes

Sleep is essential to health and well-being. After five to ten days of sleep deprivation, people become paranoid and irrational, and begin to hallucinate.[8] Longer periods of deprivation uniformly resulted in the death of experimental rats, which lost control of their metabolism and starved to death even though they tried to eat more and more food to compensate.[9] Such observations make it clear that sleep performs a vital role in maintaining perceptual and metabolic integrity. It also appears to enhance the immune system,[10] and may have many other regenerative purposes as well.

Yet, contrary to popular assumptions, according to sleep researchers the purpose of sleep cannot really be to rest either the body or the brain in general. The body should require only *inactivity* to restore its proper level of functioning, not a complex set of nervous-system changes.[11] Indeed, short-term sleep deprivation with human subjects does not produce physical symptoms of anywhere near the magnitude of the psychological disturbances incurred, merely such relatively minor discomforts as pains in the eyes and limbs.[12]

As for the brain, it remains almost as active during sleep as during waking. Only a five to ten percent decrease in neuronal activity occurs in deep sleep as compared to waking—a relatively trivial energy savings.[13] Furthermore, although selected areas like the frontal cortex seem to be deactivated during REM sleep, the brain as a whole can actually be *more* active during dreaming than during waking.[14] The electrical patterns underlying waking and dreaming look so similar, in fact, that researchers cannot easily determine which of the two states a person is in by examining brain waves alone; they must also measure certain somatic factors. High activation coupled with low muscle tone and rapid eye movements indicate REM sleep.[15]

Getting Nervy

While the overall brain remains quite active, very specific neurons within it do indeed rest during sleep, and sleep may exist, in part, to restore their efficiency. The aminergic neurons of the brainstem gradually decrease their firing rate through the first phases of sleep, and virtually turn off during REM.[16] These neurons appear to underlie the ability to pay close attention and the capacity to learn by accumulating new information in memory, and possibly function in discriminating sensory and motor signals as well.[17] They also participate in regulating metabolism, heart rate and mood, and thus play an important role in biological activity.[18] That they should require a special period of reduced activation—that is, sleep—seems reasonable since they do not have much chance to rest during waking.

In this sense, sleep is both energy-conservative and restorative, as typically believed. The major, subjective characteristics of ordinary sleep—insensibility toward the waking world and suspension of coherent thought—in fact comprise the outward aspects of the inner, biochemical process of sleep. The temporary disconnection of sensory input and the diminished memory and attentional functions we all know so well reflect the relative inactivity during sleep of the aminergic neurons of the brainstem and the probably related activational decline of the key cortical area for mediating reason and intellect.

Chemical Warfare?

Sleep physiologists have, to a fair extent, mapped out the chemical components that modulate the sleep cycle. J. Allan Hobson and his associates, for instance, found they could induce REM sleep in laboratory cats using injections of an artificial variant of the neurotransmitter acetylcholine. Similar chemicals used on humans demonstrably intensified dreams.[19]

Such observations suggested to Hobson that the brainstem's cholinergic system, which produces acetylcholine, exists in dynamic balance with the aminergic system, which produces the amines norepinephrine and serotonin. This makes for what Hobson has described as a "reciprocal-interaction" model of sleep-cycle control.[20] When the wake-enhancing aminergic system prevails, we will be awake; when aminergic activity declines sufficiently and the cholinergic system prevails, we will be in REM sleep; otherwise we will find ourselves in some stage of NREM sleep.[21] Hence, in keeping with the very low level of amines available in REM, ordinary dreaming features an inability to think and focus astutely and a lack of clear memory from one moment to the next.

The fact that *lucid* dreaming could even be possible works well with this model, which implies that our mental abilities suffer only partial impairment in sleep and that a particular chemical deficit underlies the disorientation, amnesia, and loss of self-reflective awareness characteristic of dreaming. According to Hobson these formal aspects of dreams link dreaming to psychosis, and virtually all dreams share them regardless of any specific, personal content.[22] He has suggested that lucid dreaming requires tipping the usual neurochemical balance while asleep, somehow requisitioning amines in sufficient quantities during REM to allow the improved volition, memory and critical abilities associated with lucidity, yet not enough to wake up completely.[23] This adjustment may entail "borrowing" from a regenerating supply of amines to favor the frontal cortex.

HITHER AND YAWN: THE EVOLUTION OF SLEEP

The above model of the shifts in brain chemistry underlying sleep and waking can help account for the differences in sleep habits between different kinds of animals. Almost all forms of life display circadian rhythms, patterns of activity and inactivity coordinated with periods of light and dark. This simply means that all have adapted to the earth's rotation and to the seasons. However, only those creatures with relatively complex brains unequivocally exhibit sleep, with its characteristic electrical patterns and insensibility to external stimuli; and only those with an advanced cerebral cortex show signs of REM. Thus, crocodilians and birds have well-developed NREM but only rudimentary REM sleep, while almost all mammals have the familiar, alternating REM/NREM pattern.[24]

Sleep apparently emerged evolutionarily as a requirement for the more complicated functioning of higher life forms. It may have begun as an adaptive strategy to help early reptiles, as the first wholly land-dwelling animals, to cope with the extra demands on metabolism presented by greater variations in external temperature, since the neurons involved in metabolic functions reduce output during sleep.[25] Birds and mammals, which evolved subsequently, have a decided advantage in this regard since, thanks to their feathers or fur and other adaptations, they can maintain more or less constant internal temperatures. Being endothermic lets them remain active rather than going torpid when faced with external temperature extremes as reptiles do, so they can thrive in cold climates. It also enables them to have more complex, sensitive internal organs than would otherwise be possible. The higher metabolic rate that they generate, though, requires that they not only eat a lot to fuel it but spend a fair amount of time asleep in order to lower it for a while.[26]

Another factor important in determining how sleep developed evolutionarily becomes clear when one considers how vulnerable to predation and to many other dangers a creature would be that *automatically* put all its responsive systems on hold at a particular time, regardless of its location or its activity. Closing down temporarily makes better sense when a species has enough mental flexibility to monitor its surroundings and choose a relatively safe time and place to rest. So some conscious input will almost always be involved in switching into the sleep state, however much that state may be regulated by nonconscious brainstem activity;[77] and sleep regulation, in turn, evolved hand in hand with consciousness. The more developed its cortex, the seat of conscious activity, the more likely the animal will have REM sleep. Just what REM sleep might do for the cortex, however, remains a matter of speculation.

One early idea about the purpose of the REM/NREM cycle, the "sentinel hypothesis" of psychologist Frederick Snyder, emphasized this monitoring aspect of sleep. Snyder suggested that since REM brain-wave readings look much like waking readings and since REM periods often end in brief episodes of wakefulness called microawakenings, REM may punctuate the sleep cycle precisely to keep animals aroused enough at certain intervals to be able to wake up and scan the environment for threats.[28] In evolutionary terms, since the ability to assess potential threats would have played a part in enabling the emergence of sleep, the cyclical nature of sleep could have originated as a mechanism allowing animals to do just that, since it is much easier to awaken from REM than from other stages.[29]

This hypothesis would have helped account for the increasing amount of time spent in REM over the course of the night, given that danger from the environment would likely increase the longer an animal remains asleep, assuming it sleeps exposed or otherwise accessible to predators. However, later investigation showed that those animals in the greatest danger of predation, the large hoofed mammals, actually have the *least* REM sleep.[30] The paralysis usually associated with REM might prove fatal to such beasts, who rely on quick reflexes and running for their defense. They handle their environment-monitoring needs by staying awake as much as possible and taking turns sleeping; while individuals nap at irregular intervals throughout the day and night, some members of the herd will always be awake to raise the alarm.[31]

The interplay of several variables affecting sleep can be seen in the variation in sleep patterns observed across mammalian species. Predators like the great cats, being both neurologically complex and comparatively immune to attack, sleep much longer on average than their less cunning but warier prey. They have little need to remain alert for threats, since their physical adaptations and aggressiveness place them at the top of the food chain. Animals which can create or find sheltered dwellings for sleep, such as many primates and rodents, likewise sleep relatively long, employing their agility in an adaptive behavior that keeps them safe. Sleep duration also correlates with body size, since smaller animals, probably because of their high metabolic rate, inefficient heat retention and ability to hide, generally sleep more than larger ones.[32]

Sleep at the right time in a secure place has adaptive features in and of itself. The forced inactivity conserves energy and prevents creatures, especially the young and vulnerable ones who sleep the most, from wandering about and so exposing themselves to danger unnecessarily. Yet circadian patterns of activity and inactivity should prove adequate for such purposes. Full-fledged sleep seems almost maladaptive in some ways, immobilizing creatures and robbing them of their senses for prolonged periods. The waking abilities pertaining to attention and memory which the REM stage apparently benefits could compensate for this, though. It would be logical for the sleep cycle to synchronize with preexisting circadian rhythms to achieve the triple advantage of enhanced waking awareness plus protection and better temperature regulation.

Sleep researcher Alexander Borbély, who elaborated upon the possible mechanisms affecting the peculiarities of the sleep cycle, has written, "Both the amount of time we have previously spent awake and a circadian process are responsible for regulating our sleep. . . . While the percentage of deep sleep depends mainly on the amount of prior waking time, REM sleep is largely determined by the circadian rhythm."[33] In support of this idea, even the occurrence of daydreaming seems to be subject to a ninety-minute cycle throughout the day.[34]

In any case, to emerge evolutionarily the sleep cycle must have been adaptive in some way which offset its disadvantages and which proved more useful than simple resting behaviors, and its enhancement of certain mental capacities seems the most likely reason. The first small, furtive mammals did not need to be particularly brainy to survive. Since they could sustain a viable temperature, they may well have been nocturnal, a good way to avoid primarily day-bound reptilian enemies. Still, being relatively defenseless they probably had the sense to hide themselves away securely for their rest periods. Eventually, when the mammalian branch radiated into a wide variety of ecological niches and diverse sizes and shapes with new opportunities to exploit and dangers to face, cleverness would become an asset in determining reproductive success.

Mammals enjoy a number of design advantages, one being that all but the most primitive are born live rather than incubating inside eggs, and all receive care and nourishment from their mothers after birth, as birds do too. Such advances give more complex creatures more time to develop. Virtually all reptiles come into the world equipped to fend for themselves and fixed in their perceptions and behaviors, and many birds and mammals too must at least be able to see and move along shortly after their arrival. Many others, though, undergo a critical learning period under the protection of their parents while their brains grow and their sensory pathways become permanently etched in response to environmental stimuli.[35] Young birds and mammals have more REM sleep than adults of their species; in fact many kinds of birds have REM *only* as hatchlings.[36] As a rule, the more immature a young animal's state of development at birth, the higher the percentage of REM sleep it will display at that time.[37]

REM sleep most likely, then, evolved along with the increasing capacity to model the environment. Such "modifiable awareness" would help enable sleep by letting animals learn to recognize or manufacture favorable sleeping circumstances for themselves. It would itself be further enabled *by* sleep, since they could concentrate the use of any "budget of attentional capacity" when it was most needed—during waking.[38] The complexities of sleep, with its sophisticated economizing of brain chemistry, could be seen as inevitable adaptive developments necessitated by the progressively increasing complexity of animal brain structure.

The sleep of mammals appears to have evolved to favor the specific neurons in the brain responsible for enhancing these animals' more advanced cognitive and perceptual abilities. As Hobson points out, "The more the animal is involved in critical attentional and learning tasks, the more likely it is to require adequate maintenance of the synaptic efficacy of its aminergic neurons."[39] Since those neurons also play a part in regulating metabolism, rebuilding and conserving the supply of aminergic neurotransmitters in the brain during REM may be one of the most essential purposes of sleep.[40]

CASTING YOUR NEURAL NETS: SPECULATIONS ON ACTIVATION-SYNTHESIS

The REM state has a unique physiology to match its unique biochemistry. As we mentioned in Chapter 6, REM physiology involves alternations between quiet tonic periods and active phasic periods featuring eye jerks, muscle twitches, and respiratory and blood pressure fluctuations. Vivid dreaming occurs in phasic REM, and lucidity correlates with increased phasic activity.[41] On the neurological level, REM entails activation by the brainstem of the limbic system—thought to be the seat of strong emotion and remote memory—as well as various systems of the cortex. Sensory input and motor output may be negligible in sleep, but both systems jump to life internally during REM, leading, according to the Hobson and McCarley view, to a welter of contradictory information to synthesize.

We have already discussed activation-synthesis in some detail in other chapters. Here we will attempt to explore its implications a little further with some speculations of our own towards reperceiving dream phenomena in neurological terms.

Imagine That: Data Processing and Dream Visualization

Although we disagree with some of its specifics, especially the idea that dreamed thoughts and actions are necessarily automatic and not volitional,[42] the activation-synthesis hypothesis meshes well with our own perspective overall. It would seem that any activity in the brain that affects the cortex could potentially become a suggestion factor. The brain is, at least in part, an information-processing organ that monitors, analyzes, stores and retrieves the data we all need to function in the world. Our everyday awareness directs much of this information processing, by selecting out what we pay attention to from all potential input—thoughts, emotions, physical sensations, internal drives, et cetera—and sifting it through a patterning filter of habituated responses built up from all we have paid attention to in the past.

There is, however, a neurobiological component to this processing operation that we do not consciously operate: the electrochemical deployment of our brain cells. These billions of neurons excite one another and fire in myriad conformations when triggered by various stimuli, thereby, many scientists believe, interpreting data and encoding our memories.[43] Images in the mind's eye—or ear for that matter—that we call up as thoughts and memories are, in this view, only glosses on particular patterns of neuronal activation. In conditions of sufficient arousal but attenuated awareness of the external world, such as dreaming, we may be overhearing our own nonconscious, internal processing systems on the neuronal level and inaccurately glossing the noise with seeming "meaning" through cortical networks of association.

This model would fit in with the problems and delays so often experienced when trying to produce or interact with lucid dream imagery, such as summoning an item or creating a sensation. With the right touch, of course, such effects can occur instantly, but it commonly takes some time for the desired imagery to manifest "out there" in the dream environment. The only "out there" actually available to the dreaming brain's ego-function would be elsewhere in the brain. So what goes on during such attempts at dream control?

In computer operations, a noticeable delay can occur between when the user inputs a command and when the screen produces a new image, with all manner of invisible electronic operations going on while the machine interprets the command and processes its response in a manner the user can perceive. Similarly, in the dreaming brain the lucid dreamer's directed attention, which routes the flow of the otherwise random or associational current flickering through the neuronal circuitry, may essentially send a command down to the appropriate processing system—verbal, visual, auditory, motor, and so on—to create a specific effect. From there it would eventually resurface as an illusory perception, if illusory perceptions can come *from* trying to read a neural processing system.

In other words, the dreamer has to think about what he or she wants to happen, then shift mental gears to perceive it atop all the neuronal activity that has been set off. The operation resembles struggling to remember some fact for a few moments, then giving up only to have it pop into mind after one's internal organic "computer" has scanned its data banks to retrieve the information. This would lead to such effects as the propensity Janice and Ruth both noticed for dream animals to appear shortly after abandoning trying to create them directly.

By the same principle, it would be easier for a lucid dreamer to create an image in its appropriate context than to conjure something at a whim, because associated ideas have strong links to one another in the neuronal networks of our memories. According to one account, because of chemical changes at the synapses, or nerve cell junctions, and an increase in the number of branches joining neighboring neurons that have been activated together previously, "a frequently aroused pattern of nerves is far easier to awaken than a totally fresh arrangement of cells."[44] Thus habitual neural nets will activate much more readily than novel ones, and a dream kitchen will more likely contain a refrigerator than, say, a lawnmower.

Ivan Pavlov, of conditioned learning fame, postulated that during sleep this principle may not hold, that a lower level of cortical tone in the brain allows a greater number of weak associations to activate.[45] This may be true to a point, given the frequency of odd intrusions of imagery and bizarrely strung sequences in dreams. But successful lucid dream control, at least, seems to depend heavily on common associations and expectations. Perhaps the varying degrees of stability and vividness of dream imagery also correlate to some extent with the strength of the communications between activated nerve cells.

Conversations with Ourselves

A particularly interesting delay in lucid dreams is one that can be involved when getting dream characters to answer questions. Janice and Ruth often noted a greater than normal lag between speaking to a character and receiving its answer, along with a sense of their minds manufacturing the dialogue in the pause between phrases. When Janice asked a dream neurologist about this, he disclosed that when answering questions he had to "pull ideas out of her head." This seems close to the truth of the matter. Without any deliberate attempt at influence during the pause, habitual syntax and conversational expectations would imperfectly guide the resulting speech. The dreamer in effect takes potluck on what the brain will produce, and may get nothing better than a string of random words.

At other times, the dreamer may be subliminally making up the discourse as it occurs. In a certain telling instance, Janice's perception kept alternating between hearing a nearby character somewhat haltingly and ramblingly answer a question of hers and hearing her own voice quietly continue the monologue in her head, though she was not thinking the words deliberately. Perhaps as part of the mind's overall attempt to make the dream feel more like a reality, one can dissociate from certain of one's own thoughts— which become a bit more free-form in the process—and project them outward to manifest as vocalizations from other persons in the dream. The two speech-generation mechanisms, listening to the brain and dissociated fantasy, could conceivably combine to allow a curious type of composition of which the dreamer does not have to be fully cognizant.

The neuroperceptual model mentioned above may help elucidate the quirks of dream-character talk a bit further. For instance, one way to make a dream character say specific words entails thinking over the words until the character comes out with them. This concentration might in effect set off the brain's verbal processing system, which would then send the words back up in the voice of the character, rather like a speech synthesizer. Janice saw this strikingly illustrated in one dream when she heard her own lines of dialogue before actually speaking them, probably because she was thinking them over so hard to hold them in her head while scripting the dream conversation that they came out just like speech.

When—again often after a delay—a character says only a generally appropriate response such as a pat phrase or odd remark, expectation may have set up certain associative parameters within which the verbal processor had some leeway, perhaps under the subtle guiding influence of dissociated thoughts. In the absence of sufficiently structured expectations, as when just trying to listen to a character's speech, one gets sheer nonsense or nothing, assumably due to not directing the flow of information through the processor at all. Hence the usual frustrations involved in trying to hold intelligent conversations of any length with dream characters.

It would be interesting indeed if the voices of dream people actually correspond to localized activity in the dreaming brain, if dream characters can be reduced to transiently excited neuronal nets playing through the brain's speech generators and memory stores. Laboratory science may one day be able to measure neuronal activity precisely enough to tell. Reexamining the specifics of dreams from a neurological standpoint thus offers some fascinating prospects for future research.

MATTER OVER MIND: PHYSIOLOGICAL THEORIES OF DREAMING

Hobson's observations concerning the aminergic/cholinergic dynamic may offer an important explanation of why we have REM sleep, and the activation-synthesis model may illuminate some of the neurological workings of that state. But do these constructs really answer the question of why we *dream*? Dreaming may be associated with a specific bodily state that has specific functions, yet it is not equivalent to that state, but rather a particular kind of concurrent mental activity. This fact led David Foulkes to state unequivocally that no "neurobiological description of the state of the brain during dreaming will ever prove sufficient to answer the questions of dream psychology,"[46] including the question of function. Even Hobson himself points out that since dreaming constitutes a psychological phenomenon, its own function, if it has one, must lie on a psychological and not a physiological level.[47]

So to the psychological level the discussion must turn, though guided by various physiological observations. This section will review several key scientific theories on the purpose of REM sleep and attempt to evaluate their relevance when applied to dreaming itself. These theories originally concerned themselves primarily with explaining the specifics of REM physiology and only secondarily with accounting for the psychological side of the equation, that is, with dream content and structure. Consequently, they may be valid on one level without holding up on the other.

Dreaming to Remember

One widespread theory, suggested by the late psychologist and computer scientist Christopher Evans among others, states that the distinctive electrical and chemical properties of REM somehow enable the brain to review and sort information picked up during the day in order to transfer new data into long-term memory.[48] The analogy often used is that of an offline mainframe computer system updating its files. The brain supposedly similarly needs time to consolidate experience, and when the mind catches glimpses of the underlying process it produces a dream.

Some scientists consider this theory plausible since it lends a psychological rationale both to disabling the means of picking up new sensory stimuli to process and to suspending critical attentional and short-term memory storage functions during sleep. It also seems to be upheld by certain experimental observations. For instance, people supposedly recall lists of words learned before sleep better than lists learned before a comparable waking interval,[49] and in one study subjects deprived of REM sleep did not do as well on recall tests as did those deprived only of NREM sleep.[50]

A connection between REM sleep and learning might also help explain the differential proportions of time spent asleep by individuals of different ages. Human infants and immature animals, who are just learning about the world, sleep a great deal more than the adults of their respective species. As we noted earlier in the chapter, they spend a proportionally larger amount of that time in REM,[51] when per the above theory they might be assimilating unfamiliar experiences.

We can spot certain problems with this picture, though. In the first instance cited, people may have better recall of words learned before sleep because more goes on in their minds to drive the information from memory during waking than during sleep, or because of some unaccounted-for circadian factor. And, one might possibly say that babies need more sleep than adults because their infant brains must deal with proportionally more undigested experience and so more quickly become taxed and exhausted.

Any observed increase in REM with intensive learning, then, could be a compensation to benefit an overtaxed aminergic system. Similarly, any impairment of learning with REM deprivation could simply mean that the connection between REM and memory is strictly chemical and unrelated to dreaming. Lack of REM sleep might, after all, somehow interfere with the *retrievability* or waking reiteration of new information rather than with its direct storage; one's thinking ability might be compromised if the aminergic system has not recuperated. This means the chemical modulation of sleep could have a psychological effect without itself being a psychological process.

Those who wish to extend the memory-consolidation idea to the psychological level might point to the "day residues" or traces of daily events that can appear in dream content. Yet these do not make unequivocal evidence for the model either. People may simply continue to think while dreaming about the same things they thought about during the day, or at least have those things in the back of their minds, making such thoughts and memories into suggestion factors. Or, considering this from a neurological angle, day residues may turn up fairly often because when in need of a random element to fill in a detail, the brain might tend to select out recently activated neuronal patterns that remain "lit up," as it were.

Further, while our own remembered dreams sometimes incorporate recent occurrences and ideas, we have noticed that something may occur a week or more before showing up in a dream, which hardly evidences an efficient memory-sorting mechanism.

For instance, one February Janice had a dream in which she had to let a crow out the front door of her house. She became lucid because she remembered having to let another black bird, a starling, out there the previous December in reality—a lag of two months. Likewise, our dream settings seldom keep current with changes of residence or furniture arrangements.

The memory-consolidation model does not, then, adequately explain the *content* of dreams. It does not account for the apparent nonsense and information-mangling so predominant in dreams and observable by almost anyone. Even those who do not normally recall dreams may have noticed that their sleep-onset thoughts can go over the day's events and twist them completely around. If dreams exclusively represented memory processing going on in the brain or themselves somehow sorted new material, they would assumably show a more direct correlation to ordinary experience and recent events than they normally do.

As a case in point, for several months after visiting England Janice saw London buildings in the dream version of her own hometown, a memory mix that could prove hopelessly disorienting if it indicated or caused a literal, corresponding change in her internal mental maps. Fortunately, it would seem people actually sort experience and stimulate memory formation with their waking attention and achieve the major part of learning through waking effort.

We do not believe that actions taken in dreams can have any effect on memory. We modified images in lucid and nonlucid dreams for years with no noticeable subsequent impairment of our memory abilities. This result would be expected if such dream changes take place only on the level of thought and perception and do not really affect the psyche to a significant degree. Therefore, if memory consolidation goes on during REM it would seem to do so independently of both dream content and action; in fact dreams make such muddled constructs that any positive effects REM has on memory would *have* to take place outside of the dreams themselves. After all, as we mentioned above, information processing goes on outside awareness all the time on the neurological level.

The suggestion theory does not, then, rule out the possibility that REM sleep has a connection with memory consolidation, as long as one does not specify dreams as the sorting mechanism. REM-specific neurological processes could certainly be at work. For instance, Hobson suspects that acetylcholine may reinforce new memories chemically, or that REM activation may electrically integrate new data with that already existing in a range of related neuronal circuits and action programs.[52] In this case the hyperassociative nature of dreaming might reflect the brain's making diverse connections between new information and old memories. The fact that we found ourselves virtually cut off from recent waking memories in the lucid dream experiments described in Chapter 5 may lend some credence to the idea that the brain reorganizes this material while the attention remains occupied with a dream.

But if dreaming is merely a *side effect* of memory consolidation occurring on the neuronal level during REM, as would be the case if new information were somehow electrically assimilated or chemically enhanced, this model does not provide any *psychological* explanation of dreaming because of the problem of mixing levels. If the actual process occurs neurologically and outside of consciousness, which remains engaged with dreaming, it cannot be considered a psychological process. One has to look elsewhere to find a purpose for dreaming.

Dreaming to Forget

Francis Crick, the codiscoverer of the DNA double helix, and his colleague Graeme Mitchison proposed another physiological theory of the purpose of REM sleep. They hold that we all dream not to remember but to *forget* certain useless information. According to this view, the activation of the dreaming brain discharges cortical memory buffers, clearing them of data overloads and accidental connections that would otherwise cause fantasies, obsessions, and hallucinations.[53] Hobson, observing the resemblance between certain brain-wave patterns during epileptic fits and REM sleep, has similarly suggested that REM activation might be a kind of "modified seizure" to prevent uncontrolled seizures and hallucinations in waking.[54]

Questions of course arise. Would firing off an unwanted pattern of activation not tend to *reinforce* rather than defuse its synaptic connections? And what would prevent a REM "seizure" from erasing useful connections as well as useless? Why forgetting information should have to be such an active process at all is not clear either, since we tend to forget anything not exercised by repetition. The theory seems to maintain that we pay attention to and accumulate a lot of unimportant information, when common experience shows that we pay attention only to what we judge as novel or important for whatever reason, and only *to* the extent that we judge it important. Everything else gets tuned out or forgotten long before bedtime.

Nevertheless, the notion that unwelcome "resonances" could develop out of what one *does* pay attention to and require some sort of circuit-clearing mechanism may have a certain amount of merit. But if this deletion of useless connections and data is a neurological function of REM activation, it again does not provide any explanation of the *psychological* phenomenon of dreaming, except perhaps for the appearance of bizarre images. In fact Crick and Mitchison see dream content as meaningless and not intended to be remembered.[55] We personally would concur with this in principle, but do not take their extreme view that frequently remembering dreams would be intrinsically harmful to people. The model implies not only that people who remember their dreams tend to be overimaginative and maladapted, but that they are so *because* they remember their dreams—a startling set of assumptions.

Dreaming to Develop

Another perspective on the function of REM sleep states that REM activation develops the central nervous system in early life and maintains its efficiency thereafter.[56] This would offer what might be a better explanation for the large amounts of REM experienced by babies than the memory-consolidation theory. Newborns do not have much critical attention to speak of, nor do they comprehend much of the barrage of higher-order information assailing them, being busy just getting oriented perceptually; and even unborn babies, who cannot be learning much in the usual sense of the word at all, exist almost perpetually in REM sleep.[57] Instead, then, their REM activation could represent the brain automatically creating, pruning and exercising its circuits to mature itself so it will be better *able* to process information. This work certainly involves learning, since the brain shapes itself in response to the world, but it is a developmental rather than strictly a learning process.

REM sleep does not cease after this critical developmental phase, of course, and so it may continually maintain and refine the central nervous system throughout life. One study of brain-damaged patients who had lost the ability to speak provides some interesting evidence for this hypothesis. Those individuals with better rates of improvement, which would entail active neurological restructuring as other parts of their brains took over the lost speech functions, spent proportionally more time in REM than did those recovering more slowly.[58]

Under more ordinary circumstances, REM sleep may in effect help keep the brain's "motor" running smoothly by periodically stimulating it in a stereotyped, patterned manner which ensures that all the sensorimotor circuitry remains used and exercised. It may also perform a specialized operation like testing and tuning various synaptic connections or renewing the entire memory system.[59] In this case, the purpose of REM activation may be more to prevent losing what one already knows than to store anything new.

In its general formulation this theory does not conflict with our own because it does not make any predictions about the content of dreams. It is, again, a theory of the physiological function of REM activation rather than of the psychological function of dreaming per se. One could, though, by extension say that since dreaming imposes structure on what would otherwise be unordered hallucinations, dreaming would facilitate the shift into waking's structured mentation and perception by keeping the brain's perceptual circuits and world-modeling abilities exercised. Such a process should operate regardless of the particular material dreamed, much as a muscle may be developed and maintained regardless of the particular exercise employed.[60]

Practice Makes Perfect?

A more specific variant of the above theory, supported by sleep physiologist Michel Jouvet and others, holds that REM sets off programmed reflexes and learned motor sequences to keep them exercised and to modify them according to new experience. Jouvet came to his conclusions on the basis of experiments with cats whose brainstems he surgically altered to allow motor impulses to reach the muscles during REM. He observed these sleeping animals apparently enacting their dreams by engaging in various instinctual modes of behavior such as prey stalking, even when they had never had any call to perform those behaviors in their waking lives—as if dreaming were necessary to keep their inborn survival skills in practice should the need for these ever come up.[61] This line of reasoning is not entirely clear cut, however; cats also certainly practice their predation routines through waking play, such as chasing balls, even when they have never seen nor hunted a live mouse.

Still, the above hypothesis, when applied to dream content, could account for the frequent occurrence of such significant instinctual tendencies as aggression, self-preservation and sexuality in human dreams.[62] Moreover, while cortex-memorized verbal material such as foreign vocabulary words readily decays with disuse, we can all remember habituated, brainstem-controlled motor skills like how to ride a bicycle even when we do not actually execute them for years, which suggests that running basic motor programs in REM may help us retain them. Plus the more complex the creature, the more flexible and less fixed its action patterns become, due no doubt to integrating such patterns with information in the cortex—a need perhaps served by the intense activation that is characteristic of REM.

Psychologist Nicholas Humphrey attempted to extend these ideas even further into the level of content. He suggested that dreams let us rehearse certain essential behaviors and social strategies even when they are not commonly employed in waking, to increase our adaptive facility.[63] But what about *flying* in dreams? This common dream activity could draw on various sensations learned in waking, but it has little real-world applicability itself. What about the dreamer who thinks himself a magic set of china, or the one who believes himself Elvis Presley's dog? If we rehearse as many actions and roles *without* real-world parallels as *with*, are we somehow influenced only by the useful ones and not by the useless? Again, the nonsense of dreams goes unexplained.

ANYTHING GOES: DREAM CONTENT AND THE QUESTION OF FUNCTION

All of the scientific perspectives on REM sleep considered thus far—the activation-synthesis hypothesis, the memory consolidation or memory clearance models, and the developmental and maintenance theories—have their merits on their own terms. But when stretched to explain dreaming as well, they would tend to describe dream content as somehow preprogrammed, whether by brainstem signals, or by day-to-day experiences, or by instinct. Yet our personal observations and experiments as lucid dreamers have led us to realize that dreaming is *creative*, with no necessary, preprogrammed content, except insofar as past experience informs the habit-based, associational matrix in which dreams occur. The dreamer's flexible *interpretation* of dream events seems to have at least as much of an effect on their outcome as any more mechanical sources of suggestion that may be in operation.

Although sleep physiology is complex and could have many functions, the intractable question of how anything as addled as dreaming could itself reorganize vital information or provide essential experience need not be answered from our perspective. We suggest that dream content gets structured separately from, though sometimes in concert with, certain automatic and useful physiological processes, which might include information reorganization and similar functions proposed by researchers. The substrate of REM activation does not *determine* dream content in our view, though it may supply certain suggestion factors, and may itself *be* a suggestion factor, misleading dreamers into assuming themselves awake. "The sense and nonsense of dreams," to borrow a phrase from Hobson, would reflect the indeterminacy of the mind attempting to interpret the effects of that internal activity as valid input. The representation of certain instinctual interests would result from impulses translating directly into imagined action in an area of experience where no ordinary constraints need apply in any case.

That's Entertainment: Dreaming for Creativity

A final theory that does not *seem* to conflict with or sidestep the idea of dreaming as creative states that the function of dreaming is to *be* creative, to generate novel and useful experience.[64] Dreams can be aesthetically appealing and sometimes inspirational, so why not say dreaming exists so the mind can entertain and enlighten itself during otherwise uneventful sleep? After all, even surreal mental activity is preferable to lying in a temporary coma.

Unfortunately, to say that dreams are created by the dreamer as they occur and to say that they occur for the *sake* of creativity mean two different things. If dreams are supposed to please us all, why do they so often frustrate or even frighten us? If dreams are meant to give us new, useful experiences, why should so many dreams be repetitious, confused, and mundane, and why should their content so often fall into certain definite, recurrent patterns so dissimilar from waking experiences?

The suggestion theory states that dreams reflect our own thoughts, abilities and mental habits. If our thoughts usually run to the fearful or the mundane or the fanciful, so too may our dreams, even to the point of setting up a patterned dreaming style; and creative people, or those frequently exposed to the artistic products of others, will probably have more creative dreams than most. At best one can say that the dreaming mind gives itself something to do, whether exciting or tedious, pleasant or worrisome, which might be called "entertaining" in the broad sense of engaging the attention. But it would appear to do so reflexively, not purposefully, and using the same perceptual structures developed and employed in waking modeling.

An astute investigator would also question just how useful the novel elements that do occur in dreams can be. The direction of attention may help steer dreams along, but that awareness is almost always exercised over dream-specific events and images. This makes the generated experience almost always dream-specific as well, in actions, thoughts, and emotions. Hence dreams generally provide no simulation of reality pertinent enough to the real world to be of any educational value. Instead they reflect, imperfectly, what we have *already* learned in combination with many characteristics endemic to dreams alone. If we actually learned from interacting with such confusions of fact and illusion, without reinterpreting the events after waking, we would become *less* well adapted to the real environment. Therefore, it is just as well that we usually forget them.

Dreaming Out of Habit

This brings up a crucial point. Any theory considering dreams useful on a psychological level would seem to require that the brain somehow store the experience gained in sleep, since psychological dimensions like emotion, thought and certainly memory itself depend on the storage of acquired information. Why then should we so easily forget such supposedly important occurrences—an estimated 95 percent of dreams get forgotten[65]—and so be unable to draw on them as valid experiences? Do we somehow educate ourselves *without* storing the result in memory? Invoking the concept of the unconscious here only confuses the issue. The fact that we do not readily remember dreams unless we pay special attention to them challenges the notion that their specific content could be psychologically essential.[66]

The indeterminacy observable in lucid dreams also undermines the notion that dreaming has any special psychological function. If dream creation comes down to awareness shifting between and elaborating on various suggestion factors, whether mental or physical or physiological, then dreams can have no predetermined content; and without predetermined content, there can be no function *of* specific content. In the absence of a strong candidate for any *necessary*, beneficial psychological function of dreaming, perhaps we should all seriously consider a rather less exciting alternative, then: that although sleep itself and its various phases may have any of a number of essential purposes, dreaming—the actual interplay of mentation with images and associations—may have *no* function of its own. It may be merely a by-product of sleep. Does this last theory fit all observations?

The suggestion theory of dream generation, unlike more deterministic theories based on observations of REM physiology alone, allows for NREM dreaming and can explain all the general characteristics of dream experience. It states that dreams develop when the world-modeling capacities of the mind become engaged during sleep, a state featuring both the absence of real sensory information with which to crosscheck and stabilize imaginal experiences and, more often than not, insufficient critical and memory abilities by which to put such experiences into perspective. These deficits are, obviously, exactly those thought to be caused by the resting of the aminergic neurons during sleep. With the decrease of the amines in NREM sleep the ability to direct and remember what we are thinking from moment to moment decreases, and with their near total loss in REM, and the consequent deactivation of the frontal cortex, we lose self-reflective awareness and other higher mental functions as well. This condition, coupled with sufficient internal stimulation of the brain, causes dreaming, with all its confabulatory jumbles.

David Foulkes has maintained that "dreaming does not depend on mental processes or systems that are in any way unique to sleep."[67] Indeed, while the brain's activation and modulation mechanisms obviously differ considerably in different states of consciousness, the structuring operation called "dreaming" is not exclusive to sleep at all, but essentially the same perceptual process we use throughout our daily lives. If we are aware at all, awake or dreaming, we are processing information by means of inner models. When dreaming we apply this modeling mechanism automatically, as indeed we do in waking, but now to an area where it does not fit, and with a few of the ingredients necessary for its intended functioning missing. The results differ simply because the conditions of operation differ.

By this reasoning, dreaming is not a *unique* process, and so it need not have a unique function. The suggestion theory does not require any psychological purpose for the specific content of dreams, only a biochemical purpose behind sleep. The common contemporary attitude taking dreams as not generally worth remembering or thinking about and without relevance to real-life concerns would be well in line with this perspective.

DON'T MOVE A MUSCLE: DREAMS AND EVOLUTION

Some may argue that the suggestion theory does not preclude that dreaming may have other functions, since extra evolutionary adaptations could have taken advantage of the time spent dreaming even if it initially had a biochemical origin alone. The human tongue, after all, at some point became adapted for articulate speech after originally developing for eating and tasting food. But dreaming cannot have evolved solely in conjunction with *sleep*, since the *real world* enforces the natural selection of characteristics. Dreaming would only be modified evolutionarily because of some effect it had on waking, and only to whatever extent that effect conferred an advantage favoring survival.

Yet as Foulkes has written, "It's difficult to believe that the particular contents of our dreams serve any adaptive function or play any adaptive role in nondreaming behaviors or mental states."[68] Since little that people do in dreams can significantly affect their waking chances of survival, and since dreams have no definite correlation with reality and usually go unremembered in any case, then no capacity automatically producing specific dream content on the human level of complexity would ever have been evolutionarily selected. Also, since dreamers obliviously alter their dream imagery all the time depending on how they direct their attention, no mechanism would likely evolve whereby they could easily modify, and thus possibly harm, the mind or body by doing so.

Certain observations underscore the idea that dreaming did not evolve as a separate capacity to perform a unique function. As mentioned earlier in the chapter, dreaming and waking feature essentially the same brain waves, which would imply at least a degree of similarity in their underlying neural activity; this likeness also clearly stamps dreaming as a conscious, not an unconscious activity.[69] Additionally, Jouvet's cat experiments demonstrated that REM motor inhibition exists to prevent an individual from acting out its dreams in the real world. This motor-output block is necessary since dreaming uses the same brain wiring as the neural circuitry involved with action in the external world, just as it uses some of the same sensory pathways employed during waking perception.

It makes sense that motor inhibition during REM evolved rather than the capacity to turn off the data-structuring system selectively. The paralysis is temporary and limited to times of relative immobility in any case, whereas we depend on the ability to organize data for our well-being. And since most dreams slip from our mental grasp upon awakening—or even earlier, due to the poor quality of memory in sleep—no one runs any great risk of confusing dreams with waking memories. Forgetting dreams, besides giving the aminergic neurons some time off, would have an equivalent effect to locking muscle response during sleep: preventing a creature from acting out its dreams, via memory in this case. With the addition of the motor-output block dreaming was thus rendered relatively harmless, necessitating no other adaptations to prevent it from occurring.

To suggest that dreaming has no discrete psychological function from an evolutionary point of view does not imply that dreams must remain functionless. They have proved of service to students of the mind, creative individuals, and ordinary people around the world who have learned to appreciate them for what they are—and often for what they are not, as well. The next chapter will turn a critical eye towards a variety of popularly suggested uses for dreaming lucidly.

Chapter 9

USES OF LUCIDITY

The scientific community's pioneers in lucid dream studies have offered up a wide assortment of reasons why they think developing such a talent might be useful. Lucid dreaming certainly has some practical value to sleep researchers, since it allows direct exploration of the dream universe under laboratory conditions, providing quantifiable information about the nature of sleep and dreaming. But what utility does it have for the ordinary person? Lucidity has been posited to benefit everything from creativity to physical and mental health and even psychic ability. This chapter will assess a variety of such claims, rounding them off with a discussion of how *we* think lucidity most useful on the basis of our own experience and our theoretical standpoint, the suggestion theory.

HOOK, LINE AND SINKER: LUCIDITY AND THE MASS MARKET

The publishers of books and periodicals related to lucid dreaming have quite often sought to market their efforts to a mass audience. To do so they have had to make the subject appealing and to demonstrate or assert that lucidity can be learned and applied by a fair segment of the population. Promoters have therefore dangled a number of tantalizing claims before the interested public. Those with the widest allure relate to using lucid dreams for their entertainment value, for improving creative potential and problem-solving abilities, and for practicing waking-world skills. All of these mass-market selling points have their merits, but not to anything like the extent implied in the literature.

Just for the Fun of It

The most widely appealing motivation for lucid dreaming in contemporary society would most likely be entertainment, and indeed much of the hype centers around wish-fulfillment. One of the Lucidity Institute's catalogs of products started off a list of the alleged benefits of lucid dreaming by proclaiming, "Discover the ecstasy of flying, explore strange new worlds, dare dangerous exploits (without real danger), enjoy complete sexual freedom, fulfil your wildest fantasies."[1] Similarly, the back cover blurb the publisher provided for Patricia Garfield's popular *Creative Dreaming* hooks readers with promises of "sexual union and even orgasm with the partner of your choice" and "exciting mind trips and adventures" during sleep.

We will not deny that lucid dreaming affords a superb opportunity for mental recreation. Given a strong imagination and the ability to direct that imagination positively, lucid dreaming can be great fun, being at least potentially far more vivid than ordinary fantasizing. Soaring flight, drug-free highs, sexual gratification without consequences, freedom from physical and social constraints, "magical" powers of control and storytelling—all provide a sense of pleasure and satisfaction that can linger in waking to enhance the following day.

Dreamers may actually feel more awake and alive while lucidly dreaming than they will when they wake up, when their cares and preoccupations return and their brains have the added burden of external sensory information to process. Lucidity can also inspire a sense of exploration through learning about the workings of the mind, as well as foster pleasant social interaction through the urge to share one's discoveries with like-minded others. The latter may prove somewhat difficult to locate, however. Many people consider the whole idea of lucid dreaming rather strange, and it can be hard to fit in even with those who profess an interest in it because different people typically have different agenda in their explorations.

In fact, none of the stimulating outcomes so overstressed in the promotions has any guarantee of success. Not every lucid dreamer can fly well; Janice still had trouble with it sometimes after more than a decade of practice. Dream "highs" may come easiest to those who have previously had them on drug trips. Even the erotic encounters work better for some than for others. Not everyone feels sexual sensations in dreams consistently or at all, and knowing the dream partner to be only a figment of the imagination and not a real person can detract from as easily as enhance the pleasure, depending upon one's psychology.

Force of habit, as well as limitations of the medium like instability, can override whatever freedom lucid dreamers might otherwise enjoy. Nor does everyone have much skill at dream control or the talent for scripting adventures; it takes work to make lucid dreams consistently interesting. Experienced dreamers can have long, involved saga dreams, but to create and maintain such dreams lucidly, and especially to sustain serial adventures over extended periods like Janice did, may be possible only for particularly gifted and practiced lucid dreamers. Even they will probably eventually run into something of an obstacle. Much as learning about the tricks of filmmaking can make movies lose a lot of their former impact, there is a certain tension between understanding the nature of dream creation and continuing to produce and enjoy complex lucid dreams beyond a point; they may go flat under the weight of too much technical analysis. Because of the potential problems of self-consciousness and decreased spontaneity that can come with greater awareness of the unreality of a scenario, we have known people to say they prefer to lose lucidity sometimes in order to retain their enjoyment of dream stories or sensations.

Moreover, with all the secret pleasures of lucid dreaming comes the question of how much is really appropriate. Thrilling escapades may not be all that accessible to everyone in reality, or terribly desirable, for that matter, because of the risks involved. Lucid dreaming thus makes a good outlet for a kind of virtual gaming. But those who develop elaborate dream lives because their waking ones seem too boring and ordinary should perhaps consider restructuring their lives to include at least some increase in pleasurable stimulation.

While lucid dreams can indeed be entertaining, dreamers may be overimpressed by their lucid escapades if they reflexively compare such activities only with what happens in waking, not with what happens in other, nonlucid dreams, which can also be enjoyable. Nor does it say much for the fair-mindedness of an investigation if one selects out only the most exhilarating instances to savor and share. Despite the bias of representation in the literature, lucid dreams can turn out unpleasant or dull as well as pleasant and exciting, the excitement if present might wake the dreamer up, and the novelty of it all will probably wane over time; it is easy to run out of inspiration.

A Legend in Your Own Mind: Dreams and Creativity

Some hold that lucid dreaming can animate creativity in those interested in such areas as fiction, drama, filmmaking, painting, or songwriting. This would make particular sense from the point of view of those who consider the unconscious the wellspring of creativity as well as the font of dreams. As the above-mentioned catalog says, "With lucid dreaming you can go directly to the inner source of creativity to stimulate ideas."[2] Enthusiasts frequently mention the nineteenth-century writer Robert Louis Stevenson's "Brownies" who composed his stories for him in the form of dream dramas,[3] and likewise the particular inspiring—and usually nonlucid—dreams certain other writers, painters and musicians have recounted.

Lucidity can definitely enhance enjoyment of the process of dream creation for the artistically inclined, since active creation of a dream, like any artistic product, can be more satisfying than passive appreciation. Leaving aside the aesthetic appeal of the dream medium itself, the dream world could potentially both inspire and provide an inner staging ground for dramatizing inventive work of other varieties. Some contemporary lucid dreamers have reportedly had success with this form of creativity.[4] Certainly all three of us have seen some engaging dream movies and artwork.

Yet the question arises of how often and under what conditions dream creativity can be sparked. Creative ideas certainly occur in dreams from time to time, but they do not seem to be inherent to dreaming, unless one equates bizarreness with creativity. In most cases probably only a minor portion of an artist's inspiration arrives in this way, excluding a few professionals dedicated to dream creativity like Stevenson. And just because a few professional writers and musicians who have stories and songs on their minds all the time can compose in their sleep does not mean everyone can do so. The talent belongs to the composer, not to the dream state, and in any case it may take specialized training to remember the results in sufficient detail. Although Janice figured out how to play some familiar songs in dreams, within the limits of her waking ability to play by ear, she had to compose all-new songs around the scraps of original material recalled from dreams since she could never remember an entire piece.

Moreover, there is little mention in the dream community of dream efforts at creativity which turned out to be failures, thoroughly banal, or downright nonsensical, though even Stevenson admitted that oneiric performances could be incomplete or absurd. We have heard some abysmal lyrics in our dreams, as well as suffered through some dreary presentations in the REM theater, so we know dreams are not inherently five-star productions.

Even dream material that does seem entertaining at the time may not translate into anything of value upon awakening. It may turn out to be mediocre from a waking perspective, or of good quality but still useless to the individual dreaming it. Janice sometimes dreamed of interesting scenes featuring the characters of a novel she was working on, but virtually nothing she could actually incorporate into it. Jay's moment in the spotlight ended in deflating sobriety one time when he woke and realized that the "impressive" song he had been making up in a dream had trivial, forgettable lyrics and uninspired music.

Since once in a while they *do* get something good, people sometimes wonder how their dreams can feature amazing literary, artistic or musical compositions in spite of their lack of waking talent for such endeavors, and if this indicates that lucidity can tap into unrealized potentials.[5] More likely, they automatically generate such "creative" elements in dreams from internalized patterns learned in waking as appropriate to various standard genres and styles. Remember too that the mind usually works faster and better than the hand or the mouth can convey. For example, we can all run over songs in our thoughts without necessarily being able to sing them well or to play them on instruments, so it should come as no surprise that dream compositions, which do not depend on physical skill, can exceed our normal capacity. Unfortunately, then, if we see or hear a great performance in a dream we will not necessarily have the ability to reproduce it even if we can remember it.

In any case, lucid dreaming will not confer creative ability or performance talent where none exists, or substitute for waking practice. A dreamer who rarely plays the violin during the day and hopes magically to become a virtuoso through lucid dreaming will not very likely succeed. Beyond the diversion factor, then, people can more productively pursue creative goals with their full waking faculties and powers of imagination.

"Let Me Sleep on It"

Lucidity's promoters have advertised the dream state as something of a bottle genie capable of amazing feats of creative problem-solving, again because of the supposed wisdom of the unconscious. "In our dreams we can draw upon the entire store of our knowledge; we are no longer limited to the tiny portion that we have conscious access to," Stephen LaBerge has asserted.[6] "Tackle your most perplexing daytime dilemmas and wake with those problems solved," further encourages Garfield's book cover. The most commonly cited historical example of a solution inspired in this manner might be the nineteenth-century chemist Friedrich August Kekulé's dream or hypnagogic image of a snake devouring its own tail, which gave him the idea for the structure of the benzene molecule.[7]

While such instances have occurred now and then, those successful probably worked hard over their quandaries for a considerable time, such that the synthesizing insight could have come whether they were awake or asleep. One can also agonize over some intractable issue and have the solution suddenly dawn in *waking* after an interval of ignoring it, since the brain can process some kinds of information outside awareness. But any such nonconscious processing done in sleep will not necessarily inspire concurrent dreams, and nothing inherent in the process of dream creation will ensure the relevancy of a specific dream to any waking concern. In fact people may more often simply wake up with the answer at hand rather than dream of the answer. This could also happen because the traditional wisdom of "sleeping on it" has put distance between the puzzler and the puzzle, making one's reasoning more objective, or even because one's brain chemistry has been refreshed, enabling clearer thinking.

The fact that only a small proportion of real insights have historically come from dreams, despite the famous anecdotes, indicates that the mind is normally nowhere near as potentially insightful when dreaming as when awake. More creativity will almost certainly occur in waking. People will still sometimes have creative ideas and solve problems in dreams because, after all, they *are* still thinking. Being in the dream state may even prove advantageous in some cases because one will probably be thinking somewhat differently than when awake and so come up against troubling issues from a different angle.

However, thought and memory tend to be clouded even in lucid dreams. Since becoming lucid can make people feel intellectually sharper than they had been while nonlucidly dreaming a moment before, they may assume themselves sharper while lucid than they would be if awake, but this is far from invariably the case. As the memory exercises discussed in Chapter 5 show, we do not automatically gain access to forgotten or implicit knowledge when dreaming, lucidly or otherwise, nor for that matter even retain access to everything we normally know when awake. In fact the fabrication typical of dream narratives, with their rampant non sequiturs, false memories and rationalizations, reveals instead how suggestible we all become when dreaming; we could easily enough convince ourselves we were receiving profound insights. Why should the dreaming mind with all its nonsensical muddles be inherently closer to intuitive knowledge than the waking mind?

To get around this troublesome question, dream popularizers

assume that waking-life problems must be symbolically coded in dreams, and so recommend programming oneself before sleep to receive symbolic solutions in the night's imagery.[8] However, as mentioned in Chapter 7, the dreaming mind can concoct a pictorial representation of a concern, but so can the waking mind, via metaphor; and objectifying an idea as an image still involves a kind of thought. It does not mean that symbolism is intrinsic to dream imagery nor woven into it by a wise unconscious that can prescribe a course of action. Relying on dreams rather than on reason for decision-making can amount to dodging responsibility for decisions, like depending on horoscopes or tarot cards to guide one's actions. Of course, in the process of trying to interpret the illustrated associations sometimes presented in dreams, one might reason out a decision on the original problem.

It is not clear how *lucidity* could benefit the would-be problem-solver, except insofar as asking the mind for help during the course of a dream instead of at bedtime might increase the likelihood of getting some kind of response. Some people may think that if they become lucid enough they will "know" what images represent while still dreaming. If so this "knowledge" seems like an obvious extension from waking reflection, or perhaps even a matter of naive self-conviction, considering that dream elements seldom pertain to anything at all.

Asking dream characters for their input on a problem does not necessarily make them channel intuition either. They may give reassuring platitudes or useless suggestions if they contribute at all.[9] We will have more to say about consulting with characters in later sections of this chapter.

Dress Rehearsals

Some people claim to find lucid dreaming useful for practicing skills, an application that takes advantage of the strong kinesthetic component of dreams. In the privacy of their own minds, dreamers can rehearse activities such as sporting events or social interactions, testing the outcome of various maneuvers, gearing themselves mentally to challenges, perhaps even beneficially stimulating the relevant sensory and motor systems in the brain.[10] Lucidity Institute member Brenda Giguère, for instance, reports that she learned to ride a bicycle only after first succeeding in doing so in a lucid dream, and that a friend of hers similarly used to rehearse dance routines consciously in dreams.[11]

Lucid dreaming can provide a more vivid experience than merely visualizing performances in the mind's eye as a developmental aid, but it remains far less readily controlled mentally. It is seldom easy to engage lucidity at will or to call up an appropriate scenario at need. Even then one's efforts might soon be foiled by dream instability or other distractions. When Ruth tried to practice some exercises in a dream version of her fitness gym, for example, a character representing her waking-world instructor interrupted her and rambled on frustratingly until the dream ended.

Further, some speculations regarding the efficacy of dream practice may be misguided. Athletes who dream of winning their competitions may perform significantly better in reality than those who do not, but we wonder if it is having the ability to win that makes the athletes dream about success, not the other way around. Nor has anyone compiled failed efforts at rehearsing skills through lucid dreaming, though we found we could easily do exceptionally poorly at any given activity, especially when trying to use the dream body exactly like a physical one.

Conversely, just as our dream artistic ability could be exaggerated we could sometimes perform skills vastly better when dreaming than we possibly could in waking, even do things that would be completely impossible for anyone. Jay once rode down a sidewalk and even down a stairway on a dream unicycle, ignoring the fact that it lacked one pedal and that he could not, in reality, ride a unicycle at all. Since the dream world is *not* the real world, control of one's imagination has a major impact on the action and imagery and enables results well above one's ordinary skill level. So skills practiced in lucid dreams may ultimately turn out to be worthless, and achieving them only serve to instill a false sense of confidence.

"DOCTOR, DOCTOR": LUCIDITY AS THERAPY

Proponents extol the potential virtues of lucid dreaming as a panacea for all types of physical, emotional and psychological problems. The publisher's back cover blurb for LaBerge's *Lucid Dreaming* asserts that dream control can "harness the healing power of your unconscious mind and enhance your mental and physical health." Some professionals encourage lucid dreaming as a form of therapy for overcoming nightmares, achieving psychological integration, and promoting personal growth and self-discovery. Unfortunately, most of these therapeutic uses of lucidity seem to rest on shaky ground indeed.

The Picture of Health

Some anecdotal and experimental evidence suggests that picturing healing imagery may have a positive effect on recovering from illness. In one preliminary scientific experiment, for example, some subjects showed an increased white blood cell count after receiving hypnotic suggestions to visualize these immune-system agents as sharks protecting them against invading germs.[12] Because of the particular vividness of dream imagery and the fact that certain activities in lucid dreams send corresponding signals to the real body, some think lucid dreaming may make for the ultimate inner healing milieu.[13] Changing a literal or symbolic dream image representing a disorder, whether directly or by suffusing it in healing light, partaking of a dream character's treatments, or the like can supposedly alter corresponding blocking factors in the psyche and effect or at least promote a cure.

Scattered anecdotes exist concerning successful healing which occurred after employing such methods in lucid dreams,[14] and of previously unsuspected medical problems being revealed in dreams.[15] There is, of course, no collection of anecdotes of *unsuccessful* attempts at healing through lucidity, or of flatly erroneous or absurd medical information received in dreams. Yet in our experience lucid treatments have no curative properties. When suffering from a serious health problem, Ruth tried everything from taking dream tinctures to bathing in dream spas to seeking help from dream healers, all to no avail. Nor have our dreams made reliable indicators of health. This is just as well, considering the time Jay tried using nail polish remover on some stubborn blue stains that he saw on his reflected face in a nonlucid dream and ended up turning his face into a slimy mask with one protruding, green eye.

The idea of healing through image manipulation sidesteps the fact that dream images mutate on their own all the time anyway due to instability, without any demonstrable effect on anything. Not only does the technique smack of magical thinking, advocates seem to ignore the implication that by the same logic, assuming the process did work, when healing one thing something else might get damaged by the change in balance, or that a psychosomatic symptom could simply be erased superficially only to remanifest some other way.

Most likely, though, nothing at all will result. As explained in Chapter 4, dream visuals may arise from one's mental models of the world, but changing the visuals will not automatically affect the models themselves, let alone the world. Nor could one easily hold onto a new, healthier picture of oneself once awake in the face of external conditions that have not immediately altered, as Janice found out when she tried to use dream-healing techniques to combat depression.

Even if healing does occur after any dream machinations, it is impossible to isolate *lucidity* as the deciding factor. Successful healing from such practices, whether tried in waking or dreaming, more likely results from suggestion, concentration coupled with strong motivation, or even the chemical modifications of sleep and relaxation rather than from the imagework per se, which would be at best a focusing tool. Other factors, such as chance, time, spontaneous remission, dietary and environmental changes, medication, and selective attention—learning to ignore an ailment—may also have unmeasured effects.

Then too, lucid dream imagery is by no means always as vivid as advertised, if vividness makes a difference in the efficacy of a visualization. And while certain behaviors in dreams do affect the real body in small ways, this phenomenon could well be limited to known, voluntary actions like muscle movements and to physiologically programmed sequences such as sexual response. Any assertions otherwise are premature.

Some may argue that if respected authorities lead people to believe that dream healing techniques will help cure their ills, then such techniques will more likely succeed for them. This amounts, in our opinion, to selling snake oil. If healing requires such credulity, it cannot intrinsically result from the dream efforts, but must be merely a placebo effect. It does, nevertheless, evidence the power of positive thinking in maintaining human well-being.[16] Picturing oneself getting well is healthier than picturing oneself remaining ill, not because of the picture itself changing so much as because one feels better psychologically for changing it and thus may get well faster, make other positive efforts towards regaining health, or at least be a bit more cheerful in adversity.

So, keeping this in mind, an unhealthy emotional state or the mental dimensions of an illness or injury may be alleviated temporarily by using positive role-playing in lucid dreams as something of a palliative. As an example, interacting with the images of deceased friends and relatives in lucid dreams might be helpful in coping with grief, as long as the dreamer keeps in mind that these *are* only images and not departed spirits or parallel selves. Of course, such encounters can prove unsettling as easily as comforting since nothing can guarantee how the characters will behave. But when faced with personal loss or any other unalterable condition one can certainly try to enjoy oneself while dreaming even though this will not eliminate the distressing factors from the real world.

An Armor Against Enemies: Lucidity and Nightmare Control

Lucidity can definitely help alleviate the mental distress associated with certain dreams themselves. Nightmare sufferers can lose their terror by recognizing their frightening nocturnal perils as mere dreams and therefore knowing they can wake themselves, defeat their phantasmic adversaries, turn a fall into a flight, or otherwise make their experiences more enjoyable. People could even potentially desensitize themselves to waking phobias by facing their fears in the relative safety of the dream environment, provided their dreams do not perversely exacerbate the phobia with exaggerated imagery. Although many people discover these possibilities independently, their adoption in therapeutic circles largely resulted from the controversial ethnographic research of Kilton Stewart that we mentioned in Chapter 4. Whatever the source, some dreamers find these techniques empowering and even claim to gain more self-confidence in the waking world as a result.[17]

Yet such techniques do not always prove successful. Some people, of course, find becoming lucid itself frightening. Even for those with better grounding in the concept, skill at dream control does not substitute for continuing to be lucid *about* nightmares and strange protodream phenomena after waking—that is, dismissing them as essentially meaningless and most profitably ignored.[18]

Nor will such skill necessarily banish fear forever. After becoming confident in her lucid abilities, Janice nevertheless had a bout with nightmares for a few months, largely because of irrational fears *of* those abilities. Though unafraid during the course of her dreams, whether they had any disturbing content or not she would often wake up in a fright, worrying about the possible negative portent of the imagery. Setting lucidity against nightmares resulting from a pervasive *waking* perceptual distortion attacks only the symptom, not the disease, whether it be depression, anxiety, or reading too many Stephen King novels.

For this reason many therapists take the opposing stance and caution against nightmare control tactics as escapist or worse, considering it better to work through the fear than to suppress or avoid it.[19] But in doing so they may overextend their criticism. Occasional fearful dreams in otherwise psychologically sound individuals could trace to the sheer bizarreness of dreams and the associative, hyperemotional nature of dream mentation rather than to unhealthy waking attitudes or hidden complexes. Even recurrent nightmares can result simply from preoccupation with some luridly engaging image or situation. In such cases dream control remains a satisfying, viable option.

Tag Your Id?

Although for some reason they do not always conceptualize it as control, some therapists believe that lucidity during nightmares or other stressful dreams has enormous potential for psychological conflict resolution, once more hinging on the supposed magic of symbol manipulation. Typically they eschew violence and favor befriending, transforming, or merging with dream enemies and other characters in hopes of integrating the personality, since they consider dream characters to embody subsystems of the personality.[20] LaBerge, for one, has given personal testimonials regarding the efficacy of this approach.[21]

We critiqued this standpoint at length in Chapter 4. To repeat, these techniques can give the appearance of working, during the dream at least. If one expects a positive outcome or finds playing along with such ideas intriguing, one might well get an encouraging result at times. But the effect will derive primarily from that expectation, since the behavior of dream characters can be molded in all different ways and since firmer efforts can put a stop to any unpleasantness equally well.

Reconciling with a dream enemy comes down to the same thing as imposing a reality on the character for storytelling purposes. Since it really has nothing to do with meeting symbols face to face it can work using waking suggestions too, as when certain obnoxious recurrent characters of Janice's started behaving better after she coached herself for that outcome before sleep.

If one does not expect the notion of reconciliation to work or has a strong conflicting impulse to defend oneself from dream negativity, the unprepared characters may respond to any friendly overtures with hostility anyway, spout gibberish, or simply not know what to say. When Janice resolved to be nice to the dream image of a certain contrary person and put her arm around him, he coldly ignored her, and a stray double of herself attempted to flee in terror when she wanted to round it up and merge with it. Since neither dreamer nor dream characters may have any tolerance for such ideas in a given situation, going up and asking them if they have had a bad day, as it were, can actually be intrusive on the natural flow of one's dreaming style.

We achieved no enduring effects from such behavior even when it did work, nor did we notice any personality *dis*integration after splitting into two characters on occasion. The impact must once again persist into waking only for people amenable to the suggestion. As in the case of dream healing, if the persistence of the effect depends on the dreamer's credulity, it is not inherent to the technique. So while a dream may reflect an already changing attitude or inspire an individual to adopt a new mode of behavior to overcome some personal limitation in waking life—as even watching a stirring movie can do—actions in dreams do not inherently modify mental constructs directly.

A Word from the Wise? Dreaming for Personal Growth

Some contemporary therapists encourage opening dialogues with dream characters, not only asking hostile figures what they want but seeking advice pertaining to personal development, especially from wise-seeming figures.[22] Assuming that characters have something important to teach perhaps traces back to Charles Dickens' classic story "A Christmas Carol," in which the dream ghosts of various Christmases impress on the flint-hearted Scrooge his lessons in charity. In any case, the assumption essentially inflates them. Dream advisors may seem sagacious and have a certain power over the imagination because they literally "know" one's own mind and repeat what one might want or expect them to say, which can include points of view that may be familiar from other belief systems. Yet some people have a real tendency to judge their percipience by waking standards and take them as independent intelligences rather than as mouthpieces for the dreamer's own thoughts.

For the more skeptical inquirer, querying dream characters about personal issues may yield only fanciful nonsense, or they may not be very forthcoming with their answers. Even when they spell out their ideas and contrary opinions of the dreamer explicitly, would-be dream advisors may offer little of any real value, only meaningless critiques and bad advice. Their opinions can also conflict; one character apparently thought Janice crazy for writing the present book, while another in a later dream told her that he thought writing it was an excellent idea.

So while befriending and talking to dream characters make valid response options, a dreamer cannot depend upon getting useful information from them. It would probably be more telling to ask friends, relatives, and coworkers to point out one's personality problems instead. For the most part the only useful insights we received from characters were hints to become lucid.

Ruth introduced us to the idea of trying to accelerate personal growth in dreams by asking the dreaming mind for images that represent things one needs to learn or improve about oneself. This approach presupposes that dreams come from a wise unconscious source that wants to help people better themselves, and it can also be attempted by programming before sleep for a relevant nonlucid dream.[23] Yet these responses too may turn out to be silly, completely useless, or things one already knows. When Ruth decided that she would find emblems of her temporarily blocked creativity in one dream apartment, the door bumped against something as she opened it, a nice literalization of her request. The items she found behind the door, however, seemed only to comprise an intriguing but ultimately useless sequence of mental connections to her topic of inquiry. Again, some waking investigation and effort might be more appropriate.

The Light of Experience: Dreams and Self-Discovery

Lucid dreaming does allow more direct self-exploration, without bothering with characters or puzzling over symbols. It fosters a *general* type of integration of disparate aspects of self: that of the waking self and the dreaming self or selves. Even merely remembering dreams brings something of dream experience into waking, enhancing one's self-knowledge. Becoming lucid in effect brings something of waking experience into dreaming, and is thus integrative in and of itself, although the effects of bridging the gap between the selves in this way are usually only temporary or partial like lucidity itself.

Still, dreamers can when lucid study their own behavior in a variety of unfamiliar contingencies, including when enacting impulses they may reject or have little opportunity to express in the outer world.[24] This could give warning of possible problems or enrich their range of experience. Of course, they could accomplish the same goal by reviewing their nonlucid dreams.

However, many thoughts, emotions and behaviors in dreams simply have no relevance to waking life. Because of this, dreams have limited diagnostic value, and naturally one does not have to start reacting as strangely in waking as one does when dreaming. Also, some dreamers may be unduly limited by cultural ideals concerning which sentiments to inculcate and which to avoid, regardless of the fact that different rules apply in the dream world, and thus end up dwelling on the import of their dreamed actions in a very nonlucid way, as Janice can attest. Investing dreams with too much significance in this way can promote a morbidity and self-absorption contrary to good mental health.

Some of a therapeutic bent go further and maintain acting out impulses in lucid dreams to be somehow cathartically beneficial. Thus they may recommend safely unleashing socially unacceptable feelings such as aggression by taking them out verbally or physically on characters and settings. For instance, Ann Faraday, author of some very popular works on self-awareness and dreaming, recounts a lucid dream in which she gleefully beat up a critic of her popularizing tendencies. She then made up with the character and awoke to a strong sense of mental and physical well-being that she took as indicative of a "release of energy through new integration."[25]

Perhaps, though, since dreaming often magnifies emotions people can mistake satisfaction at a successful dream achievement for something more significant, or take a transient feeling of empowerment for a more enduring change. While venting a little pique in a lucid or nonlucid dream may feel good and temporarily alleviate stress, it can hardly eliminate the factors that caused the stress to begin with, and the dreamer may wake up regretting his or her excesses. The stress of one's own inadequate control over dreams might be an exception. Janice found it helpful to indulge in gratuitous dream violence in the face of other people's contrary opinions about such behavior as part of overcoming her phase of regressive fear of lucid dreaming. She did sometimes regret it afterwards, and of course it did not stop people from having their own opinions, but it did demonstrate her reassertion of authority over her own dreams and thoughts.

SUPERNATURAL DELIGHTS: ARCANE APPLICATIONS OF LUCIDITY

Some individuals come to lucid dreaming with expectations that seem even harder to credit than those of the people who hope to put it to therapeutic use. They choose to indulge their fascination with occult, mystical, and psychic phenomena. In fact many people, even those who know little about the field, seem to have an automatic association between lucid dreaming and the paranormal.[26] This association is as unfounded as it is unfortunate for lucid dreamers with more mundane intentions, who may end up prematurely typecast.

Revelation or Recreation?

Believers in matters arcane may learn lucid dream techniques in order to leave their bodies for travel to the astral plane, blocking themselves, in our view, from *really* realizing that they are only dreaming. They may want to live out past or parallel lives, perhaps taking false memories and role-playing as indicators of these. Maybe they desire to seek enlightenment, or talk to the dead, or meet aliens, angels, spirit guardians and other entities. Their dreams, as we have already mentioned, could comply with relevant imagery fed by their preoccupations, making it relatively easy to simulate the encounters desired.

These dream simulations allow certain people to satisfy their cravings for anomalous experiences, perhaps without the anxiety that doing such fantastic things for real might evoke. From any truly critical perspective they can only be seen as autosuggested perceptions. Even an "archetypal" dream image, after all, is only an image, and if anyone could glimpse a higher dimension in a dream the result would still be prone to subjective distortions since it would be produced by the same suggestion mechanism as all dreams. If we cannot reliably interpret the ringing of an alarm clock in a dream, how can we hope to perceive Truth?

Needless to say, such endeavors did not work well for the three of us. As skeptics lacking sufficient motivation, we could not easily structure our requests in ways to which our dreaming minds could convincingly respond. Our attempts at experiencing mystical states of consciousness and "seeking the Highest" when lucid did not meet with much success either, our minds seemingly taking the commands too literally for one thing; we tended to soar upwards then hit a ceiling limit. Janice did use to have protodreams along lines that might excite would-be mystics early on when she mistakenly conceived of these as trances, experiencing such oddities as being filled with fire and floating through realms of flame and mist. Even then, though, the sensations left no noticeable transcendent effects.

I'll See You in My Dreams

One major preoccupation amongst members of the dream community, called shared or mutual dreaming, concerns meeting up with fellow sleepers while dreaming and hopefully later remembering parallel experiences. Like certain young children do with their waking imaginings, some adults find it tempting to believe that their vivid dream imaginings could somehow be external to themselves. Perhaps a deeper desire even comes into play, a desire not to be the lone living soul in a universe of shadows. In any event, such people may profess to seek the challenge of demonstrating the connectedness of all consciousness and the fun of participating in dream activities together.[27]

Shared dreaming aficionados tend to interpret characters as the literal dream selves of the real people represented, or at least as aspects of the real people. They may arrange to "meet" with specific individuals on designated nights, later comparing accounts for congruent images and themes. Those who find the idea compelling often find it easy to simulate, creating characters with the illusion of independent existence.

Ruth and Janice experimented with shared dreams when they belonged to a correspondence dream group. Each succeeded in installing the other as a recurrent character in her respective local lucid dream setting, and they dreamed of one another in other contexts too. But while they sometimes experienced similar themes on a given night, they never simultaneously dreamed of the same events; in fact, when Ruth produced her most convincing simulation of a dream meeting with Janice, the latter had no corresponding dream and was probably even awake. The impersonating dream characters showed no signs of knowing anything about the real women beyond what the dreamers already knew of each other, when they even got *that* right. Of course, the fantasy remained quite enjoyable even so.

If shared dreaming ever occurs as anything more than fantasy or coincidence, as some anecdotal evidence suggests it might,[28] it would of course not reveal the dream world to be an objective plane of existence where people's astral doubles meet. The congruities would most logically result from commonality of experience, from similar mindsets in operation, or, more remotely, through a form of empathic bonding not currently understood. Even in the latter case, the visible representations of people would still be suggested constructs of the dreamer connecting with those people.

The existence of shared dreaming in any more literal sense would, in any case, negate what many enthusiasts equally value in lucid dreaming. Their freedom from social constraints would disappear if other characters were somehow real and could suffer from their actions.

Hits and Misses: The Psychic Dimension

Some adherents approach lucidity to develop psychic abilities, from telepathy to clairvoyance and precognition.[29] It strikes us that many hunger for such incidences before they even grasp the basic skills and implications of lucid dreaming. While the dream community circulates some amazing claims of such phenomena, of course one hears little about failed or inconclusive attempts at having psychic dreams. Yet while Janice dreamed all the time about certain celebrities, she never dreamed of any correspondences to aspects of their lives or careers that would make convincing evidence for a psychic connection.

She and Ruth did, however, have a number of other dreams that might fall into the "psychic" category, usually containing trivial or easily coincidental predictions such as the contents of the next day's mail. For example, Ruth had one lucid dream in which a woman came up to her with a hug and the cryptic comment, "Rosemary has no meaning to you until tomorrow." The next day she was surprised to receive a notice from a former classmate named "Rose Marie" about an upcoming high school reunion.

Our experiments did not demonstrate the existence of shared or other forms of psychic dreaming to our satisfaction so much as how easy it is to recast one's dreams as evidence of psychic contact or awareness. Because of the biases of human psychology, people will be more likely to remember their few striking "hits" than their many misses, and so tend to consider themselves gifted. Believers will also tend to pick out the dream elements with the closest correspondence to their associates' dreams or to the eventually revealed reality; stretch the imagination to cover dissimilar elements as symbolic parallels; and overlook discrepancies in their own memories to make a cleaner image. So when several members of her dream group reported train imagery on a night scheduled for a shared dreaming experiment, Janice excitedly tied this to the fact that she was up working on a model railroad layout while everyone slept. Later she realized that the image, if not just coincidental, most likely evolved from a shared association: they were all trying to make *connections* with one another.

Why, indeed, should lucid dreaming have anything to do with psychic ability or unusual percipience? Surely any such capacity, if it existed at all, would exist independently and lucid dreams be merely one medium in which it could manifest, since impressions and premonitions apparently surface in nonlucid dreams and in waking as well.[30] Possibly, as we have already indicated, intuitions about people or the likely course of the future will sometimes be more easily noticed in dreams, where less filtering of stray impulses occurs and where thoughts and feelings may become objectified as images.[31] Nevertheless, most people's dreams probably less often reveal upcoming events or hidden information than they do mere worries and suspicions that turn out to be unfounded.

Bewitched, Bothered and Bewildered

Psychic dreaming has another, more occult aspect. Such is the continuing power of the idea of sympathetic magic that some people want to influence others via dreams rather than just receive information, and believe that manipulating objects or characters in the dream world will have repercussions affecting the real world. They may attempt to help or indeed to harm others through working with dream images, as if lucidity were a special ingredient making dream actions supernaturally effective. Others try to set up reality in their favor more generally, on the supposition that dreamed occurrences prefigure waking ones yet to come.

Whether or not anyone has such talents we cannot say, but they cannot be inherent to dream replica manipulation. Janice and Jay have each dismembered the other in effigy in their lucid dreams without doing any genuine damage; and for all Janice's years of horseback riding in her local lucid dreams she has yet to see an equestrian infestation in her real town. In any case, the same criticisms and cautions apply to those who try to be dream healers for others as to those who attempt self-healing through lucid dreams. Unfortunately, these and other New Age applications of lucid dreaming, while often considered by their adherents to foster spiritual growth, seem to us to be far more often diversionary than spiritual in nature.

THE BENEFIT OF THE DOUBT: LUCIDITY AND SPIRITUALITY

Can lucidity offer anything to spiritual development beyond the airy-fairy? This rather depends on definitions. If improving one's quality of awareness and learning to distinguish truth from falsehood are considered spiritual endeavors, and if becoming lucid means to perceive the unreality of dreams and the implications of that unreality, then lucid dreaming counts as a spiritual activity. Lucidity may, then, be of some value as a mental exercise or as a tool to help one understand the nature of perception. These applications too present a certain number of problems, but they have a firmer foundation than other approaches and may ultimately prove more useful, not only to spiritual seekers but to the sciences of the mind.

A Watchful I: Lucidity as a Mental Exercise

Lucidity can confer certain advantages with long-term practice. Judging by Janice's experience, it is possible to develop enough talent that lucidity tends to arise automatically and naturally, without extensive waking preparation or reflecting on dreamsigns. Even before that point, the confidence that the frequent lucid dreamer gains from handling troubling scenarios with competence can percolate into ordinary dreams, leading to a more satisfying overall dream life for as long as interest in lucidity remains high. Eventually we found it increasingly difficult to distinguish tacit from partial lucidity or to define the point when a dream actually became lucid, because the techniques and activities associated with our lucid dreaming styles had become pervasive.

Can people benefit in any way in *waking* from practicing lucid dreaming? Lucidity, after all, means clear thought, and requires alertness and a quick wit to sustain itself, all inarguably useful when awake. Though one wonders how often it occurs given all the less than clear-headed approaches to lucid dreaming out there, if a certain mindfulness or keener awareness rubs off on waking experience because of paying more attention when dreaming, then the exercise will have had a positive result. The same holds if lucid accomplishment extends into waking a sense of confidence in one's ability to handle oneself or of taking responsibility for one's thoughts and actions.

Yet people can achieve mindfulness, self-confidence and

personal responsibility through waking practice without bothering with lucid dreaming at all. Lucid dreaming may even prove somewhat detrimental to waking awareness in certain ways. LaBerge has emphasized that if we all must sleep through a third of our lives, we may as well be aware during that time,[32] but this seems ingenuous, since the awakening of critical attention throughout sleep would probably inhibit the restorative function of sleep needed for full engagement with the waking world. Further, for the leisurely at least, lucid dreams can result from staying in bed too long, when one really may as well be awake.

Dreaming in the Real World

Perhaps we should all be more interested in applying the lessons of lucid dreaming to the subject of waking perception. Some people have used becoming lucid as an analogy for a spiritual awakening, for seeing the unreality and relativity of what had been taken as real and absolute in one's life. The Tibetan Buddhist scheme of development, for instance, uses lucid dreaming to teach the initiate, among other things like practice for lucid dying, about the illusory nature of the world.[33] Such statements do not necessarily mean that reality does not exist, as they are often literally interpreted, but rather that whether we admit it or not our perceptions of reality are incomplete and seen only through our personal psychological filters.[34]

Perception depends on suggestion to build up information from partial cues, so it takes many shortcuts. On the sensory level, we do not always recognize the constructed aspects of personal reality and the great extent to which our conditioned assumptions influence our perceptions of everything around us. But we can come to appreciate this better through the experience of observing and controlling dream imagery, of struggling to penetrate the illusions of dreaming. On the psychological level, we project and rationalize and behave without reflection most of the time in our waking lives, just as in dreams. But we can learn to see these distortions of reality and see how we affect our experience of the world with our thoughts more clearly in dreams, where our thoughts *create* what passes for the world.

Ibn El-Arabi, a thirteenth-century master of the Sufi tradition of spiritual development, recommended the exercise of controlling one's thoughts in dreams. He said this would "produce awareness of the intermediate dimension," which he considered greatly beneficial.[35] Leaving aside obvious occultist readings, this may simply mean that with training in lucidity one can see the way in which one's thoughts and emotions select out and attach meaning to experience. Intermediate between the real world and our reactions to it is an interpretive gap, and interpretations can highly color or even warp what we perceive. Much as we can change events in dreams by controlling our interpretations of them, we can alter the impact and sometimes even the outcome of waking events by modifying our interpretations. We may for instance mature in our understanding of adolescence by realizing that our parents felt concern for our welfare rather than simply enjoyed ordering us around, or learn to give people the benefit of the doubt when they make mistakes instead of jumping to conclusions about their motivations. This awareness gives us greater flexibility in our choices of reaction and lets us break bad perceptual habits.

In other words, just because we perceive something as true does not mean that it *is* true, either in dreams or in waking. We are often fooled by appearances and driven by assumptions in waking in essentially the same manner as we are deceived nightly in our dreams. Becoming sensitive to this fact, whether inside or outside of a spiritual discipline, must be basic to self-observation and self-development, since one can improve as a person by better attuning oneself to the truth, even truth in the mundane form of facts. Learning to become lucid in dreams, then, can be a step towards learning to refine our models of reality rather than simply being confused that they *are* reality.

The Impossible Dream? Becoming Lucid About Lucidity

The uses of lucidity discussed in this section, though subtle, may be among the most reasonable, but even the basic perceptual benefits can be obtained through other methods such as a good liberal arts education. In fact, for those who do not have a natural talent for it, because of the time and effort consumed in trying to learn lucidity, the unreliability of its induction techniques, and its variability from dream to dream, it will not generally be "cost-effective" for *any* of its proposed benefits compared to addressing them in the real world. Moreover, most of the benefits claimed by researchers and promoters are so speculative and based on such questionable theories that they seem destined to remain not only unproven but largely unapplied, at least by critically-minded lucid dreamers. Still, the three of us do hope that more dreamers will become interested in lucidity *for its own sake* or to verify less exotic claims like the ones made in this book.

The idealistic explorers can be excused for treasuring lucid dreaming as the El Dorado of conscious states, with the whole area still relatively uncharted by scientific research. The high hopes surrounding lucidity parallel early, eventually disproven expectations of electricity, say, or hypnosis. Many experimental psychologists once thought the hypnotic state conferred unusual abilities in sensory discrimination, physical strength, and memory until later research demonstrated only that the power of suggestion influenced the performance of hypnotized subjects.[36] Since suggestion similarly affects what people think is happening in or because of their lucid dreams, the time seems right to temper that enthusiasm with a reality check.

When approached experimentally and without expectations of fantastic results, lucid dreaming largely debunks its own legend. A major theme of this book has been the importance of learning to be lucid about dreaming, to understand dreams as both unreal and without any necessary relevance *to* the real world. People also need to be lucid regarding lucidity. Becoming lucid about dreams, and subsequently understanding more about the way the mind works, seem to us to be the most important and perhaps the only real uses of lucidity. Becoming lucid *in* a dream appears, by itself, to confer no automatic benefit.

THE BURDEN OF TRUTH

In conclusion, just as one must understand how dreams are created before deciding what, if anything, they may mean, so one must know what dreams really are before considering any approach to using them. Yet in a desire to be open-minded and inclusive of all opinions and possibilities regarding lucid dreaming, people have tended, paradoxically, to discard the one thing that would help them sort through the confusion: critical thinking. Because those different points of view can be mutually exclusive, they cannot possibly all be right.

In coming up with an explanation for the full range of our observations, it has become clear to us that certain ideas about lucid dreaming, and indeed dreaming in general, *cannot* be correct or complete. This caveat carries back to the original assumptions on which those ideas rest. If most of the extraordinary speculated benefits of lucid dreaming have been based on either the unconscious model of the mind or on outdated occultist models, as certainly seems to be the case, then on that basis alone they should be considered suspect, since those formulations do not fit in the neurophysiological picture of the brain developing today. In turn, if virtually *none* of those benefits is consistently attainable in practice, as our own efforts have displayed, it would appear to be time to adopt a more reasonable model of dream creation.

Chapter 10

UNANSWERED QUESTIONS

A great deal of the recent burgeoning of interest in lucid dreaming has been devoted to dubious propositions and applications. As serious dream explorers, we find the point of view presented in this book sufficient armor against the more obvious pitfalls of other perspectives. But while the suggestion theory can account for much about the nature of dreaming, lucid or otherwise, questions do remain which we cannot adequately answer at this time given the limitations of our own experience. This chapter will look at several aspects of the phenomenon that we hope will receive further investigation. These include the efficacy of lucid dream induction techniques, the prospect of harming oneself physically or psychologically through lucid dreaming, and the origins of protodream experiences, as well as assorted possibilities for future laboratory research.

THE YAWNING GULF: OVERCOMING NONLUCIDITY

The most fundamental problem facing the lucid dreamer is that of induction, of how to surmount the mental deficiencies that are characteristic of nonlucid dreaming. Popular works on the subject often confidently claim to be able to teach anyone picking up the book how to start having lucid dreams.[1] But can just anyone learn lucidity? According to our survey of sixty lucid dreamers, the younger the individual at the time of his or her first lucid incident, the greater the ease of learning lucidity and the higher the current frequency of lucid dreams experienced. This suggests that proficient lucid dreaming takes a certain amount of natural talent.

Apparently most people who become interested in lucid dreaming as adults do not find it easy to pick up. If such people have a few lucid dreams a month, they do well. Many have far less, perhaps a handful a year; the median number of lucid dreams per year for our survey respondents was only 12. Even beyond the difficulty of acquiring the skill itself, because lucid dreaming builds on a foundation of waking memory and awareness it requires a level of dedication, attention and time many people simply do not have to spare. When real-life preoccupations arise during busy weeks or months, or when serious induction attempts stop, lucid dreaming frequency usually drops off. In essence, then, lucid dreaming is a skill likely to be of interest only to a limited segment of the population, and it will only be adequately learned by a much smaller group.

Only ten percent of our survey respondents felt they could induce a lucid dream whenever they wanted, which shows that induction techniques often fail when confronted by the inertia of nonlucidity. Recognizing a dream in progress is no easy matter, since although surreal indicators of one's true state appear throughout most dreams, the mind's sensitivity to these is quite undependable. Even at our peak the three of us surprised ourselves with the frequency of undetected false awakenings, missed clues and forgotten intentions. Our receptivity to autosuggestive programming for lucidity before sleep was also irregular, and even reentering a dream right after awakening from it, although relatively simple, could lead as easily to a nonlucid continuation as a lucid one. Entering a dream through the protodream state with a continuing thread of awareness from the moment of going to bed appears to be difficult to master without considerable mental discipline. Jay, who falls asleep almost upon hitting the pillow, found it nearly impossible, and even Janice and Ruth found the ability waned with disuse.

At present, then, no lucidity induction technique can be guaranteed successful even when taking a daytime nap or using a mechanical induction device for assistance, and although some individuals may find one or another method especially effective we doubt if anything could be counted upon to make lucidity more than partial and temporary once attained. As mentioned in Chapter 8, being "awake" in one's dreams may amount to something of a juggling act with one's brain chemistry, requiring the use of amines, the neurotransmitters associated with memory storage and focused attention, in a higher proportion than usually occurs during dreaming. The aminergic system must, even so, remain at a relatively low level of activity in order to sustain sleep. People may not ever reliably overcome the problems of inducing and maintaining lucidity, then, as long as there is no reliable way to alter and stabilize brain chemistry in the necessary balance. Perhaps someday scientists will be able to isolate and supplement artificially the relevant neurochemicals needed to overcome these limitations, as a fringe benefit of more practical uses for neuropharmacological research in such areas as treating sleep disorders.[2]

SIDE EFFECTS: THE CONSEQUENCES OF DREAMING LUCIDLY

Having critiqued numerous ideas about how lucid dreaming may be useful in the last chapter, it seems appropriate here among the unanswered questions to consider ways in which it might possibly be harmful. Some psychophysiological consequences that seem plausible include adverse effects on sleep needs and a certain amount of confusion between states of consciousness. This section will evaluate these possibilities plus some additional odd claims put forth by a few New Age lucid dreamers.

Getting Some Shuteye? Lucidity and Sleep Needs

One question that immediately comes to mind, after having mentioned sleep disorders and neurochemistry, is whether trying to be extra alert while dreaming could lead to a reduction of the alertness level possible in waking. If lucidity reactivates the aminergic neurons, which normally rest and recharge during dreaming to recuperate from the day's waking activities, it may use up replenishing stores of aminergic compounds. This would seem likely to make lucid dreamers need more sleep to make up the chemical debt thus incurred.

However, after a few hours of sleep the brain should have some leeway for the chemical fluctuation that would allow periods of greater critical awareness in dreams. In most cases people probably do not spend enough time lucid to wear themselves out any more than they would do by spending a few extra minutes awake at night or getting up a few minutes early. Besides, as Stephen LaBerge points out, it seems more wearisome to fret over a nonlucid dilemma—expending *ineffective* mental effort—than to abandon it for some more pleasurable, lucid activity.[3] We have even known some people to claim that paying extra attention in their lucid dreams makes them more inclined to pay attention to the waking world as well. Nevertheless, Janice did often feel impelled to take a nap to recuperate from hours-long stretches of lucid dreaming, so lucidity *in excess* could have certain repercussions on sleep needs.

Janice and Ruth both tended towards light sleep with frequent wakings and bouts of insomnia, a condition that can promote impaired mental functioning the following day but which also seems to help promote lucid dreams because of the high degree of alertness involved. Ruth's insomnia often led to lucid protodreams, while Janice sometimes resignedly prepped herself for a lucid dream as the only way to drop off into some semblance of sleep after hours of lying awake. In Janice's case, waking up very frequently, whether due to a noisy environment, illness, preoccupation, or writing down dreams, could lead to almost every dream being lucid, and consequently to quite a bit of fatigue. For a while she used to coax her mind to *suppress* what had become a virtually automatic semilucidity, so she could sleep better. This is admittedly a rare problem, though even Ruth found that her brain seemed to take breaks from lucid dreaming after a few nights of intense involvement, and when overtired she made no effort to encourage lucidity, preferring to sleep soundly.

Other than in this matter of alertness level, it is unclear whether the increased activation and control characteristic of lucidity would have positive or negative impacts on any of the various functions REM sleep might have—or any effect at all. But if the brain does something on the physiological level to benefit itself during REM, and if dream control does, as we have suggested, involve directing the flow of information through neural processing systems to achieve desired effects, it would be reasonable to wonder if dream control could interfere with the brain's agenda. Presumably, though, even nonlucid dreams driven chiefly by association would involve at least some degree of command-and-response interaction with the processing systems, since dreamers always interpret events and decide on courses of action that will influence the imagery turning up from moment to moment. Therefore those systems must be able to respond to world modeling in addition to anything else they may be doing, and dream control comes down to an exercise in flexible modeling.

Can such practices as sleep-onset initiation or prolonging and reentering dreams via lucidity significantly disrupt the balance of the sleep cycles by producing too much REM? If so the brain would almost certainly compensate subsequently with more of the shortchanged phases, to judge by experiments in selective sleep deprivation showing such a rebound effect.[4] The phenomenon of sleep-onset lucid dreaming does raise the question of how people with this ability manage to throw the various systems involved in falling asleep out of sync in order to remain relatively aware internally while becoming insensible to the world, and what repercussions this might have. Janice eventually abandoned the practice when she began noticing uncomfortable physiological changes such as an exaggerated startle reaction, as well as disagreeable alterations of consciousness. It seemed preferable to sleep through the transitional phase, especially since she had plenty of lucid dreams regardless.

Breaking Barriers

We have described lucid dreaming as a paradoxical state: being awake when asleep, breaking down the traditional wall between the waking and the sleeping minds. Yet such integration could, in a certain light, be seen more as *disintegration* of a natural, useful barrier. Hence some may wonder if lucid dreaming may eventually lead to a problem with inadequate differentiation between dreaming and waking.

One lucid dreamer reportedly experimented with maintaining awareness of and continuing to move his physical body while sleeping to the point of becoming confused as to whether he was asleep, awake, or lucidly dreaming.[5] However, we have experienced simultaneous awareness of two body images while falsely taking one of these to be a movable physical body. The individual in question may have had an unclear understanding of protodreaming, then, or may have been experiencing NREM lucid dreams that allow physical movement rather than actually overcoming REM motor inhibition and blurring all the boundaries between physiological states.

We know of only one case in which an active lucid dreamer started to have prolonged, vivid intrusions of dreamlike mentation and imagery in waking. She ultimately encouraged rather than feared such waking dreams, considering them episodes of heightened awareness, the natural outgrowth of developing her awareness in lucid dreams. Whether or not this impression was correct, the alteration of perception and sense of unreality she has described resemble those associated with the dreamy auras of temporal lobe epileptic seizures,[6] so similar experiences can result from causes other than practice of lucidity.

Plugged In: Energy Aberrations

This brings up an important observation. While lucid dreamers may be less likely to have unreasoning fear of unusual perceptions and sensations than the average person, they sometimes go to the opposite extreme of valuing what may be unhealthy manifestations as somehow "spiritual." Patricia Garfield, for example, has described how she cultivated a vibratory buzz first noticed in her lucid dreams through both acupuncture and Taoist meditation, magnifying it into a powerful charge of energy surging through her body. Eventually this became so uncontrollable she had to consult a meditation master to learn how to regulate it.[7]

Scott Sparrow, a therapist and dream researcher, has also published a warning regarding the supposed deleterious effects of dreaming lucidly without a spiritual guide.[8] Apparently, Tibetan sources advise against attempting dream yoga unaided because of the risk of awakening this energy, known by the term "kundalini" in the New Age literature, which can purportedly lead to mental illness as easily as to higher consciousness.

We must point out, again, that such symptoms can have other than spiritual causes, such as metabolic or hormonal problems or megadoses of caffeine. The overwhelming electrical current suggests overstimulation of the nervous system, perhaps a neurochemical fluctuation due to intense excitement or anxiety, which stimulates the production of adrenaline, an aminergic compound.[9] If there is a causal connection between lucid dreaming and "kundalini" at all, a scientific explanation might lie in sleep physiology, in a forced neurotransmitter imbalance that results in unusual nervous activity or sensitivity—such as too many amines, the modulators of consciousness.

Since such electrical sensations often occur during protodreams, the problem may have more to do with particular ways of incubating lucidity, with being lucid in certain sleep phases, or simply with trying to spend too much time highly aware, than with lucidity itself. Few dreamers are talented or zealous enough to be at risk of producing serious aberrations by this means in any case. Vibrations that we ourselves experienced in conjunction with OBEs and such usually disappeared within moments of awakening, and any similar but more persistent sensations developing in waking would also most likely disappear with time as the body's regulatory systems balance themselves out.

Dark Nights of the Soul: Lucidity and Depression

Sparrow's cautionary note also mentions a "course correction" he experienced at the height of his lucid dreaming endeavors. He recommends that people be advised of the painful, but psychologically necessary, developmental ordeal awaiting them should lucidity make them aware of their repressed complexes, or should any abuse of "power" in their lucid dreams ultimately incite such complexes to strike back via negative incidents.[10] However, people commonly enough suffer depression and nightmares without being involved in lucid dreaming or dream control, so these activities cannot be isolated as the causes of such problems. In fact those preoccupied with self-development, who sometimes try to pursue that goal through lucid dreaming, can easily tie themselves in emotional knots around their failings, especially since lucid dreaming does not guarantee progress.

Interestingly, though, research with depressive patients has shown them to be oversensitive to acetylcholine, the neurotransmitter that activates REM sleep. They have earlier, longer, and more intense REM periods than normal subjects.[11] Because aminergic activity diminishes in both states, dream sleep and depression share a similar biochemistry as well, although, surprisingly, dreams seldom reflect the emotional affects of depression.[12] Depressives also experience the same light, disturbed sleep pattern that helps some people have lucid dreams, and altering their rhythm of sleep and waking can produce a marked, though temporary, alleviation of their symptoms.[13]

All this suggests that if there is some *biological* correlation between frequent lucid dreaming and depression it would again probably be a matter of upsetting the individual's neurochemistry. Spending an excessive amount of time dreaming now and again will not likely predispose a person to depression, since sleep-phase imbalances are largely self-correcting. But making a habit of sleeping at irregular intervals or trying other disruptive techniques in order to have lucid dreams might throw off one's circadian rhythms or otherwise make matters worse for anyone who *has* for some reason become depressed. Any increase in REM would create yet more acetylcholine, which depressives already have a hard time counteracting because their aminergic systems have become ineffective.

According to one chemical model, an extended period of anxiety—such as anxiety about one's lucid dream experiences?—can overproduce amines to the point of exhausting the ability of one's neurons to receive any more of these chemicals, resulting in a state of depression.[14] This would suggest a model for how a "kundalini" crisis could progress from feeling extremes of energy to adverse mental health effects. It is harder to account for why adherents also claim that the energy can beneficially transform awareness. Perhaps the initial flood of amines, if not too destructive, can unleash significant changes in the metabolic activity of the brain cells which route cognitive processes,[15] but even so it seems unlikely that such experimentation could of itself provide more than an initial rush of elation and clarity. Thus, while some may approach lucid dreaming in the hopes of encouraging such "mystical experiences," these would seem to have little to recommend them.[16]

DIVERS ALARUMS

Some factions within the dream community speculate about a variety of other unpleasant consequences that may follow upon pursuing lucidity. Jayne Gackenbach, most notably, emphasizes a few instances where people suffered negative psychological effects in connection with it, which can hardly be representative of lucid dreamers as a whole. She has interpreted such incidents as "quasi-psychotic splits with reality,"[17] bolstering her fears with the admonitions of certain psychotherapists who reject lucid dreaming as escapist, delusory and narcissistic. In the absence of a sufficient number of long-term, well-documented case studies, we see little justification for classifying lucid dreaming as inherently harmful psychologically, but a few reasonable points of inquiry might be raised.

A Snare and a Delusion?

If someone has elaborate, conscious dream adventures, will his or her engagement with the waking world suffer? The potential for obsession certainly exists. One lucid dreamer admitted in *Lucidity Letter* to becoming so addicted to the state as to sleep in public, miss work, and eventually stay in bed for several days straight.[18] Needless to say, this person may have had other, more telling reasons for his behavior than the insidiousness of lucid dreaming, such as a lack of compelling social responsibilities.

Very few people even have the ability to incubate quite so much lucid dreaming as to chance that degree of self-absorption, and most people know how to regulate their pleasures well enough. Janice and Ruth have both, though, felt a degree of "withdrawal" during times when their lucid dream frequency or control ability dropped off, followed by a lifting of their spirits upon its return. So one can certainly come to identify a bit heavily with being a lucid dreamer.

Some people have unhealthy psychological repercussions from lucid dreaming simply because they do not understand it. Since virtually none of the mental processes characteristic of lucid dreaming fall outside the range possible in ordinary dreaming, the problem would not seem to lie in lucidity per se but in one's reaction to it. Another contributor to *Lucidity Letter*, for example, panicked in one incident because it became so vivid it felt physically real,[19] an anxiety attack that a better understanding of lucid dreams could probably have prevented.

Many lucid dreamers appear to us to have let themselves be deluded in various ways about the meaning of their experiences, fearing or revering them due to a lack of critical thinking about the subject when awake. Some can even wax evangelical, wanting to spread the word about lucidity or considering themselves experts after having a few impressive experiences. In this way lucid dreaming can unfortunately lead to greater self-deception rather than greater self-awareness, to enhancing one's suggestibility rather than improving one's understanding of how suggestion works.

Overdoing It

Could a person potentially overdo dream control? Some lucid dreamers at a certain stage find their newly gained powers of control so compelling that exercising those abilities dominates their lucid experiences, and they command dream elements to their own satisfaction by force of will and adopted persona. They may at whim take on grandiose pretensions, such as being a wizard or minor deity, to overawe troublesome characters and the dream environment. LaBerge reports the case of one individual who took his "power" so seriously he inflated himself to the status of god of the dream world, such that one of his characters eventually reminded him that he was as unreal as them.[20]

This not only exemplifies how a conflicting idea can become

embodied in the actions and conversations of dream characters, it shows another facet of the common difficulty with inappropriate conceptualization of dream experience. Letting oneself identify beyond a point with the dream ego and conceiving its abilities in terms of "magical powers" rather than of control of one's thoughts can lead to some overserious role-playing. A dreamer who conceptualizes his or her exploits too heavily in fantastical terms can promote partially lucid confusion, half thinking he or she really *is* a demigod or magician. Such a situation is relatively harmless, though, as long as the individual remains rational in waking and does not consider his or her influence to extend to the real world.

To Be of Two Minds

What of the dream-specific personality, the temporary ego adapted to a given dream and its special circumstances? Accomplished lucid dreamers who sustain virtual dream lives apart from their waking ones might end up developing strong, recurrent DSPs with attitudes and inclinations counter to their waking personalities. This could potentially create a certain amount of psychological tension, and did lead to occasional conflicts of interest in Janice's lucid soap opera dreams between her waking plans and her dream impulses.

But again, few people attain the level of skill needed to become lucid often or consistently enough to form a stable fictional version of themselves. Even then, in most cases doing so should pose no more threat than acting a part normally does to actors. It depends on how emotionally involved one becomes with the dream world. For anyone unstable enough for intensive lucid dream make-believe to be harmful in this way, probably any similar preoccupation, such as participating in medieval dungeon adventure games, would be harmful. As always, having a little lucidity about dreams makes an important asset.

CHARTING THE BORDERLAND: OBSERVING SLEEP TRANSITIONS

However mysterious it may seem at times, the transitional zone between sleep and waking can be useful for inducing lucid dreams because of the relatively high level of mental arousal that potentially pervades it. Although probably not all sleep-onset lucid incidents take place in REM sleep, they still reveal much about the early stages of dream generation that would otherwise go unobserved. This section will delve into the internal roots of various sleep-border phenomena associated with OBEs and sleep paralysis experiences, as well as consider the possible origins of hypnagogic dream content, a matter of some controversy. A close look at sleep-onset hallucinations and their subsequent vignettes will show how these experiences too tend to support the suggestion theory of dreaming.

Neither Here Nor There: The ABCs of OBEs

As we have mentioned, light sleep can generate "out-of-body" experiences in some sensitive individuals. These most plausibly occur, according to one contemporary theory, because internal models of the body and environment have replaced those based on real, current perceptual input.[21] Virtually deprived of contact with the outside world when the sensory systems shut down for sleep, the brain may if otherwise relatively aware automatically resurrect an impression of oneself lying in bed—a false awakening of a sort. The result will not necessarily be well resolved visually nor accurate as to actual body position, and quite often the individual will feel paralyzed because of what can be detected of the immobile physical body.

Lack of information, marginal lucidity, and putting up a struggle to awaken can cause people to elaborate a simple case of sleep paralysis into a dreadful ordeal that they may interpret as a death struggle or even a spectral assault. But if sleep deepens and calmness prevails, as the dreamer attempts to move around consciousness may gradually switch attachment from the impression of a body lying in stasis to a new dream body that is not so restricted. With nothing to put it in perspective, the imagined environment, whether it be the bedroom or some other scene, becomes more and more convincing; the illusion becomes "real," the model substitutes for reality. OBEs occurring during waking, after accidents, or under anesthesia probably have a similar origin, with regular models breaking down due to such factors as acute stress, exhaustion, and monotony.[22]

Barring a negative reaction from the experient, the transitional state can drag along as a rather boring stretch of darkness and the occasional snore, save for some specific odd sensations that may occur.[23] Without resorting to the arcane, we can identify the probable roots of these eerie effects in sleep physiology. For example, the feelings of floating or falling that we have described as sometimes leading into OBEs may come from losing tactile contact with the outside world, or from the relaxed state of the muscles in sleep. The condition of the muscles also obviously connects to the usual difficulty moving and speaking during a sleep paralysis experience; the cognitive and sometimes even the perceptual systems of the brain are somehow activated without being in proper coordination with muscle tone.[24] Additionally, breathing slows at the beginning of sleep and becomes shallow and irregular during REM,[25] which might cause the feelings of trouble breathing or a heaviness on the chest often reported with sleep paralysis.

The roaring sounds, buzzing noises, gusts of "wind," and tingling currents or vibrations that some people experience might arise from such sources as changes in blood pressure, alterations in the electrical activity of the brain, lowered body temperature, and heightened awareness of circulation or of activity in the nerves.[26] Such normally small stimuli might magnify in a person's awareness as other perceptions become less noticeable. Any excitement or panic would tend to increase adrenaline levels and heart rate, possibly increasing the strength of these sensations. Both Janice and Ruth noticed a lessening in the frequency and intensity of all such discomforts over time as they became used to protodreaming, lost their fears and learned to focus on other things.

Listening In: The Question of Hypnagogia

Other kinds of sleep-border hallucinations occur besides OBEs, of course, and these too reflect the processes involved in producing dreams. Researchers continue to speculate about what causes the hallucinatory mental processes of sleep onset.[27] Does ordinary thought drift into a muddy, fluid state due to the ebbing of awareness and the loss of sensory anchors to the real world? Or do hypnagogic effects surface from a continuously present, subliminal mental flow of which people only become aware when outside stimuli and their own thoughts grow sufficiently quiet? The second conception lends itself too easily to the overworked model of the unconscious mind repressed by the conscious mind, so the first conception seems more likely in terms of our own theoretical structure, but each may explain part of the picture.

In our experience, as concentration lapses during a prolonged sleep-onset period, thought structure often shifts back and forth along a continuum, progressing towards the increasingly associative. The fact that Janice occasionally, with lucidity, remained aware *of* a garbled stream of consciousness through an extended narrative while falling asleep does not necessarily support the idea of two parallel thought streams, as it might appear. It may only indicate that she managed to detach a degree of awareness from her own thoughts and fancies. Such listening in on oneself is difficult to do because people usually identify heavily with their verbal thinking. Far more often, when nodding off Janice simply caught herself now and again being tugged away in the undertow of little thought-dreams—on the order of the Joycean "Ride, Liffey! It has but taken a crow to overkill his name"—and waded back out.

Since it is difficult to remain lucid during such dreamy narratives, both Janice's and Ruth's protodream transitions usually involved sensory hallucinations of one sort or another—when not OBE sensations, then chaotic audio and/or visual perceptions. With the eyes closed and the mind relaxed, luminous blurs and lines in the visual field can reform into tiny, vivid patterns or scenes. Muted visual impressions may fleetingly appear and vanish like glimpses of life in the depths of a murky pond. Images at this stage tend towards the unusual and bizarre, like a man surfacing in a swim mask or people riding a dinosaur.

Audio hypnagogia ranges from jangles of noise to complete phrases that can sound like utter nonsense or almost like real conversation, as in Janice's "What do you want for $28.00 apiece?" The fact that the phrases can occur in a variety of voices other than one's own suggests that the brain perceives their source as separate from ordinary awareness.

Sometimes such material clearly springs from the sleeper's own thoughts, muzzy though those might be. As an example, on one occasion when Janice lay thinking about a sketch of a skunk that Jay had recently drawn, she saw a vision of a skunk walking out of her former bedroom. Such microdreams show how in a condition of reduced awareness one's thoughts start to become "realities."

Even when hypnagogic hallucinations seem not to originate in thought, the possibility of dissociated thoughts comes to mind, since certainly people *can* think in mental pictures or in vocal patterns besides their own. Yet often this perceptual variety of hypnagogia seems so incongruous and intrusive that it would be hard to maintain that it must come from thought destructuring into hallucinatory form. Furthermore, we could easily continue thinking during the visual variety at least, and sometimes found it possible to control the hallucinations mentally. Paranormal explanations aside, exactly where, then, do they originate?

Since the external perceptual system all but shuts down at sleep onset, disjunctive perceptual hypnagogia might stem partly from transformed, incorrectly perceived sensory stimuli, and partly from the brain attempting to read internal data instead of external. Communications on the neuronal level might be rendered unpredictable due to the decrease in amines and, particularly for those subject to sleep-onset REM, to bursts of altered brain waves. Activity in the sensory and verbal interpretive systems of the cortex, its patterning unconstrained either by coherent thought or the real environment, could conceivably replace normal input and scan like loosely strung bits of nonsense.[28] Plus, it may be that any information-processing operation, including thought, can generate some extraneous but often readable data in the richly interconnected neural matrices of the brain. As in the "parallel thought-stream" hypothesis mentioned above, such stray signals would indeed be continuously present and only noticeable in the absence of stronger competing signals from within or without, but devoid of especial relevance. They are normally drowned out because they *should* be disregarded, though they can sometimes turn into little dream fragments.

Hallucinations built around the background noise of the brain would predominate in sleep-onset mental content because that noise is the only variable thing going on at the time, with both the environment and one's thoughts gone dull. Attention naturally lights on changes while disregarding steady input. People would tend to tune out the clamor of random neurological suggestion factors better during the later dreams of the night, as they habituate to it and become more heavily involved in the dream creation process. In fact Janice has deliberately silenced intrusive verbal protodreams not only by concentration but by imaginally getting up to craft a "local lucid," forcing a more complete dream setting to develop and occupy her attention.

Nonlucid laboratory subjects also display a return to fairly normal mentation and mundane dream content in Stage 2 sleep after a wildly hallucinatory period in Stage 1. Some researchers have considered this a defense against the dissolution of higher cognitive functioning and, perhaps, against the surfacing of unacceptable impulses from the "unconscious."[29] However, while the mind may well have a certain aversion to mental chaos in general, the eventual restitution of order could be more reflexive than defensive, the automatic provenance of the world-modeling function. If one were, atypically, aware enough of hypnagogic activity to feel threatened by it, the normal reaction would be to wake up startled, not to build a dream around it.

Early hypnagogic content is usually benignly ridiculous, however much it may annoy the lucid protodreamer waiting for a real dream to start. Admittedly, though, we have found that due to suggestion the character of hypnagogia can change in conjunction with one's emotional state and one's ideas about the nature of such hallucinations. And since blurry bedtime musings often relate to waking preoccupations—such as, in some cases, notions about having unacceptable impulses—unwelcome thoughts may cause alarm when they spring an ambush at this unguarded juncture. Nevertheless, once a person gets past the initial jumble of unstructured thought and hallucination caused by the loss of contact with reality, the world-modeling function would not likely care whether the stuff at hand were pleasant or unpleasant, so long as it could order it enough to enable relatively coherent thinking again.

Ins and Outs: Hypnagogic Bridges

Both one's own thoughts and the chatter of the dozing brain, then, can apparently externalize into pictures or voices around which characters may generate and dreamlets form. Occasionally when very tired Janice would miss most of the preliminaries and jump right into a nonlucid dreamlet within moments of going to sleep, vague and disjointed perhaps but complex enough to include vision, sound and motion from the outset. Sometimes her awareness level would be so low that she did not feel much connection to these experiences, in which case they may have originated from something already running in her brain, relatively divorced from her thoughts. Other such dreamlets most definitely related to her thoughts, as in the time she lay thinking about some shopping she had done during the day and then seemed to be walking through the store in question. Quite often the sudden changeover to dream perception startled her enough to bring the experience to a quick end, because she would realize she was dozing off and pull herself more alert.

When lucid during the protodream stage, of course, Janice could stay asleep and deliberately assemble sleep-onset dreams. Retaining awareness throughout the process of falling asleep presumably occurs when the brain's external sensory and motor systems wind down while the cortical centers involved in higher cognition asynchronously stay on. Although lucidity may distort the typical nonlucid process to an extent, remaining unperturbed and watchful during this phase has allowed us to observe the development of full-fledged dreams from scratch. While sinking into light sleep, pay just the right attention for long enough and a dreamlet will often become a dream. Any missing perceptual elements will eventually fill in, such that imaginary sounds or movements generate relevant visual imagery, or a dream body and appropriate soundtrack attach to a vision. This again demonstrates the constructing power of suggestion at work, of building more complete realities from minimal information.

Something comparable to this process presumably happens throughout the sleep cycle, as sleepers switch from the typically thoughtlike mentation of NREM sleep into REM dreaming. Even seemingly automatic dreams that do not initially relate to any obvious thoughts would have to be affected by the attention paid to them if allowed to run on long enough, especially if they progress to the point where the dreamer starts to take a selective interest in specific components or to participate in the ongoing action. At this point, without sufficient lucidity to provide a proper perspective, the displaced mind will add the final component to the illusion, making its best guess as to what in the world the experient is doing and why based on the apparent context. So if Jay were to find himself in school and not know which class to attend, he might decide he left his schedule in his locker and go looking for it. If he finds the locker empty, he might assume someone stole all his books, then raise a fuss trying to get them back. The dream is on; one's very fantasies have externalized.

One can likewise learn to watch the dreaming process deconstruct into hallucinated visions, sounds, and sensations, or perhaps loosely woven narratives and songs, upon slowly awakening back through the protodream level again. Sensory suggestion factors seem particularly likely to take hold during this phase. For instance, the marauding insect crawling on the bed, wall or ceiling that Janice and many others have occasionally glimpsed in panic for a few moments after waking probably originates in the spidery pattern of blood vessels in the eye, which, as a constant stimulus, normally gets tuned out of the visual field.[30]

The fragmentation process may also unmask sensory suggestion factors that had been influencing the fully realized dream that just ended, since persistent external stimuli often become incorporated into a dream before waking one up. And although we do not concur with the views of the nineteenth century researchers who considered all dream imagery to arise from excitation of the retina, on several occasions Janice observed what might have been retinal phenomena linking directly to dream images. For instance, during one false awakening she went downstairs and saw a man in a red shirt seated on a chair in her living room. After waking up a few moments later, she could hypnopompically see a red blur against her eyelids, equivalent to the red-shirted man, get up and "walk" away.

It is also possible to rouse with a single dream sense of totally mental origin continuing after the others have shut off. One may briefly see a nonexistent figure in the room, or continue to hear a snatch of imagined conversation or music. Familiar things could take on interesting new guises when Janice woke incompletely during the night; unknown cats in a variety of conformations might appear on her bed for a minute before slowly resolving into the shape and color of her own pet. A person's thoughts can remain muddled at first, too, as evidenced by still believing some false supposition of the preceding dream, feeling an unreasoning impulse, or speaking in a dazed, rambling stream of consciousness. Even after ostensibly waking, then, the brain may take a while to shift states completely, revealing dreaming and waking as a lively continuum.

Back to Basics: Hallucinations Within Dreams

Hypnagogic-type hallucinations are not limited to the edges of sleep. We have known fragmentary visual and audio images, free-form thought and speech, and even complete OBEs to occur during false awakenings or frame dreams in which we only *believed* ourselves to be falling asleep, as well as to persist way beyond their usual provenance into more obvious dreams. In addition, Janice could deliberately "back out" of a lucid dream temporarily, turning off the imagery by an act of will and switching herself closer to the waking state. In this way she could often determine the external source of her imagery. Closing her eyes while dreaming also sometimes sent her back to the protodream level with accompanying visions, voices, sensations, or narrative thinking. Janice occasionally used such intradream hallucinations as the basis for generating new scenes or characters, as when she would envision a hypnagogic horse against her closed dream eyelids as a preliminary to fashioning a full-sized animal in the actual setting.

Either we were simulating hypnagogic and OBE imagery due to long experience—that is, *dreaming* about it—or such hallucinations depend more on a disruption of sensory input than on being in a particular phase of sleep. This would be consistent with the waking hallucinations sometimes caused by sensory deprivation, during which the brain seems to fabricate stimuli to make up for the absence of real perceptions.[31] Then too, the activation-synthesis hypothesis describes dreaming itself as an hallucinatory process enabled, in large measure, by the brain's acute insensitivity to real sensory input during sleep.[32] The resulting loss of orientation to the external world seems even more vital to creating a dream experience than does memory loss, since it is possible to enter a dream consciously from the waking state with one's memories more or less intact. Apparently, even *imaginally* blocking out the resulting *imaginal* perceptions can set the whole process going again.

THE FRONTIERS OF DREAM RESEARCH

The suggestion theory of dreaming and its explanation of the dynamics of dream creation may be of interest to professionals from a number of disciplines. In this section we will discuss a few ways in which an understanding of lucid dreaming could prove fertile of research possibilities in various academic fields. Next we will list a number of areas where experimentation utilizing people trained to be aware in their dreams could help test and clarify different hypotheses about dream creation by providing quantifiable correlations between dream mentation and sleep physiology. And since particular dreams may remain difficult to explain even using the suggestion theory approach because of factors related to remembering and recording them, we will close by recommending a few ways to enhance the vital subjective component of dream research.

Open Secrets: Dreams in an Interdisciplinary Context

In order to resolve the seeming paradox of the possibility of being awake in our dreams, we all have to extend our notions of what constitutes a dream. Visions and reveries, sightings of bedside apparitions, and out-of-body sensations, often regarded as exceptional because the experient professes full consciousness, can now be seen as protodreams from the edge of sleep that form a continuum with lucid dreams in sleep. Dream lucidity, in turn, constitutes little more than a reconceptualization of what is already a conscious state and already largely under our personal control. Scholars, humanistic and scientific alike, would benefit by understanding that protodream experiences and lucid dreams are of themselves neither paranormal nor abnormal, and that they provide a key to understanding other aspects of human experience.

Folklorists, for instance, would find within the dream community a rich field of shared folk belief to harvest. They have already realized that protodream phenomena can provide insights into the experiential core of certain traditions, since folklorist David Hufford has postulated that the sleep paralysis nightmare is the basis of numerous superstitious beliefs in vampires, incubi, witches and other supernatural beings assailing sleepers.[33] A thorough study of the nature of hypnagogic hallucinations, which Janice knows for a fact can be projected into the external environment, would go a long way towards explaining supposed encounters with ghosts, fairies, and aliens. Anthropologists could similarly examine dream and hypnagogic image manipulation as the phenomenological basis for the shamanistic techniques of many cultures.

Theologians, in turn, may come to understand more about the nature of visionary encounters by seeing how people can create realistic dream imagery reflecting virtually any belief system. Parapsychologists could approach waking, near-death and other out-of-body experiences from the same standpoint as dream OBEs, as resulting from a person's models of self and environment being disrupted in certain circumstances rather than as evidence of a separable soul or advanced psychic capacity. It might also be illuminating to reexamine the phenomenon of channeling "entities" in terms of creating dream characters, given that Janice and others have been able to sustain complex recurrent characters with distinctive voices and personalities in lucid dreams. Such a study would also no doubt provide insights into the inner dynamics of multiple personality disorder.

Voicing Opinions

In the psychiatric fields, the observations of lucid dreamers, if widely known, could expand the concept of possible and normal human experience, so that mental health professionals need not diagnose problems where none exist, or at least not where they are sought, in "aberrant" dream experience. The folklorist Hufford strongly advised his readers to resist sleep paralysis attacks rather than pursue them into OBEs, which he took as potential forerunners of identity disintegration. "I have spoken with people who have reported years of anguish," he wrote, "some of it involving symptomatology much like some of the features of psychosis, after having intentionally cultivated this experience."[34] Psychiatrist and lucid dreamer Andrew Brylowski has reported the chilling case of a man actually committed for talking about having OBEs.[35]

Schizophrenia can indeed produce symptoms that bear some resemblance to out-of-body experiences. However, these form part of a broad spectrum of pervasive and obviously delusional psychotic perceptions.[36] It is also true that misunderstood conscious sleep phenomena like OBEs can be quite upsetting. Yet the mental imbalance does not lie in *having* OBEs, episodes of sleep paralysis or sleep-onset voices and visions, but in the individual's negative reaction *to* such phenomena; they do not have to provoke crippling fear or unhealthy fascination.

In any case, a clearer understanding of hypnagogia and dream construction in general may shed light on certain forms of mental illness featuring persistent hallucinations, which might be seen as dreamlike mental processes that continually intrude on waking experience. Many such psychoses have been linked to organic defects or chemical imbalances in the brain, but an additional factor suggests itself. If hallucinatory material is in effect present all the time if only we listen for it in the chatter of our own neurons, the "voices" heard by schizophrenics and the severely depressed may result because their inward focus makes them prone to heed aspects of their internal information processing to which most people remain oblivious.

Recall the model discussed in Chapter 8 for generating the speech of dream characters by concentrating attention on specific words or general expectations to activate the neural processing networks associated with speech, then reading the result as a verbal perception. In some individuals, an overload of inwardly directed attention in waking could conceivably cause "spikes" in the circuitry that get read back as verbal microdreams of their own thoughts sounding aloud or being replied to, a common complaint of schizophrenics.[37] More complex productions like disparaging critiques could result from making a habit of dissociative fantasy; more random ones, from simply skimming the surface of the neurological pond, as it were. Schizophrenics, whose neurological structure may be more disordered than normal to begin with,[38] perhaps pay *so* much attention to such material that it comes to dominate their experience and they lose control of their own thought processes. In fact the illogical speech of patients with advanced cases of schizophrenia recalls the ramblings of undirected dream characters.

Bearing all this in mind, it would make sense for psychiatrists to try encouraging patients whose only complaint is hearing the occasional voice to disregard the sounds and to establish a more stimulating environment to give the brain more external input to process. This would make a more conservative starting point for treatment than automatically diagnosing them as schizophrenics or dissociatives and dosing them with drugs, committing them to institutions, or probing what may be only externalized signaling noises for "meaning." Lack of lucidity regarding what could be dismissed as mere dream fragments might in effect *create* an unbalanced mental condition when none need develop, and preoccupation with the voices would only tend to enhance them. Careful study of the natural hallucinatory processes appreciated by otherwise quite rational lucid dreamers in controlled circumstances might ultimately help in understanding and treating the disturbing hallucinations of those less fortunate.

Perhaps something could be learned from lucid dreamers that would also help illuminate the phenomenology of certain sleep disorders. Consider narcolepsy, a largely hereditary condition involving sudden, involuntary bouts of sleep during the day, often sparked by strong emotion. Narcoleptics, like many lucid dreamers, commonly suffer from sleep paralysis and vivid hypnagogic hallucinations, and enter the REM state directly from waking during their attacks.[39] At the least, narcoleptics who become aware that others without their condition not only have but often welcome similar experiences when falling asleep might feel less anxiety about them.

Coming Full Circle: Lucidity in the Laboratory

The potential contributions of lucid dream research to the study of psychoses and sleep disorders may seem intriguing, but many other aspects of lucidity are worthy of future investigation as well. In fact insofar as the scientific findings in the field remain largely unintegrated with mainstream sleep research, the entire range of phenomena associated with lucid dreaming could stand further objective verification, even if this means repeating and reexamining the pioneer work comparing lucid and nonlucid dreaming on such measures as REM intensity and brain-wave signatures.[40] Scientific inquiry first proved the validity of claims of being awake within dreams, and sleep-laboratory experimentation with subjects connected to physiological monitors promises to continue to provide useful data.

In a 1993 issue of his newsletter, Stephen LaBerge announced that he had begun work on a computerized glove containing sensors to pick up the fine movements of the physical hand corresponding to gestures made with the dream hand.[41] Such a device would enable subjects to communicate directly from their lucid dreams with more complicated signals than the traditional controlled eye movements. LaBerge also announced plans for a detailed analysis of electroencephalogram (EEG) readings to map the differential electrical activation of various brain regions during lucid dreaming. Using more modern computerized imaging technology to scan the brains of skilled lucid subjects would relate neurological activity to specific behaviors in dreams in considerably more detail than has yet been possible.[42]

Laboratory tests could objectively demonstrate the volitional control possible with lucidity, as well as help elucidate the limiting factors affecting that control. Remember for instance the Lucidity Institute experiment suggesting that lucid dreamers sometimes could and sometimes could not observably increase the lighting level in their dreams. Since dream lighting level might correlate with the degree of brain activation, which is a measurable quantity, "A prime target of research would be to discover what the brain is doing under both circumstances," as the experiment reviewers comment.[13] Neurophysiological measures might help explain variations in the successfulness of other dream control techniques as well, showing, for instance, whether consistently different types of brain activity occur when phasing through "solid" objects seems easy or difficult, which can change from night to night.

It may even be possible to correlate major dream instabilities, such as scene shifts, with changes in brain activity or other factors. Once when she was very lightly asleep Janice found that she could lucidly make scenes change merely by stamping her foot or shaking her head in the dream, the actions causing a brief jolt of wakefulness and thus discontinuity. It would be interesting to see if ordinary scene shifts in REM can correlate with slight movements or microawakenings.

A series of experiments could certainly determine if the unexpected blank spots sometimes noticed during lucid dreams correlate with tonic episodes within REM or with more pronounced shifts in level of sleep. This might also reveal to what extent the alternation between phasic and tonic periods is a preprogrammed, biological function and to what extent it can be influenced by the dreamer's variable attention to dream visuals, given that the three of us could also induce blank spots by performing disruptive actions or by becoming less engaged with the imagery. The alternation may, like breathing, be automatic to an extent yet largely controllable as well.

The suggestion theory puts more emphasis on attention chasing dreams along than on randomly generated dream elements attracting the attention, though it would be difficult to pin down such subtleties of thought in a laboratory. Nevertheless, we would be curious to know what proportion of dream content gets suggested by the state and what by the dreamer's mental activity. Dream content often correlates with physiological indicators like eye movements, middle ear muscle twitches, and facial and limb twitches. But how much do these phasic components of REM sleep *cause* such content as opposed to being *caused by* the dreamer's volitional actions— looking, listening, talking, moving around?

Some of LaBerge's "oneironauts" deliberately initiated sexual activity while lucid, which led to appropriate and measurable physiological changes.[44] This demonstrated at least one instance in which specific dream activities created specific somatic effects rather than the reverse. Also, a series of experiments with lucid dreamer Alan Worsley showed that activity in Worsley's eyes, larynx and various muscles correlated quite well with the intentional dream activities he reported.[45] Similar laboratory experimentation might be able to tell if changing the experienced temperature in a lucid dream, something the three of us sometimes found it possible to do, can produce measurable corresponding effects on the physical body.

We do not presently know just how fully activated a lucid dreamer's critical faculties and memories can be while in various stages of sleep, but we would obviously predict that the areas of the brain involved in reasoning and memory show more activation during lucid than during nonlucid dreams. Further study could also more clearly determine what physiological differences might pertain between REM and NREM lucid dreams. Do people who have "wake-initiated" lucid incidents usually enter the REM state directly, or do those dreams normally take place in NREM Stage 1 and 2? How soon do their dreams begin after sleep onset, or resume after attempted dream reentry? Does the sleeper typically miss transitional gaps, such as the dreamlets Janice sometimes remembered only after waking from a lucid dream that she thought at the time proceeded directly from waking consciousness?

We would also like to see further work with advanced meditators who claim to be able to remain aware all night through all stages of sleep,[46] to see how meditative lucid dreaming might differ from ordinary lucid dreaming in terms of eye movements, brain-wave patterns and other physiological measures. One experiment might involve having a meditative lucid dreamer close his or her dream eyes for an extended period and otherwise attempt to suppress dream content, with the cortex all the while being monitored for changes in activation. If the presence of dream imagery is determined solely by self-regulating brainstem pulses or involuntary rapid eye movements stimulating the visual cortex, how could anyone voluntarily make a dream disappear by the willful act of closing imaginary eyes?

As something of an obstacle to any of these proposed investigations, researchers would have to locate a number of dedicated lucid dreamers having the necessary background and technical knowledge to make good test subjects. Volunteers would have to be sensitive enough to control induction reliably yet flexible enough to do so under laboratory conditions. Sleeping comfortably while wired with electrodes seems difficult enough; the close confinement and clangor of some brain-scanning machines might prove intolerable, not to mention the injections required for certain imaging processes. Moreover, subjects would need to live near fully equipped sleep laboratories staffed by interested researchers and technicians, or at least be able to travel and visit these for extended periods.

Not all empirical work requires a laboratory, however. The most complex of LaBerge's lucidity induction devices, as well as a more research-oriented tool developed by J. Allan Hobson and associates,[47] detect and digitally record data about the wearer's eye and head movements, which can be used to identify sleep stages in conjunction with mentation reports collected in the comfort of one's own home. Such devices are at least somewhat less unpleasant than more sophisticated equipment, though still too disruptive for ultrasensitive sleepers such as Janice. Researchers could also undertake comparative analyses of the physical and psychological profiles of lucid dreamers of differing skill levels, looking for correlations with such factors as sleep disorders, psychiatric problems and health conditions as well as with indices of creativity, intelligence, perceptual skills and the like.[48]

The Art of Lucid Dreaming

We have described the dream creation process as being more creative than deterministic. Just as science as presently constructed cannot encompass other creative human activities like the fine arts, neither can it fully encompass dreaming and lucid dreaming when these are redefined as creative acts. Quantitative investigation aside, then, lucid dreaming will probably always remain more of an art than a science.

Most of our claims regarding what we found possible with lucidity are anecdotal and probably not verifiable scientifically, at least in the short run within the limitations of present technology. As subjective impressions, many aspects of lucid dreaming may *never* lend themselves to external verification, even with improved methods. Many people view personal experience as more valuable than anything else, but although personal experience informs all the observations in this book, the usual lack of lucidity *about* dreaming points to the inadequacy of relying on anecdotes alone. Hence the need for science to verify, to the extent possible, such claims and ideas.

The observations of lucid dreamers might themselves be considered scientific evidence, as long as the veracity of their dream reports can be credited. It may take special training to bring dream reporting up to a certain necessary standard, since at present much of the literature and quality of thought on the subject remain inferior. Dreamers often describe things in idiosyncratic terms, mixing waking interpretations with dream descriptions to such an extent that it becomes difficult to say, from an external vantage point, what they actually experienced. Some, for instance, feel impelled to cloak their descriptions of dream control with the trappings of occultism or magic, as an applicable but less than lucid frame of reference. Such biases often make reports overly selective and more reflective of the dreamer's personal tastes or assumptions about dreaming than of the original dreams themselves.

Further, being relatively unaware of the nature of dream phenomena can cause people to transpose or skip certain details in their reports. A sudden transition might be remembered as a division separating two dreams and so be dropped from either account; indistinct imagery might be described as distinct; the lack of narrative consistency might be overlooked as too difficult to put into words; and so on. What the dreamer thought or expected at a critical point, which can often explain why a change in imagery occurred, might not even be observed, since dreamers typically focus on "external" occurrences without heeding their own input.

People recording or talking about dreams also have a temptation to describe the effects they *tried* to get or *assumed* they got rather than the ones actually achieved. For instance, they might gloss over major instabilities of time and motion that took the place of an action. A dream event like leaving a shopping mall and suddenly finding oneself at the image of one's car might end up as the realistic but inaccurate, "I crossed the parking lot to my car." This tendency can make dreams look much more naturalistic than they really are.

Dream accounts often confuse dream characters and places with their waking correlates even though the images may have been far from authentic. In fact the lack of a special vocabulary to describe dream phenomena leads people to describe almost everything in accordance with descriptions of waking reality. Whether or not one thinks of dreams as real while they occur, one will perceive dreamed events in the same way as waking events, and tend to recount them in the same kind of language: "I flew over New York with my sister" rather than "I had the impression of flying over what I took to be New York with a dream character resembling my sister." While oversimplification makes sense for brevity's sake, these naive descriptions can subtly affect a person's thinking, reinforcing the tendency to think of dreams as real and making lucidity both during and after dreams hard to develop or sustain. This indiscrimination about describing dreams in waking terms may also help explain why people commonly assume dreams must be relevant to their waking lives.

A certain lack of lucidity, then, is embedded in the average dream account. Biasing effects occur with the transcriptions of both lucid and nonlucid dreamers, including ourselves; Janice started writing down dreams to entertain her correspondents, not to provide scientific data. However, lucid dreamers will probably be more likely to notice such things as sudden transitions, surreal discrepancies and the effects of their own thoughts, since they can learn to watch for these in action.

We do hope that more people will take science into consideration when planning and recording their lucid dreams. Obviously more people need to experiment and compare notes, in order to verify our claims and to work out individual differences. Negative results in any dream-control experiment are suspect; anything that seems impossible to do within a lucid dream may be merely a matter of varying dispositions or talents. We do credit, for instance, that other lucid dreamers can summon up the extremes of bliss that we cannot.

Although consensus is important when assessing subjective experiences, if a significant minority report certain divergent effects these should be credited and the differences explored. An investigator seeking to understand the totality of lucid dream experience would be remiss to focus on the pleasures of a group of shared dreaming enthusiasts while ignoring the terrors of a Father "X." Unlike in waking science, repetition of observations does not necessarily constitute confirmation when it comes to lucid dreaming phenomena. Dissimilar results can be as interesting as similar ones, since all often result simply from expectation. Nevertheless, the investigator has to exercise some caution, since rogue accounts may otherwise go unchallenged.

THE LAST WORD

We believe our personal testimony valuable not because people must believe our reports, but because the explanation of dreaming that we learned through our experiences seems unusually clear and sensible for this area of inquiry, as well as integrative of various perspectives. Anyone can approach lucid dreaming in terms of the biases of a pet preoccupation, be that meditation, shamanism, occultism, parapsychology, or psychoanalysis. We have attempted to counterbalance the presiding interpretations of lucid dreaming by showing how it looks from such underrepresented points of view as the psychology of perception and modern neuroscience, and to apply the insights gained towards a new understanding of ordinary dreams as well.

Still, we do not want to set up a doctrinaire explanation of dreaming which cannot be questioned and tested. The suggestion theory as presented here only describes how dreams are created *in general*. The way in which such a mechanism creates individual dreams may be much more complicated and detailed, and efforts to understand that process may lead to some surprising developments.

We have not written the last word on lucid dreaming. Almost undoubtedly, future researchers, scholars and dreamers will improve on our observations. Many more experiments will be devised and performed, further illuminating various aspects of the dreaming process. Such a continuing endeavor will hopefully make a clearer understanding of dreams available to many more people. But whatever the detailed explorations yet to come, our own forays into the world of lucid dreaming have helped us discover at least one essential point. However intriguing, however striking, however vivid or lucid, *a dream is just a dream*.

Notes

Chapter 1: Exploring Dreams Lucidly

1. For a more detailed review, see Stephen LaBerge (1988a), in Gackenbach and LaBerge (1988).

2. Hervey de Saint-Denys (1982) [1867].

3. Frederick van Eeden [1913], in Tart (1990).

4. Arnold-Forster (1921).

5. Fox (1962) [1920].

6. Ouspensky (1971) [1931], p. 242–50, 252.

7. Green (1968). Green came out with a second book on lucid dreaming a quarter century later to update her presentation in light of new findings; see Green and McCreery (1994).

8. Garfield (1976).

9. See LaBerge (1986a), p. 67–77. Even people who think they never dream reputedly recall dreams if awakened from REM.

10. See Alan Worsley's description of their early studies in Gackenbach and LaBerge (1988), p. 322–24.

11. Such as LaBerge (1986a).

12. These are sometimes called *hypnopompic* instead when they occur just before awakening.

13. LaBerge and Rheingold (1990), p. 91–92.

14. See Shah (1964), p. 141.

15. Arnold-Forster (1921), p. 54, remarks on the limitations of studying dreams in isolation.

16. This behavior was apparent at the annual meeting of the Lucidity Association in Santa Cruz, California, June 1992.

17. See Fox (1962) [1920].

18. See LaBerge (1986a), p. 240–41.

19. For a relatively innocuous example see Harary and Weintraub (1989b).

20. See "Dream Soul" in Leach and Fried (1984), p. 325.

21. For dream examples, see Ryback (1988).

22. See Magallón (1997).

23. For example, see Sparrow (1982).

24. Castaneda (1972); Castaneda (1993). For a collection of essays on the Castaneda phenomenon, see DeMille (1990).

25. Roberts (1986).

26. See Paul Tholey, in Gackenbach and LaBerge (1988), p. 269–72.

27. See for instance Malamud (1982).

28. See for instance Harary and Weintraub (1989a), p. 76–77.

29. See Gawain (1978).

30. LaBerge and Rheingold (1990), p. 152–80.

31. Such as described in Garfield (1979).

32. J. Allan Hobson, personal communication.

33. LaBerge and Rheingold (1990), p. 33–38.

34. For much more detailed descriptions of these and other induction techniques, see LaBerge and Rheingold (1990), p. 48–98.

35. A number of Lucidity Institute experiments have suggested that naps of various kinds increase the likelihood of having lucid dreams; see for instance LaBerge et al. (1994)

36. LaBerge and Rheingold (1990), p. 79–80.

37. See Stephen LaBerge (1988b), in Gackenbach and LaBerge (1988), p. 146–47.

38. Hobson (1988), p. 211, notes the likelihood that the brain "uses its own eye movement data in dream scene elaboration."

39. A full eighty percent of the respondents to an informal survey we conducted reported flying as a common experience in their lucid dreams.

40. Ouspensky (1971) [1931], p. 251; Green (1968), p. 157.

41. Garfield (1976), p. 143.

42. LaBerge (1986a), p. 113–14.

43. Green (1968), p. 56, 63.

44. As for instance Gackenbach and Bosveld (1989).

Chapter 2: Levels of Lucidity

1. Tart (1990).

2. Tart (1984).

3. Gillespie (1983).

4. Gillespie (1984b).

5. Frederick van Eeden [1913], in Tart (1990), p. 181–86.

6. See for example Gebremedhin (1990), p. 43–44.

7. An observation also noted by Hervey de St. Denys (1982) [1867], p. 47.

8. See for example MacTiernan (1987); Gebremedhin (1990).

9. Van Eeden, in Tart (1990), p. 180.

10. Father "X" (1990), p. 56; Father "X" (1989), p. 42.

11. Green (1968), p. 23.

12. Such as Barrett (1992–93).

13. For instance Moss (1986).

14. Lucid dreamer Alan Worsley makes a similar observation about the variability of his lucidity in Gackenbach and LaBerge (1988), p. 326.

15. Tart (1985), p. 13.

16. Hewitt (1988), p. 64.

17. See Arthur J. Deikman [1966], in Tart (1990).

18. Gackenbach and Bosveld (1989), p. 136–38 and 182–95.

19. Arnold-Forster (1921), p. 64–69, describes a process of increasing her dream flight skills over a period of years.

20. LaBerge and Rheingold (1990), p. 119–20.

21. Arnold-Forster (1921), p. 55–56, describes how she at first used to wake herself up from nightmares then found doing so to be unnecessary.

22. Hervey de Saint-Denys (1982) [1867], p. 58–59, describes an interesting example.

Chapter 3: The Suggestion Theory of Dreaming

1. James (1950) [1890], 2 vols.

2. Ornstein (1986); Ornstein (1991).

3. See Ornstein (1985), p. 178–79.

4. James (1950) [1890], vol. I, p. 402.

5. James (1950) [1890], vol. II, p. 604.

6. Taylor (1984), p. 15–34.

7. Although LaBerge has articulated a perceptual model of dream generation very similar to parts of the suggestion theory, he does not seem to have followed through on many of its most important implications. See especially LaBerge (1996a); also Foulkes (1985), p. 5–7 and 76–77.

8. Hervey de Saint-Denys (1982) [1867], p. 39 and 52–53, anticipated James' ideas on dreams. Arnold-Forster (1921), p. 130, 135, and 138, came to similar conclusions.

9. Some researchers have suggested that even many of the *physiological* attributes of hypnosis may themselves be the result of suggestion by the hypnotist, expecting and coaching all subjects to conform to standard expectations of the state. See James (1950) [1890], vol. II, p. 598–99.

10. See Hilgard (1968), p. 5–10.

11. O. L. Zangwill, in Gregory (1987), p. 330.

12. James (1950) [1890], vol. II, p. 289.

13. Ornstein (1991), p. 193.

14. See Freud (1952) [1901], p. 35 and 70.

15. For a review of the REM memory-consolidation idea, see Hobson (1989), p. 197–99.

16. For more information on how dream stories follow standard narrative structures, see LaBerge and Rheingold (1990), p. 109.

17. LaBerge (1986a), p. 107.

18. See for example Gillespie (1984a), p. 88; Stephen LaBerge in LaBerge et al. (1986), p. 95.

19. Tholey (1989), p. 15.

20. Taylor (1984), p. 27–28.

21. See Hobson (1988), p. 206–7.

22. Also, occasionally the ability to block muscle movement during REM fails due to old age or neurological disease, and the afflicted subjects consequently act out their dreams. See Hobson (1994), p. 136–37.

23. Arnold-Forster (1921), p. 141.

24. Levitan (1991b); Levitan (1993).

25. To the best of our knowledge neither urination nor ejaculation in dreams typically leads to a corresponding physical event, at least for adults.

26. Hobson (1988), p. 203–22.

27. Barrett (1987), p. 36.

28. LaBerge (1986a), p. 208.

29. Bogzaran (1990), p. 28.

30. James (1950) [1890], vol. I, p. 13.

31. James, vol. I, p. 8.

32. James, vol. I, p. 162–76. For a detailed explanation of how habit can produce the same phenomena attributed to the unconscious, see p. 145–82.

33. Hobson (1988), p. 53.

Chapter 4: Dream Control

1. Walter Bonime, in Bonime et al. (1990), p. 31.

2. See Dane et al. (1987), p. 70–76.

3. Patricia Garfield, in Bonime et al. (1990), p. 33–34.

4. For example, Harary and Weintraub (1989a), p. xi, advise lucid dreamers to employ control skills only temporarily and sparingly.

5. One of its earliest critics was Alfred Adler, a psychoanalyst who had been one of Freud's associates. See Van de Castle (1994), p. 178–79. Hobson (1988), p. 52–68, gives a scientific criticism of the theory of the unconscious.

6. LaBerge and Rheingold (1990), p. 26.

7. Gebremedhin (1992–93), p. 97, noted as much with regard to one of her own lucid dreams.

8. Paul Tholey, in Gackenbach and LaBerge (1988).

9. LaBerge (1986a), p. 117.

10. See Father "X" (1985), p. 65.

11. Tarab Tulku XI (1989), p. 54–55, discusses Tibetan Buddhist ideas regarding modifying one's psychology by confronting, giving in to, or changing lucid dream images.

12. LaBerge (1986a), p. 179.

13. Van de Castle (1994), p. 449.

14. Kilton Stewart [1951], in Tart (1990), p. 194.

15. For an exposé of Stewart, see Domhoff (1986).

16. Garfield (1976), p. 112–15.

17. See Stanley Krippner (1990b), in Krippner (1990c), p. 191–92.

18. Johanna King, in Bonime et al. (1990), p. 36.

19. Harary and Weintraub (1989a), p. x, note that becoming lucid involves realizing how one is already controlling the dream, though they still manage to caution against dream control.

20. Levitan et al. (1992), p. 9–11.

21. LaBerge (1986a), p. 267, notes that the dream ego "is just another dream figure" and that the "actual creator of the dream is not a part of the dream at all—being, in fact, the sleeping self," but he fails to reconcile these observations with his earlier commentary.

22. It is interesting to note that damage to a particular area of the brain involved in attention can result in either increased dream vividness or the absence of dreaming. See Hobson et al. (1998), p. R9.

23. Frederik van Eeden [1913], in Tart (1990), p. 183.

24. Gackenbach and Bosveld (1989), p. 166.

25. Lucid dreamer Bruce Marcot (1987), p. 68–69, reported a similar effect.

Chapter 5: Emotions, Thoughts and Memories in Dreams

1. Hobson (1994), p. 152 and 157–60.

2. Hobson (1988), p. 7–8.

3. Hobson (1994), p. 42.

4. Hobson et al. (1998), p. R3 and R7, discussing the work of Allen Braun and several other researchers.

5. A fact noted in Hobson (1994), p. 155.

6. Subjects did report emotion and public self-consciousness significantly more often, and deliberate choice significantly less often, in conjunction with dreams. See Kahan and LaBerge (1994), p. 249.

7. See Gillespie (1986), p. 30.

8. See Garfield (1979).

9. See Hewitt (1988), p. 64.

10. LaBerge (1986a), p. 107.

11. For an accessible discussion of the scientific understanding of memory, see Schacter (1996).

12. See for instance Gillespie (1984c), p. 104.

13. Levitan and LaBerge (1993b), p. 12.

14. Excerpt previously published in Levitan and LaBerge (1993b), p. 13.

15. An idea going back to Sigmund Freud, according to Hobson (1988), p. 44.

16. Levitan and LaBerge (1993b), p. 12.

17. See Schacter (1996), p. 156–57. Not surprisingly, the frontal lobes have been found to be inactive in REM sleep; see Hobson et al. (1998), p. R3 and R9.

18. See Evans (1983), p. 179.

19. As in Freud's conception of the censorship mechanism that alters the repressed content of the unconscious into less disturbing symbolic form before presenting it as a dream. See Freud (1952) [1901], p. 63.

Chapter 6: The Origins of Common Dreams

1. For a version of the activation-synthesis hypothesis geared to a more general audience, see J. Allan Hobson, in Krippner (1990c).

2. Hobson (1988), p. 238–39.

3. Hobson (1988), p. 245.

4. See Rivlin and Gravelle (1984), p. 161.

5. Hobson (1988), p. 210.

6. Hobson (1994), p. 61.

7. Hooper and Teresi (1986), p. 295.

8. Hervey de Saint-Denys (1982) [1867], p. 141.

9. Green (1968), p. 90.

10. Hobson et al. (1998), p. R10–R11. For the effects of brain damage to the frontal cortex, many of which resemble certain mental characteristics of dreaming, see Hooper and Teresi (1986), p. 41–42; also Ornstein (1991), p. 150–55.

11. See Hobson (1988), p. 214.

12. See McCrone (1992), p. 91.

13. Ouspensky (1971) [1931], p. 247–48.

14. As discussed in Borbély (1986), p. 50.

15. Stickgold et al. (1994), p. 114.

16. Such as Alan Worsley, in Gackenbach and LaBerge (1988), p. 336–37.

17. Worsley, in Gackenbach and LaBerge (1988), p. 336.

18. Levitan and LaBerge (1993a).

19. Ian Oswald, in Gregory (1987), p. 202.

20. Hobson (1988), p. 166.

21. Ouspensky (1971) [1931], p. 246.

22. Although one usually associates dreaming with visual imagery, the congenitally blind reportedly have no visual images in their otherwise vivid dreams, because the vision centers in the brain do not develop in the absence of stimuli. People who become blind later in life, however, can have visual dreams. See Foulkes (1985), p. 37–38.

23. Hobson (1988), p. 255.

24. Hobson (1988), p. 206–7.

25. Hobson (1988), p. 171.

26. Hobson (1989), p. 162–63.

27. Stephen P. LaBerge [1981], in Ornstein (1986), p. 176.

28. Sagan (1977), p. 144, 147.

29. LaBerge (1993), p. 5. LaBerge suggested that the left-hemisphere activation at lucidity onset comes from thinking, "This is a dream"; but becoming lucid by no means requires such an articulation.

30. LaBerge (1996b), p. 18, notes that reading is such a complex perceptual process that it should be especially tricky to replicate normally in dreams.

31. Hemispheric specialization is itself a more complex matter than many realize, certain aspects of it being culturally rather than biologically determined, for instance. For a review of developments in this area of research, see Ornstein (1997).

32. Tholey (1989), p. 15–16.

33. Many of the interpretations for common dream themes cited in this chapter were derived in part from Faraday (1976), as representative of a popular perspective.

34. Gackenbach and Bosveld (1989), p. 47.

35. Gackenbach and Bosveld, p. 47.

36. Hobson (1989), p. 175.

37. Ouspensky (1971) [1931], p. 247.

38. See Hobson (1989) p. 109–10.

39. LaBerge (1986a), p. 94–95.

40. See Levitan (1991a), p. 10.

41. Hobson (1989), p. 186–87.

42. Foulkes (1985), p. 200–201.

43. Hobson (1994), p. 43.

Chapter 7: Dream Interpretation

1. Such as Van de Castle (1994).

2. Domhoff (1986), p. 23.

3. For shamanistic beliefs and practices relating to dreams, see Stanley Krippner (1990b), in Krippner (1990c).

4. See Van de Castle (1994), p. 73–84.

5. For a Christian perspective on the role of dreams, see John A. Walsh, in Ullman and Limmer (1988).

6. Van de Castle (1994), p. 56–57.

7. Miller (1995) [1900], p. 295.

8. Krippner (1990b), in Krippner (1990c), p. 190–91.

9. For a more accessible version of his ideas about dreaming, see Freud (1952) [1901].

10. Van de Castle (1994), p. 141.

11. Jung [1960], in Lindzey and Hall (1965). For a collection of his major writings on dreams, see Jung (1974).

12. Van de Castle (1994), p. 175–76.

13. Van de Castle, p. 187–91.

14. Van de Castle, p. 191–95.

15. See Ullman and Zimmerman (1979).

16. See Hobson (1988), p. 23–51, 69–81.

17. Stanley Krippner (1990a), in Krippner (1990c), p. 173.

18. Wilse B. Webb, in Krippner (1990c), p. 181–82.

19. See Van de Castle (1994), p. 207–19.

20. See Van de Castle, p. 241–64.

21. Foulkes (1985), p. 174.

22. Foulkes, p. 191.

23. Hobson (1988), p. 44–45.

24. Hobson (1988), p. 139–40.

25. Hobson (1988), p. 15 and passim.

26. Hobson (1988), p. 50–51.

27. See Deborah Jay Hillman, in Krippner (1990c).

28. OBE enthusiast Robert Monroe, for instance, not only wrote books on the subject beginning with Monroe (1973), but started a foundation to instruct those similarly interested.

29. Wilhelm Stekel, one of Freud's dissenting pupils, noted that patients have dreams in the form most pleasing to the analyst, who invariably reads into them. See Van de Castle (1994), p. 181.

30. Webb, in Krippner (1990c), p. 175–78.

31. Webb, in Krippner (1990c), p. 181.

32. Foulkes (1985), p. 39.

33. Meuris (1994), p. 120.

34. See Foulkes (1985), p. 137–39.

35. There is some indication in Jung's writings that, in keeping with certain early anthropologists, he considered the mentality of "primitive" and "civilized" people vastly different. Perhaps he could more easily account for commonalities of imagery as coming from a shared outside dimension impinging itself on consciousness rather than from human minds everywhere having the same basic *conscious* structure and producing similar motifs. See Jung (1958) [1949], p. 116.

36. One has only to remember the "Paul Is Dead" craze, in which Beatles fans combed the group's songs and album covers for supposed clues concerning Paul McCartney's fictive premature demise, to see this interpretive tendency in action.

37. Hobson (1994), p. 113–14.

38. Paul Tholey, in Gackenbach and LaBerge (1988), p. 270.

39. Tholey (1989), p. 16–17.

40. Hervey de Saint-Denys (1982) [1867], p. 77–78.

41. Hobson (1988), p. 258.

42. See for instance Maguire (1989), p. 13–14.

43. See Ullman and Zimmerman (1979), p. 12–13.

44. See for instance Langs (1990), p. 8–9.

45. Arnold-Forster (1921), p. 83–84.

46. An approach popularized in Faraday (1976).

47. Amy Tan, in Epel (1993), p. 282.

48. See Ullman and Zimmerman (1979), p. 13.

49. Shulman (1979), p. 147–48.

50. For a concurring therapeutic opinion, see Malamud (1982), p. 30.

51. See Hobson (1994), p. 43–45.

52. Ian Oswald, in Gregory (1987), p. 203.

53. See Hobson (1988), p. 214–22 for a discussion of the differences between Freud's perspective and his own.

Chapter 8: The Functions of Sleep and Dreaming

1. Hobson (1989), p. 154–56.

2. Hobson (1988), p. 5.

3. LaBerge (1986a), p. 52–53.

4. Borbély (1984), p. 25. Eventually researchers coined other terms, but the REM/NREM terminology persisted.

5. LaBerge (1986a), p. 54.

6. See Hobson (1988), p. 140.

7. See Hobson (1989), p. 117–25, for a detailed description of sleep physiology.

8. Hobson (1989), p. 4. The psychological effects of depriving people of REM sleep alone are not as dramatic as once commonly assumed. In the 1960s sleep researcher William Dement posited that REM deprivation could cause mental unbalance, though his results were not upheld later and he himself retracted his conclusions. See Borbély (1984), p. 166; Evans (1984), p. 131.

9. Hobson (1989), p. 114–15, describing the work of Allan Rechtschaffen.

10. Hobson (1994), p. 188–90.

11. Hobson (1988), p. 286–87.

12. Borbély (1984), p. 157.

13. Hobson (1988), p. 289, describing his work with Mircea Steriade.

14. Hobson (1988), p. 17.

15. Hobson (1988), p. 136.

16. See Hobson (1994), p. 59–60.

17. Hobson (1988), p. 289–90; Hobson (1989), p. 132–34.

18. Hobson (1988), p. 122.

19. Hobson (1988), p. 193.

20. Hobson (1988), p. 31. Although the neurological details have had to be revised since its original formulation, the basic tenets of

the reciprocal-interaction model still appear to be true. See Hobson et al. (1998), p. R3–R7.

21. Hobson (1994), p. 14–15.

22. See Hobson (1988), p. 229–31.

23. Hobson (1994), p. 173.

24. Hobson (1989), p. 52–53.

25. Hobson (1989), p. 55–56.

26. Hobson (1989), p. 61.

27. Hobson (1988), p. 173–74.

28. See Borbély (1984), p. 203.

29. Hobson (1988), p. 145.

30. Hobson (1989), p. 69.

31. See Borbély (1984), p. 204.

32. Hobson (1989), p. 60–69.

33. Borbély (1984), p. 194–97.

34. Ian Oswald, in Gregory (1987), p. 202.

35. See McCrone (1992), p. 37–39.

36. Hobson (1989), p. 57.

37. Borbély (1984), p. 110.

38. See Hobson (1988), p. 112–13.

39. Hobson (1988), p. 290.

40. See Hobson (1989), p. 191–92.

41. Stephen LaBerge (1988b), in Gackenbach and LaBerge (1988), p. 138.

42. See Hobson (1994), p. 61 and 139.

43. See Hobson (1994), p. 103.

44. McCrone (1992), p. 63.

45. LaBerge and Phillips (1994), p. 3.

46. Foulkes (1985), p. 55.

47. Hobson (1988), p. 286.

48. Evans (1984), p. 140–41.

49. Hobson (1988), p. 295.

50. Tamkins (1995), reviewing the work of Avi Karni.

51. Hobson (1989), p. 72.

52. See Hobson (1994), p. 114–17. Hobson et al. (1998), p. R12, suggest that in REM the brain consolidates information from waking, perhaps in conjunction with emotion, while discarding the dream information it generates in the process.

53. Hobson (1988), p. 296; Herbert (1983).

54. Hobson (1994), p. 134–36.

55. See Van de Castle (1994), p. 275–76.

56. See Hobson (1988), p. 291–93.

57. Hobson (1988), p. 292.

58. See Evans (1984), p. 158–59.

59. See Hobson (1988), p. 291. See Hobson (1989), p. 199 for a discussion of the latter intriguing possibility, based on the work of Bernard Davis.

60. Foulkes (1985), p. 203–4, similarly suggests the possibility that "dream processing can have adaptive effects, even when . . . the particular mnemonic elements being processed are haphazardly selected."

61. See Evans (1984), p. 151.

62. See Hobson (1988), p. 294–95.

63. Evans (1984), p. 151–53.

64. See Hobson (1988), p. 296–97.

65. Hobson (1988), p. 7. One wonders, though, how much of waking experience is actually remembered.

66. Or as Hobson et al. (1998), p. R12, put it, "Because dreams are so difficult to remember it seems unlikely that attention to their content could afford much in the way of high-priority survival value." See also Hobson (1994), p. 282.

67. Foulkes (1985), p. 1.

68. Foulkes, p. 201.

69. See LaBerge and Levitan (1996), p. 3, discussing the ideas of the neurologist Rodolpho Llinás.

Chapter 9: Uses of Lucidity

1. The Lucidity Institute, Inc. (1994), p. 2.

2. The Lucidity Institute, Inc. (1994), p. 2.

3. See Shulman (1979), p. 119–20.

4. See for instance Bogzaran (1987).

5. See for instance Giguère (1995).

6. LaBerge (1986a), p. 186.

7. See Garfield (1976), p. 44, citing Norman MacKensie.

8. As in Faraday (1976), p. 142–56.

9. Although she interprets the results differently than we personally would do, lucid dreamer Barbara Olsen gives an amusing account of the difficulties involved in asking dream characters for advice in Olsen (1992–93).

10. See for instance Tholey (1990).

11. Giguère (1995), p. 13–14.

12. David Sobel, in Ornstein and Swencionis (1990), p. 72.

13. See LaBerge (1986b).

14. For instance Kellogg (1989).

15. Several examples are listed in Gackenbach and Bosveld (1989), p. 109–11.

16. For a collection of scientific papers concerning the importance of mental factors in maintaining health, see Ornstein and Swencionis (1990).

17. Gackenbach and Bosveld (1989) list several anecdotes attesting to this effect, p. 83–86.

18. A therapist identifies taking dreams too seriously as a major cause of her clients having undue problems getting over nightmares in Belicki (1989).

19. See for instance Delaney (1991), p. 365.

20. See Tholey (1989), p. 15–16.

21. For his favorite example, see LaBerge (1986b), p. 10.

22. See Harary and Weintraub (1989a), p. 72–73.

23. See Faraday (1976), p. 156–60.

24. See Malumud, in Garfield et al. (1986), p. 232–34.

25. Faraday (1980), p. 300–301.

26. Godwin (1994) perpetuates this misunderstanding by discussing lucid dreaming in the context of world shamanistic and mystical traditions.

27. See for instance Linda Lane Magallón and Barbara Shor, in Krippner (1990c).

28. Fox (1962) [1920], p. 47, describes a classic example.

29. Interestingly, of a sample of professed psychics, 93 percent of those who had intentionally tried to become psychic were lucid dreamers. Millar (1992–93), p. 137.

30. For a relatively balanced discussion, see Jon Tolaas, in Krippner (1990c).

31. Faraday (1980), p. 180–81, cautions her readers to consider seemingly "paranormal" impressions in dreams as ordinary, overlooked perceptions.

32. LaBerge (1986a), p. 20.

33. Garfield (1976), p. 154–55 and 161–64, discusses the Tibetan Buddhist view of the afterlife and how lucid dreaming could provide practice in facing fearful apparitions like those that supposedly appear at that time. George Gillespie, in Gackenbach and LaBerge (1988), p. 30–33, reviews yogic teachings on dream control, meeting religious figures in lucid dreams, and meditation while lucid.

34. Tarab Tulku XI (1989), p. 49–51, discusses the Tibetan Buddhist conception of perception.

35. Cited in Shah (1964), p. 141, quoting Ibn Shadakin.

36. O. L. Zangwill, in Gregory (1987), p. 328.

Chapter 10: Unanswered Questions

1. And how to become masters within a month, in one case: Harary and Weintraub (1989a).

2. The only scientific efforts at pharmacological enhancement of lucidity that we know of were some inconclusive Lucidity Institute experiments with the hormone melatonin and an acetylcholinelike compound.

3. LaBerge and Rheingold (1990), p. 28.

4. For a review, see Hobson (1989), p. 113.

5. Marcot (1987), p. 72.

6. See John Oxbury, in Gregory (1987), p. 225.

7. Garfield (1979), p. 173–82.

8. Sparrow (1988).

9. Hobson (1994), p. 74.

10. Sparrow (1988).

11. Hobson (1994), p. 195.

12. Hobson (1988), p. 230.

13. See Borbély (1986), p. 168–69 and 198–99, for a discussion of sleep deprivation therapy with depressive patients.

14. Hobson (1994), p. 195–96.

15. See Hobson (1994), p. 72. See Hooper and Teresi (1986), p. 328–32, for ideas on how epilepsy and lowered serotonin levels can induce "mystical" states of consciousness.

16. For a description of one lucid dreamer's "kundalini" experience and its aftermath, see Kelzer (1987), p. 118–38.

17. Gackenbach and Bosveld (1989), p. 79–99.

18. Barroso (1987).

19. MacTiernan (1987).

20. LaBerge (1986a), p. 265–67, discussing the lucid dream life of the early twentieth century Indian physician Ram Narayana.

21. Susan J. Blackmore, in Gregory (1987), p. 573. Blackmore (1982), p. 279–80, gives a more detailed discussion of how OBEs originate in the breakdown of mental models.

22. Sue Blackmore, in Gackenbach and LaBerge (1988), p. 380.

23. See Levitan and LaBerge (1991), p. 2.

24. Hobson (1989), p. 175.

25. Hobson (1989), p. 183.

26. Body temperature, blood pressure, and pulse rate drop at sleep onset and fluctuate afterwards. See Borbély, p. 30.

27. For a review of the scientific debate on this subject, see Robert F. Price and David B. Cohen, in Gackenbach and LaBerge (1988), p. 106–9.

28. Hobson (1989), p. 153, similarly posits that the lingering waking activation of the brain enables a kind of miniature activation-synthesis for a short time at sleep onset.

29. See Gerald Vogel, David Foulkes, and Harry Trosman, in Tart (1990).

30. Retinal neuritis can similarly cause hallucinations of spiders. See Derek Russell Davis, in Gregory (1987), p. 300.

31. See the description in Evans (1984), p. 119–21.

32. Hobson (1994), p. 73.

33. Hufford (1982), written without reference to lucidity.

34. Hufford, p. 243.

35. Andrew Brylowski, in a discussion following the original presentation printed as Dane et al. (1987), p. 86–87.

36. See Baker (1996), p. 266–67; also R. E. Kendell, in Gregory (1987).

37. See Davis, in Gregory (1987), p. 300.

38. See Hooper and Teresi (1986), p. 113; for examples of schizophrenic speech, see p. 108.

39. Borbély (1984), p. 98–101.

40. For a summary, see Stephen LaBerge (1988b), in Gackenbach and LaBerge (1988).

41. LaBerge (1993).

42. One possibility would be positron emission tomography (PET) scans, which were used to discover the differential activation of various brain regions in REM. These scans measure sugar consumption in the brain, an indicator of the metabolic activity needed to support neural activity. Hobson (1994), p. 171.

43. Levitan and LaBerge (1993a), p. 9.

44. LaBerge (1986a), p. 89–94.

45. See Morton Schatzman et al., in Gackenbach and LaBerge (1988).

46. For a review of preliminary quantitative studies of meditation, see Meirsman (1990).

47. Hobson and Stickgold (1994), p. 9–10.

48. See the summary of Jayne Gackenbach's research along these lines in Gackenbach and Bosveld (1989), p. 166–176.

References

Arnold-Forster, Mary (1921). *Studies in Dreams*. London: George Allen & Unwin Ltd.

Baker, Robert A. (1996). *Hidden Memories: Voices and Visions from Within*. New York: Prometheus Books.

Barrett, Deirdre (1987). "Flying Dreams and Lucidity: An Empirical Study of Their Relationship." *Lucidity Letter* 6(2): 33–37.

Barrett, Deirdre (1992–93). "Just How Lucid Are Lucid Dreams?" *Lucidity* 11(1–2): 17–26.

Barroso, Mark A. (1987). "Letter to the Editor." *Lucidity Letter* 6(2): 156–57.

Belicki, Kathryn (1989). "Limitations in the Utility of Lucid Dreaming and Dream Control as Techniques for Treating Nightmares." *Lucidity Letter* 8(1): 95–98.

Blackmore, Susan J. (1982). *Beyond the Body: An Investigation of Out-of-the-Body Experiences*. Chicago: Academy Chicago Publishers.

Blackmore, Susan J. (1987). "Out-of-the-Body Experience." In Gregory (1987), p. 571–73.

Blackmore, Susan J. (1988). "A Theory of Lucid Dreams and OBEs." In Gackenbach and LaBerge (1988), p. 373–87.

Bogzaran, Fariba (1987). "The Creative Process: Paintings Inspired from the Lucid Dream." *Lucidity Letter* 6(2), p. 61–64.

Bogzaran, Fariba (1990). "Experiencing the Divine in the Lucid Dream State." *Lucidity Letter* 9(1): 22–31.

Bonime, Walter, Jayne Gackenbach, Patricia Garfield, Eugene Gendlin, Johanna King, and Jane White Lewis (1990). "Panel Discussion: Should You Control Your Dreams?" *Lucidity Letter* 9(2): 29–44.

Borbély, Alexander (1986). *Secrets of Sleep*. New York: Basic Books. Trans. from German by Deborah Schneider.

Carroll, Lewis (1978). *Alice's Adventures in Wonderland & Through the Looking Glass*. London: Octopus Books Limited. Originally published separately in 1865 and 1872.

Castaneda, Carlos (1972). *Journey to Ixtlan*. New York: Simon and Schuster.

Castaneda, Carlos (1993). *The Art of Dreaming*. New York: HarperCollins Publishers.

Dane, Joseph, P. Eric Craig, and Morton Schatzman (1987). "Ethical Issues for Applications of Lucid Dreaming." *Lucidity Letter* 6(2): 70–93.

Davis, Derek Russell (1987). "Hallucination." In Gregory (1987), p. 299–300.

Deikman, Arthur J. (1966). "Deautomatization and the Mystic Experience." *Psychiatry* 29: 324–38. Reprinted in Tart (1990), p. 34–57.

Delaney, Gayle (1991). *Breakthrough Dreaming: How to Tap the Power of Your 24-Hour Mind*. New York: Bantam Books.

DeMille, Richard, ed. (1990). *The Don Juan Papers: More Castaneda Controversies*. Belmont, California: Wadsworth Publishing Company.

Dickens, Charles (1984). *A Christmas Carol. In Prose. Being a Ghost Story of Christmas*. New York: Penguin Books. Originally published 1843.

Domhoff, G. William (1986). *The Mystique of Dreams: A Search for Utopia through Senoi Dream Therapy*. Berkeley and Los Angeles: University of California Press.

Epel, Naomi, ed. (1993). *Writers Dreaming*. New York: Carol Southern Books.

Evans, Christopher (1984). *Landscapes of the Night: How and Why We Dream*. New York: The Viking Press. Ed. by Peter Evans.

Faraday, Ann (1980). *Dream Power*. New York: Berkley Books.

Faraday, Ann (1976). *The Dream Game*. New York: Harper & Row/Perennial Library.

Father "X" (1985). "Lucid Dreams and Out-of-Body Experiences: A Personal Case." *Lucidity Letter* 4(2): 62–67.

Father "X" (1989). "Reflections on Lucid Dreaming and Out-of-Body Experiences." *Lucidity Letter* 8(1): 35–45.

Father "X" (1990). "Reflections on 20 Years of 'Conscious' Sleep Experiences." *Lucidity Letter* 9(2): 53–57.

Foulkes, David (1985). *Dreaming: A Cognitive-Psychological Analysis*. Hillsdale, New Jersey: Lawrence Erlbaum Associates.

Fox, Oliver (1962). *Astral Projection*. New Hyde Park, New York: University Books. Originally published ca. 1920.

Freud, Sigmund (1952). *On Dreams*. New York: W. W. Norton & Company. Trans. and ed. by James Strachey. Originally published in German in 1901.

Gackenbach, Jayne and Stephen LaBerge, eds. (1988). *Conscious Mind, Sleeping Brain: Perspectives on Lucid Dreaming*. New York: Plenum Press.

Gackenbach, Jayne and Jane Bosveld (1989). *Control Your Dreams*. New York: Harper and Row.

Garfield, Patricia (1976). *Creative Dreaming*. New York: Ballantine Books.

Garfield, Patricia (1979). *Pathway to Ecstasy: The Way of the Dream Mandala*. New York: Prentice Hall Press.

Garfield, Patricia (1988). *Women's Bodies, Women's Dreams*. New York: Ballantine Books.

Garfield, Patricia, Judith Malamud, Jean Campbell, Ann Sayre Wiseman, and Gordon Halliday (1986). "Mental Health Applications: A Panel Discussion." *Lucidity Letter* 5(1): 230–49.

Gawain, Shakti (1978). *Creative Visualization*. New York: Bantam Books.

Gebremedhin, Elinor (1990). "Differences Between Lucid and Nonlucid Ecstatic Dreaming." *Lucidity Letter* 9(1): 36–48.

Gebremedhin, Elinor (1992–93). "Invited to Dream: Of Dream Control and Lucidity." *Lucidity* 11(1–2): 95–104.

Giguère, Brenda (1995). "Piano Dreams: Lucidity and the Mozart Conundrum." *NightLight* 7(2): 11–14.

Gillespie, George (1983). "Memory and Reason in Lucid Dreams: A Personal Observation." *Lucidity Letter* 2(4), as reprinted in their *Back Issues*, p. 76–77.

Gillespie, George (1984a). "Problems Related to Experimentation While Dreaming Lucidly." *Lucidity Letter* 3(2–3), as reprinted in their *Back Issues*, p. 87–89.

Gillespie, George (1984b). "Can We Distinguish Between Lucid Dreams and Dreaming-Awareness Dreams?" *Lucidity Letter* 3(2–3), as reprinted in their *Back Issues*, p. 95–97.

Gillespie, George (1984c). "Statistical Description of my Lucid Dreams." *Lucidity Letter* 3(4), as reprinted in their *Back Issues*, p. 104–8.

Gillespie, George (1986). "Ordinary Dreams, Lucid Dreams and Mystical Experiences." *Lucidity Letter* 5(1): 27–31.

Gillespie, George (1988). "Lucid Dreams in Tibetan Buddhism." In Gackenbach and LaBerge (1988), p. 27–35.

Godwin, Malcolm (1994). *The Lucid Dreamer: A Waking Guide for the Traveler Between Worlds*. New York: Simon & Schuster.

Green, Celia (1968). *Lucid Dreams*. Oxford: Institute for

Psychophysical Research.

Green, Celia and Charles McCreery (1994). *Lucid Dreaming: The Paradox of Consciousness During Sleep.* New York: Routledge.

Gregory, Richard L., ed. (1987). *The Oxford Companion to the Mind.* Oxford University Press.

Harary, Keith and Pamela Weintraub (1989a). *Lucid Dreams in 30 Days: The Creative Sleep Program.* New York: St. Martin's Press.

Harary, Keith and Pamela Weintraub (1989b). *Have an Out-of-Body Experience in 30 Days: The Free Flight Program.* New York: St. Martin's Press.

Herbert, Wray (1983). "Forgotten Dreams." *Science News* 124(12): 188.

Hervey de Saint-Denys (1982). *Dreams and How to Guide Them.* London: Duckworth. Trans. by Nicholas Fry, ed. by Morton Schatzman. Originally published in French in 1867.

Hewitt, Daryl E. (1988). "Induction of Ecstatic Lucid Dreams." *Lucidity Letter* 7(1): 64–67.

Hilgard, Ernest R. (1968). *The Experience of Hypnosis.* A shorter version of *Hypnotic Susceptibility.* San Diego: Harcourt Brace Jovanovich.

Hillman, Deborah J. (1990). "The Emergence of the Grassroots Dreamwork Movement." In Krippner (1990c), p. 13–20.

Hobson, J. Allan (1988). *The Dreaming Brain.* New York: Basic Books.

Hobson, J. Allan (1989). *Sleep.* New York: Scientific American Library.

Hobson, J. Allan (1990). "Dreams and the Brain." In Krippner (1990c), p. 215–23.

Hobson, J. Allan (1994). *The Chemistry of Conscious States: How the Brain Changes Its Mind.* Boston: Little, Brown and Company.

Hobson, J. Allan and Robert Stickgold (1994). "Dreaming: A Neurocognitive Approach." *Consciousness and Cognition* 3(1): 1–15.

Hobson, J. Allan, Robert Stickgold, and Edward F. Pace-Schott (1998). "The Neuropsychology of REM Sleep Dreaming." *NeuroReport* 9(3): R1–R14.

Hooper, Judith and Dick Teresi (1986). *The Three-Pound Universe.* New York: MacMillan Publishing Company.

Hufford, David J. (1982). *The Terror That Comes in the Night: An Experience-Centered Study of Supernatural Assault Traditions.* Philadelphia: University of Pennsylvania Press.

James, William (1950). *The Principles of Psychology*, two vols. New York: Dover Publications. Originally published in 1890.

Jung, C. G. (1958). "The Psychology of the Child Archetype." In *Psyche and Symbol: A Selection from the Writings of C. G. Jung,* ed. by Violet de Lazlo, p. 113–47. New York: Anchor Books. Essay previously published in 1949.

Jung, C. G. (1960). "Patterns of Behavior and Archetypes." In *The Collected Works of C. G. Jung, Vol. 8: The Structure and Dynamics of the Psyche*, trans. by R. F. C. Hull, ed. by Herbert Read, Michael Fordham, and Gerhard Adler, p. 200–34. New York: Pantheon. Reprinted in Lindzey and Hall (1965), p. 59–76.

Jung, C. G. (1974). *Dreams*. Selections from *The Collected Works of C. G. Jung*, Bollingen Series XX, trans. by R. F. C. Hull. Princeton, New Jersey: Princeton University Press.

Kahan, Tracey L. and Stephen LaBerge (1994). "Lucid Dreaming as Metacognition: Implications for Cognitive Science." *Consciousness and Cognition* 3: 246–64.

Kellogg III, E. W. (1989). "A Personal Experience in Lucid Dream Healing." *Lucidity Letter* 8(1): 6–7.

Kelzer, Kenneth (1987). *The Sun and the Shadow: My Experiment with Lucid Dreaming*. Virginia Beach, Virginia: A.R.E.® Press.

Kendell, R. E. (1987). "Schizophrenia." In Gregory (1987), p. 697–99.

Krippner, Stanley (1990a). "Dreams in Different Times and Places." In Krippner (1990c), p. 171–74.

Krippner, Stanley (1990b). "Tribal Shamans and Their Travels into Dreamtime." In Krippner (1990c), p. 185–93.

Krippner, Stanley, ed. (1990c). *Dreamtime and Dreamwork: Decoding the Language of the Night*. Los Angeles: Jeremy P. Tarcher.

LaBerge, Stephen P. (1981). "Lucid Dreaming: Directing the

Action as It Happens." *Psychology Today* (January): 48–57. Reprinted in Ornstein (1986), p. 171–79.

LaBerge, Stephen (1986a). *Lucid Dreaming*. New York: Ballantine Books.

LaBerge, Stephen (1986b). "Healing through Lucid Dreaming." *Lucidity Letter* 5(2): 9–13.

LaBerge, Stephen (1988a). "Lucid Dreaming in Western Literature." In Gackenbach and LaBerge (1988), p. 11–26.

LaBerge, Stephen (1988b). "The Psychophysiology of Lucid Dreaming." In Gackenbach and LaBerge (1988), p. 135–53.

LaBerge, Stephen (1993). "Lucidity Research, Past and Future." *NightLight* 5(3): 1–6.

LaBerge, Stephen (1996a). "Dreaming and Consciousness." *NightLight* 8(1–2): 4–11.

LaBerge, Stephen (1996b). "To Sleep, Perchance to Read: The Re-Reading Reality Test and the *Traumdeutung* Quest," *NightLight* 8(1–2): 17–21.

LaBerge, Stephen, Beverly Kedzierski, Kenneth Moss, Jill Gregory, George Gillespie, and Henri Rojouan (1986). "Personal Exploration of Lucid Dreaming: A Panel Discussion." *Lucidity Letter* 5(1): 75–103.

LaBerge, Stephen and Lynne Levitan (1996). "Toward a Science of Consciousness: Tucson II, 1996." *NightLight* 8(1–2): 1–3.

LaBerge, Stephen and Leslie Phillips (1994). "Word Association

Tests and Brain Functioning in Waking and Dreaming." *NightLight* 6(4): 1–4, 9.

LaBerge, Stephen, Leslie Phillips, and Lynne Levitan (1994). "An Hour of Wakefulness Before Morning Naps Makes Lucidity Likely." *NightLight* 6(3): 1–4, 9.

LaBerge, Stephen and Harold Rheingold (1990). *Exploring the World of Lucid Dreaming*. New York: Ballantine Books.

Langs, Robert L. (1990). *Decoding Your Dreams*. New York: Ballantine Books.

Leach, Maria and Jerome Fried, eds. (1984). *Funk and Wagnalls Standard Dictionary of Folklore, Mythology, and Legend*. San Francisco: Harper and Row. Originally published in 1949.

Levitan, Lynne (1991a). "'Sleep on the Right Side, as a Lion Doth': Tibetan Dream Lore Still True after 10 Centuries." *NightLight* 3(3): 4, 9–11.

Levitan, Lynne (1991b). "Day of the DreamLight." *NightLight* 3(4): 1–3, 13.

Levitan, Lynne (1993). "Welcome NovaDreamers!" *NightLight* 5(4): 1–2.

Levitan, Lynne and Stephen LaBerge (1991). "In the Mind and Out-of-Body: OBEs and Lucid Dreams, Part I." *NightLight* 3(2): 1–4, 9.

Levitan, Lynne and Stephen LaBerge (1993a). "Through the Glass Lightly, Testing the Limits of Dream Control: The Light and Mirror Experiment." *NightLight* 5(2): 5–10.

Levitan, Lynne and Stephen LaBerge (1993b). "Dream Times

and Remembrances." *NightLight* 5(4): 9–14.

Levitan, Lynne, Stephen LaBerge, Jeanette Edelstein, and Jennifer Dole (1992). "The Look and Feel, and Sound of One Hand Dreaming." *NightLight* 4(3): 4, 9–11.

Lindzey, Gardner and Calvin S. Hall, eds. (1965). *Theories of Personality: Primary Sources and Research*. New York: John Wiley & Sons.

Lucidity Institute, The (1994). *Winter Catalog*.

MacTiernan, Vincent (1987). "Letter to the Editor." *Lucidity Letter* 6(2): 157–60.

Magallón, Linda Lane and Barbara Shor (1990). "Shared Dreaming: Joining Together in Dreamtime." In Krippner (1990c), p. 252–60.

Magallón, Linda Lane (1997). *Mutual Dreaming: When Two or More People Share the Same Dream*. New York: Pocket Books.

Maguire, Jack (1989). *Night and Day*. New York: Simon & Schuster/Roundtable Press.

Malamud, Judith (1982). "Training for Lucid Awareness in Dreams, Fantasy and Waking Life." *Lucidity Letter* 1(4), as reprinted in their *Back Issues*, p. 27–31.

Marcot, Bruce (1987). "A Journal of Attempts to Induce and Work with Lucid Dreams: Can You Kill Yourself While Lucid?" *Lucidity Letter* 6(1): 64–72.

McCrone, John (1992). *The Ape that Spoke*. New York: Avon Books.

Meuris, Jacques (1994). *Magritte*, trans. by Michael Scuffil. Wittingen, Germany: Benedikt Taschen.

Meirsman, Jan M. R. (1990). "Neurophysiological Order in the REM Sleep of Participants of the Transcendental Meditation and TM-Sidhi Program." *Lucidity Letter* 9(2): 88–112.

Millar, Charles R. (1992–93). "Reports of Psychics on Lucid Dreaming and Psychic Experiences: A Study." *Lucidity* 11(1–2): 123–39.

Miller, Gustavus Hindman (1995). *Ten Thousand Dreams Interpreted*. Chicago: Rand McNally & Company. Originally published in 1909.

Monroe, Robert A. (1973). *Journeys Out of the Body*. Garden City, New York: Doubleday & Company/Anchor Press.

Moss, Kenneth (1986). "The Dream Lucidity Continuum." *Lucidity Letter* 5(2): 25–28.

Olsen, Barbara (1992–93). "Using Lucid Dreams in Decision Making: No Symbols or Metaphors, Please—Just Tell Me Yes or No." *Lucidity* 11(1–2): 39–44.

Ornstein, Robert (1985). *Psychology: The Study of Human Experience*. San Diego: Harcourt Brace Jovanovich.

Ornstein, Robert, ed. (1986). *The Psychology of Consciousness*, Second Revised Edition. New York: Penguin Books.

Ornstein, Robert (1991). *The Evolution of Consciousness*. New York: Prentice Hall Press.

Ornstein, Robert (1997). *The Right Mind: Making Sense of the Hemispheres*. New York: Harcourt Brace & Company.

Ornstein, Robert and Charles Swencionis, eds. (1990). *The Healing Brain: A Scientific Reader*. New York: The Guilford Press.

Oswald, Ian (1987). "Dreaming." In Gregory (1987), p. 201–3.

Ouspensky, P. D. (1971). *A New Model of the Universe*. New York: Random House. Originally published in Russian in 1931.

Oxbury, John (1987). "Epilepsy." In Gregory (1987), p. 223–25.

Price, Robert F. and David B. Cohen (1988). "Lucid Dream Induction: An Empirical Evaluation." In Gackenbach and LaBerge (1988), p. 105–34.

Rivlin, Robert and Karen Gravelle (1984). *Deciphering the Senses: The Expanding World of Human Perception*. New York: Simon and Schuster.

Roberts, Jane (1986). *Seth: Dreams and Projection of Consciousness*. New York: Stillpoint Publishing.

Ryback, David and Letitia Sweitzer (1988). *Dreams that Come True: Their Psychic and Transforming Powers*. New York: Doubleday & Company.

Sagan, Carl (1977). *The Dragons of Eden*. New York: Random House.

Schacter, Daniel L. (1996). *Searching for Memory: The Brain, the Mind, and the Past*. New York: BasicBooks.

Schatzman, Morton, Alan Worsley, and Peter Fenwick (1988). "Correspondence During Lucid Dreams Between Dreamed and Actual Events." In Gackenbach and

LaBerge (1988), p. 155–79.

Shah, Idries (1964). *The Sufis*. London: The Octagon Press.

Shulman, Sandra (1979). *Nightmare: The World of Terrifying Dreams*. New York: MacMillan Publishing Co.

Sobel, David S. (1990). "The Placebo Effect: Using the Body's Own Healing Mechanisms." In Ornstein and Swencionis (1990), p. 63–74.

Sparrow, G. Scott (1982). *Lucid Dreaming: Dawning of the Clear Light*. Virginia Beach, Virginia: A.R.E. Press.

Sparrow, G. Scott (1988). "Letter from Scott Sparrow." *Lucidity Letter* 7(1): 6–8.

Stewart, Kilton (1951). "Dream Theory in Malaya." *Complex* 6: 21–33. Reprinted in Tart (1990), p. 191–204.

Stickgold, Robert, Cynthia D. Rittenhouse, and J. Allan Hobson (1994). "Dream Splicing: A New Technique for Assessing Thematic Coherence in Subjective Reports of Mental Activity." *Consciousness and Cognition* 3(1): 114–28.

Tamkins, Theresa (1995). "Learning While You Sleep." *American Health* January/February 1995: 46.

Tan, Amy (1993). "Amy Tan." In Epel (1993), p. 282–88.

Tarab Tulku XI (1989). "A Buddhist Perspective on Lucid Dreaming." *Lucidity Letter* 8(2): 47–57.

Tart, Charles (1984). "Terminology in Lucid Dream Research." *Lucidity Letter* 3(1), as reprinted in their *Back Issues*, p. 82–84.

Tart, Charles (1985). "What Do We Mean by 'Lucidity'?" *Lucidity Letter* 4(2): 12–17.

Tart, Charles, ed. (1990). *Altered States of Consciousness*, Third Edition. HarperCollins/HarperSanFrancisco. Originally published in 1969.

Taylor, Eugene (1984). *William James on Exceptional Mental States: The 1896 Lowell Lectures*. Amherst, Massachusetts: The University of Massachusetts Press.

Tholey, Paul (1988). "A Model for Lucidity Training as a Means of Self-Healing and Psychological Growth." In Gackenbach and LaBerge (1988), p. 263–87.

Tholey, Paul (1989). "Overview of the Development of Lucid Dream Research in Germany." *Lucidity Letter* 8(2): 6–30.

Tholey, Paul (1990). "Applications of Lucid Dreaming in Sports." *Lucidity Letter* 9(2): 6–17.

Tolaas, Jon (1990). "The Puzzle of Psychic Dreams." In Krippner (1990c), p. 261–70.

Ullman, Montague and Claire Limmer, eds. (1988). *The Variety of Dream Experience: Expanding Our Ways of Working with Dreams*. New York: Continuum.

Ullman, Montague and Nan Zimmerman (1979). *Working With Dreams*. Los Angeles: Jeremy P. Tarcher.

Van de Castle, Robert L. (1994). *Our Dreaming Mind*. New York: Ballantine Books.

Van Eeden, Frederik (1913). "A Study of Dreams." *Proceedings of the Society for Psychical Research* 26: 431–61. Reprinted in Tart (1990), p. 175–90.

Vogel, Gerald, David Foulkes, and Harry Trosman (1966). "Ego Functions and Dreaming during Sleep Onset." *Archives of General Psychology* 14: 238–48. Reprinted in Tart (1990), p. 94–113.

Walsh, John A. (1988). "Myths, Dreams and Divine Revelation: From Abram to Abraham." In Ullman and Limmer (1988), p. 82–104.

Webb, Wilse B. (1990). "Historical Perspectives: From Aristotle to Calvin Hall." In Krippner (1990c), p. 175–84.

Worsley, Alan (1988). "Personal Experiences in Lucid Dreaming." In Gackenbach and LaBerge (1988), p. 321–41.

Zangwill, O. L. (1987). "Experimental Hypnosis." In Gregory (1987), p. 328–30.

Index

acetylcholine, 205, 218, 264, 312n
activation-synthesis, 61–64, 130, 146, 170, 210, 276, 314n
  speculations on, 210–14
Adler, Alfred, 296n
adventures, dream, xv, 11, 22, 28, 230–31, 265
altered state of consciousness, xvi, 10, 21, 34–35, 43, 113
Alzheimer's disease, 160, 197
amines, aminergic, 204–5, 210, 216, 225–27, 258–59, 263–64, 271
Arabi, Ibn El-, 2, 6, 253
archetypes, archetypal imagery, 167–68, 176, 187, 195, 246
Aristotle, 2, 172
Arnold-Forster, Mary, xiii, 2, 59, 190, 290n, 293n, 294n
Aserinsky, Eugene, 170
astral plane, astral projection, 8–10, 82, 246–48
attention, interaction of dream imagery with, 53–58, 85–86, 90–99, 132–34, 156–57, 175, 211
autosuggestion, 3, 13–14, 52, 258

bizarreness, 13, 93–98, 104, 117–18, 149, 186, 212, 271
  origins of, xvi, 63, 89–90, 130–35, 185, 219
blank spots, 38, 56, 94–95, 144–46, 281
body:
  images and models of, 5, 8, 30, 261–62, 268–69
  effects on dreams, 38, 58–61, 129, 152, 268–69, 314n
  affected by dreams, 146, 238–40, 261–62, 282
  sleep needs of, 203, 207–8
Borbély, Alexander, 208
brain:
  brain chemistry, 119, 139, 197, 205–6, 209, 235, 258–59
  brain functions, 49, 74, 168, 210, 233, 235
  brain waves, 3, 227, 271, 280, 283
  disorders of, 125, 197, 220, 278–80, 299n
  activation and effects on

dreaming, 49–52, 62, 102, 130, 134, 144–47, 149–50, 154, 170, 181, 205, 210–22, 280–82, 291n, 297n, 300n
  in NREM sleep, 158, 202–6
  in REM sleep, 123, 130–32, 146, 154, 202–7, 210, 214–22, 227, 260, 308n
  in transitional states, 268–75, 314n
  regions of, 149–50, 199, 281, 315n
  scans of, 283, 315n
brainstem, 62–64, 131, 138, 146–47, 170–71, 203–7, 210, 221–22, 283
Braun, Allen, 298n
Brylowsky, Andrew, 278, 315n
buzzing sensations, 262, 269

Calloway, Hugh, *see* Fox, Oliver
Carroll, Lewis, 15, 121
Castaneda, Carlos, 9
cholinergic, 205, 214
"Christmas Carol, A" (Dickens), 243
Cicero, 172
cognitive functioning, 99–100, 103–4, 174, 183, 210, 265, 269, 272
consciousness, 12, 33, 69, 207, 247, 259
  higher, 8, 17, 34–35, 113, 247, 263, 313n
  in dreaming, 69, 87, 135, 160, 218, 225
  in lucid dreams, 14, 21–22, 32, 86–87, 97–98
  in transitional states, 261, 270–71, 274–76, 283–84
cortex, 130, 206–7, 210, 221, 271, 283
  frontal, 138, 204–5, 225, 299n
  motor, 147
  visual, 131, 283
Creative Dreaming (Garfield), 3, 230
creative visualization, 10
creativity, 244, 284
  in dreams, 36–38, 52, 56, 97–99, 111, 115–16, 223–24
  enhanced by dreams, 10, 67, 72, 178, 229, 232–34
Crick, Francis, 218–19
cues, cueing, 47–49, 92, 120, 138, 197, 252
  in dreams, 69, 98, 124–25, 133, 138, 155, 177–78
  lucidity, 13, 60, 180
  sensory, 49, 58–61, 128, 140

Dahomey, 8
day residues, 52, 170, 216

depression, dreaming and, 263–64, 313n
detachment, 24, 30, 34, 102, 10–11, 117
  from own thoughts, 270
Dickens, Charles, 243
Don Juan, 9
dreams, dreaming:
  purpose of, 163–227
  as omens, 165–66
  speech in, 17, 102, 149, 213–14
  reentering, 13, 258, 261
  recurrent, 27, 80–81, 157, 187–88, 241
  styles of, 52, 157, 187, 223
  dream research, xvii, 1, 12, 64, 70, 141, 169
dream accounts, biases in, 7, 16–18, 130–31, 141, 195, 284–86
dream body, 58–59, 84, 88–89, 151–52, 153, 237
  movement of, 62, 146–48
  creating, 13–14, 50–51, 153, 268–69, 274
dream characters, 95–97, 104, 141, 278–79, 310n
  controlling, xv, 38, 76–83, 96–97, 278
  interacting with, 27–28, 39, 114, 240
  therapeutic dialoguing with, 10, 75, 78–81, 242–44
  awareness of, 96, 151, 183–85, 236, 243–44, 310n
  speech of, 104, 150–51, 213–14, 279
dream community, 4, 8–10, 11, 67, 71–72, 74, 171, 247–49, 265, 277
dream control, xiii, xv, 7, 15–18, 25–30, 35–37, 57–58, 63–66, 71–100, 101, 105–9, 181, 195–96, 238, 260–61, 296n, 297n, 312n
  limits to, 97–99, 125, 129, 142–51, 211, 281, 286
  overdoing, 266–67
  opposition to, 11, 17, 71–72, 74–75, 81–82, 106, 183, 195–96, 296n, 297n
dream ego, 50–51, 84–90, 94, 115, 143, 151–54, 184, 196, 267, 297n
  movement of, 146–48
dream interpretation, 10, 70–75, 79, 151–59, 163–200, 236
dream generation, xv, 48–49, 58, 61–69, 99–100, 126–28, 160–61, 163–78, 191, 224–26, 276, 293n
dream objects, 37, 54, 91–93, 98, 104, 130, 144
  controlling, xv, 91, 92–95, 250, 281

dream recall, 12, 25–26, 32, 37, 73–74, 88, 104, 139–42, 145, 177, 224–27, 234, 289n, 309n
  of lucid dreams, 23, 67, 119, 233
  during dreams, 107, 122–24, 157, 181–82, 187
  as harmful, 218–19
dream scenes, 14, 23, 50, 53–55, 62, 92–93, 113, 138, 291n
  controlling, xv, 50, 56, 64, 86, 93–95, 108, 148
  scene shifts, 28, 37–38, 51, 93, 98, 116, 281
dream sensations, xv, 22–23, 34, 90–92, 97, 130–32
  sensory intrusions, 58–61, 69, 151–54, 169, 271, 274
dream-initiated lucid dream (DILD), 14
dream-specific focus, 66–67, 104, 126, 177–78, 187, 197–98, 224
  dream-specific personality (DSP), 179–82, 185, 190, 267
dreaming-awareness dreams, 21–22
Dreaming Brain, The (Hobson), 68, 141
Dreams and How to Guide Them (Hervey de Saint-Denys), xiii, 2

dreamsigns, 13, 14, 37, 251
dreamwork, 82, 171, 198

emotions:
  in dreams, 101–6, 117–18, 126–28, 135, 179–81, 187–89, 224, 241, 245, 264, 298n, 308n
  in lucid dreams, 4, 24, 31–35, 61, 88–89, 105–113, 117–18, 196
  in transitional states, 272
  as suggestion factors, xvi, 52–58, 67, 77–80, 133, 157–60, 170, 175, 185, 189, 191–95, 250
entertainment, lucid dreaming for, xv, 24, 89, 95–97, 108, 230–32
Evans, Christopher, 215
expectations:
  as suggestion factors, xvi, 55–57, 69, 76–81, 84–85, 140–41, 147, 156, 175–77, 212, 285–86
  lack of guiding, 56, 107, 156
  controlling, 40, 57, 76–78, 93–97, 201
  of lucid dreams, 16–17, 35, 40, 43, 65–67, 113, 246
  of dream characters, 76–78, 83, 242–43

false awakenings, 13–14, 28–29, 37, 56, 60–61,

63, 88, 125, 143, 258, 268, 275
false memories, 26, 32, 87, 125–28, 136–37, 182, 235, 246
Faraday, Ann, 245, 301n
Father "X", 24, 286
flying dreams, xv, 15, 36–40, 62, 72, 86, 92, 129, 147, 181, 187, 191, 222, 230–31, 291n
  physiological origins of, 62, 152
  as escapism, 72
  Amy Tan's, 190–91
folk belief about dreams, 73, 165–72
forebrain, 64
Foulkes, David, 48, 160, 170, 173, 214, 225–26, 309n
Fox, Oliver, 3
frame dream, 29, 275
Freud, Sigmund, 2, 52, 66–69, 154, 167–74, 186, 189, 193–94, 197–99, 296n, 299n, 303n, 305n
full lucidity, 29–30, 111

Gackenbach, Jayne, 4, 34, 265
Garfield, Patricia, 3, 17, 72, 82, 109, 230, 262
Gassendi, Pierre, 2
Giguère, Brenda, 237
Gillespie, George, 21
Green, Celia, 3, 17, 27, 137

Hall, Calvin, 141
hallucination, 48, 160, 203, 218–20, 276, 278–80, 314n
  hypnagogic, 5–6, 14, 30, 55, 158, 270–76
  hypnopompic, 289n
  kinesthetic, 13, 143, 268–69
healing dreams, 10, 65–66, 80, 238–40, 243, 250
Hearne, Keith, 3, 144
hemispheric specialization, 148–50, 301n
Hervey de Saint-Denys, xiii, 2, 134, 169, 185, 294n
Hobson, J. Allan, 62–65, 68, 102, 130–31, 138, 146–47, 152, 160, 170–71, 186, 205, 210, 214, 218, 223, 283, 291n, 308n, 309n, 314n
Hoffman, Edward, 130
Hufford, David, 277–78
Humphrey, Nicholas, 221
hypnosis, 48–49, 238, 254, 294n
hypothalamus, 154

impulsiveness:
  in dreams, 103, 122–23, 147, 154, 175–76, 179–80, 189, 223, 250
  in lucid dreams, 39, 98, 112, 116–17, 180, 196, 295n
insomnia, 6, 260

instability:
  in dreams, xv, 17, 51, 80, 93, 98, 105, 129–33, 143, 175–76, 239, 285
  in lucid dreams, 23–25, 37, 86–88, 100, 118, 132, 142, 150, 231, 237, 281
integration, psychological, 72, 78–82, 90, 168, 196–97, 238, 242–45
interpretations:
  as suggestion factors, 50, 53, 100, 113, 134, 194, 222, 252, 261
  controlling, 76, 97, 107, 175, 195, 253
Interpretation of Dreams, The (Freud), 167, 171
irrationality in dreams, 39, 103–4, 116–17, 128

James, William, 44, 46, 48–49, 68, 127
Jouvet, Michel, 221, 227
Jung, Carl, 67, 167–68, 171, 176, 194, 197, 304n

Karni, Avi, 308n
Kekulé, Friedrich August, 234
Kleitman, Nathaniel, 170
kundalini, 262–63

LaBerge, Stephen, 3–4, 12–14, 17, 38, 48, 56, 60, 64, 73, 115, 144–49, 234, 238, 242, 252, 260, 266, 280–83, 293n, 301n
  on dream control, 75–81, 89, 297n
light-switch phenomenon, 27, 91, 144
Llinás, Rodolpho, 310n
local lucid, 13, 60, 80, 248–50, 272
Locke, John, 169–70
lucid dreams, lucid dreaming:
  definition, xv
  history of, 2–4
  speculation about, 7–12
  inducing, 12–15, 88, 254, 257–59
  at sleep-onset, 91, 203, 261, 268, 273, 282–83
  induction devices, 4, 60, 258, 283
  levels of, 16–35
  magical solutions in, xv, 26, 36–37, 76–80, 86–87, 230, 267
  pleasurable, 11, 15, 24, 28, 34, 109–13, 117, 229–32
  improving skills with, 36–40
  experimenting with, xv, 4, 6, 15, 52, 88–99, 108, 115, 119–20, 196, 254, 276–86

conceptualizing, xvi–xvii, 21–22, 106–9, 114–15, 267
and dream interpretation, 192–96
uses of, 229–55
potential consequences of, 259–67
lucid dream research, 1–4, 7, 11, 22, 31, 214, 229, 254, 257, 276–86
Lucid Dreaming (LaBerge), 6, 238
Lucid Dreams (Green), 3, 5
Lucidity (Letter), 4, 21, 24, 30, 33, 265
Lucidity Association, 4, 290n
Lucidity Institute, 4, 86, 88, 103, 122–23, 158, 230, 237, 281, 291n, 312n

Magritte, René, 174
Maury, Alfred, 58, 169
McCarley, Robert, 62–65, 130, 170–71, 210
McCartney, Paul, 304n
meditation, 17, 34–35, 108, 262, 283, 287, 312n
melatonin, 312n
memory:
  in dreams, 84, 93–96, 100, 102, 104, 118–24, 127–29, 135–38, 160, 176–82, 204–5, 225–27
  in lucid dreams, xv, 23, 40, 88–90, 98–101, 105, 118–25, 135–38, 205, 235, 276, 282
  of dream characters, 183
  as suggestion factor, 50, 52, 77, 140, 151–57, 170–72, 184, 187, 216
  possibly served by dreaming, 52, 208, 215–19
metabolism, 203–10, 263–65, 315n
microawakenings, 207, 281
Mitchison, Graeme, 218–19
Monroe, Robert, 303n
multiple personality disorder (MPD), 197, 278
mutual dreaming, *see* shared dreaming
Myers, Frederic W. H., 2
mystical experiences, 8–9, 21, 34, 66, 164, 246–47, 265, 313n

napping technique, 13, 203, 258, 291n
Narayana, Ram, 314n
narcolepsy, 62, 280
neuronal activity:
  influences on dreams, 62–63, 69, 80, 93, 130–33, 146–47, 170, 210–14, 216, 281
  influences on hallucinations, 271–72, 279
neurotransmitters, 203–5, 210, 258, 263–64

New Age beliefs, xiii, 8–11, 83, 171, 250, 259, 262–63
Nietzsche, Friedrich, 2
night terrors, 158
NightLight, 4, 144
nightmares, 24–25, 145, 157–58, 179, 263, 277, 311n
 lucidity for coping with, 10, 32, 36–38, 196, 238–42, 293n
nonlucidity, 25–26, 84–87, 100, 120–24, 140, 196, 257–59, 272
 blending with lucidity, 31–34, 86, 89, 103, 110, 117, 135, 235, 261
non-REM sleep (NREM), 3, 15, 59, 144, 158, 202–5, 206–7, 215, 225, 262, 274, 282, 305n
norepinephrine, 205

occultist views of dreams, 8, 33, 53, 65, 164, 172, 246–50, 284
Olsen, Barbara, 310n
On Dreams (Aristotle), 2
Ornstein, Robert, 44, 49
Ouspensky, P. D., 3, 17, 140, 145, 153
out-of-body experience (OBE), 3, 8–9, 60, 118, 124–25, 263, 268–70, 277–78, 303n, 314n
 developing into lucid dreams, 14, 50, 143, 147, 276

Pavlov, Ivan, 212
perception, 44–54, 74, 84–87, 105, 127, 129–36, 146, 153, 172–74, 195, 209–12, 220, 225–27, 251–53
 habits of, xvi, 49, 55, 68, 84, 94, 129, 132–34, 156, 159, 194, 223–25
Perls, Fritz, 168, 197
personal growth, 188, 238, 243–46, 250
postlucidity, 27–28
prelucidity, 27
Principles of Psychology (James), 44
problem solving in dreams, 72, 178, 190–92, 229, 234–36
protodreaming, 14–15, 30, 241, 247, 257–58, 260, 262–63, 269–77
protolucidity, 30–31
psychic dreaming, 8–9, 80, 172, 178, 246–50, 311–12n
psychoanalytic theory, 66–69, 74–75, 128, 154, 166–72, 176–77, 184–85, 197–99
psychotherapeutic uses of dreams, 10, 71–83, 168, 183–92, 197–99, 242–45

rapid-eye-movement sleep
(REM), 3, 15, 58–63,
100, 123, 130, 132, 138,
144, 146–47, 154, 158,
170, 201–5, 210, 227,
260–64, 268–82, 289n,
294n, 298n, 305–6n,
308n, 315n
  phasic vs. tonic, 145, 210,
    282
  evolution of, 206–10, 227
  functions of, 214–26, 260
rationalization in dreams,
  25, 87, 96, 103, 116,
  126–28, 134–37, 143,
  182, 189–90, 235
reading in dreams, 13, 27,
  148–50, 301n
reality test, 13, 27, 28, 151–52
Rechtschaffen, Allan, 306n
reciprocal-interaction model,
  205, 306–7n
rehearsing skills in dreams,
  10, 236–37
Reid, Thomas, 2
Roberts, Jane, 9
role-playing in dreams, 26,
  28, 56, 89, 107–8, 113–15, 140, 177, 190, 240,
  267

Sagan, Carl, 148
schizophrenia, 278–80
semilucidity, 28–29, 39,
  111–13, 116, 125
Senoi, 82

sentinel hypothesis, 207
serotonin, 205, 313n
Seth, 9
sex:
  in dreams, 61, 131, 154,
    165, 175, 180, 221
  in lucid dreams, 11, 82,
    112, 230–31, 240, 282
shamanism, 8–9, 82–83,
  164, 277
shared dreaming, 9, 164,
  247–49, 286
Shopenhauer, Arthur, 172
sleep, sleeping:
  stages of, 3, 201–5, 272,
    282–83
  functions of, 203–5, 210
  evolution of, 206–10
  disorders, 43, 259, 280
  sleep research, xiii, 48,
    102, 169–71, 201–5,
    264, 280
sleep-border phenomena, 5,
  159, 268–76
sleep deprivation, 203, 215–16, 261, 306n, 313n
sleep laboratory, 3, 131,
  145–47, 205, 229, 272,
  280–83
sleep onset, 5, 13–15, 30,
  62, 152, 158, 202–3,
  217, 268–75, 278, 282,
  314n
sleep paralysis experiences,
  5–6, 13–14, 39, 53,
  268–69, 277–80
Snyder, Frederick, 141, 207

Society for Psychical Research, 2
Sparrow, Scott, 262
St. Augustine, 2
St. Thomas Aquinas, 2
Stekel, Wilhelm, 303n
Steriade, Mircea, 306n
Stevenson, Robert Louis, 232
Stewart, Kilton, 82, 241
Studies in Dreams (Arnold-Forster), xiii, 3
suggestion in dreams, 16, 49, 83–84, 99, 164, 247
   suggestion factors, 51–69, 98–100, 142, 151, 159, 170, 178, 187–88, 211, 216, 222, 272–74
   suggestion theory of dreaming, 44, 65–70, 73, 81, 83–84, 128, 131–33, 159–78, 186, 192, 197, 217–18, 223–26, 227, 268, 276, 280, 287, 293n
supernatural beings in dreams, 65, 82–83, 164, 277
symbolism in dreams, 10–11, 66–67, 72, 165–69, 173–74, 184–86, 191, 194, 197, 236, 299n
   symbol manipulation, 10, 78–80, 238–43

tacit lucidity, 26–30, 86, 89, 102–3, 125–26, 135, 179–81, 189, 251
Tan, Amy, 190–91
Tart, Charles, 21, 33
Temiar, 164
Tholey, Paul, 4, 57, 75, 150, 183
thoughts:
   in dreams, 85, 101–6, 120, 126–28, 133–41, 210, 245
   in lucid dreams, xv, 23, 57–58, 61, 63, 77, 88, 105–9, 113–18, 126, 195–96, 201, 235
   in transitional states, 13, 217, 270–76
   as suggestion factors, xvi, 50–55, 69, 77, 85, 100, 130, 134, 156–60, 170–72, 175, 185–96, 216, 223, 250, 285
Through the Looking Glass (Carroll), 15
Tibetan Buddhism, 2, 252, 262, 296n, 312n

Ullman, Montague, 168
unconscious, unconscious mind, xvi, 43, 65–69, 71–74, 85, 99, 123, 166–71, 182, 185–91, 196, 232–38, 270, 272, 295n, 296n, 299n
   collective unconscious, 167, 176

About the Authors

Janice Brooks and Jay Vogelsong are a wife-and-husband team who were brought together by their mutual interest in lucid dreaming. Janice, who has enjoyed frequent lucid dreams and related experiences since childhood, is an honors graduate of the University of Pennsylvania's programs in folklore and anthropology. Jay is a long-term private student of psychology who taught himself to dream lucidly as an adult out of curiosity. Their researches for this project were enhanced by the efforts of a third experienced lucid dreamer, Ruth Sacksteder. All three contributors have participated in various dream study groups and specialist publications, but the bulk of their labor and thought on the subject has gone into the production of the present book and its forthcoming companion volume, *Dream Control*.

Printed in the United States
103598LV00001B/5/A